AFTER REPEAL

About the editors

Kath Browne is a Professor of Geographies of Sexualities and Genders at University College Dublin. She has worked on Heteroactivism, LGBT equalities, lesbian geographies, gender transgressions and women's spaces. Her other publications include *Ordinary in Brighton: LGBT, Activisms and the City* (with Leela Bakshi, 2013), *Queer Spiritual Spaces* (2010), and the co-edited collections *Lesbian Feminism* (2019), *Geographies of Sex and Sexualities* (2016) and *Lesbian Geographies* (2015).

Sydney Calkin is a Lecturer in Geography and a Leverhulme Early Career Fellow at Queen Mary University of London. Her current research investigates the changing geographies of abortion access and the impact of transnational feminist social movements for reproductive justice. She is also the author of *Human Capital in Gender and Development* (2018).

AFTER REPEAL

Rethinking Abortion Politics

EDITED BY KATH BROWNE AND SYDNEY CALKIN

ZED

After Repeal: Rethinking Abortion Politics was first published in 2020 by Zed Books Ltd, The Foundry, 17 Oval Way, London SE11 5RR, UK.

www.zedbooks.net

All author royalties on behalf of Kath Browne and Sydney Calkin and creative royalties on behalf of Anna Cosgrave donated to the Abortion Support Network.

Typeset in Bulmer by Swales and Willis Ltd, Exeter, Devon
Cover design by Burgess and Beech
Cover photo © Anna Cosgrave

Printed and bound by CPI Group (UK) Ltd, Croydon, CR0 4YY

A catalogue record for this book is available from the British Library

ISBN 978-1-78699-717-3 hb
ISBN 978-1-78699-718-0 pb
ISBN 978-1-78699-720-3 pdf
ISBN 978-1-78699-719-7 epub
ISBN 978-1-78699-721-0 mobi

Contents

List of contributors

Kate Antosik-Parsons is a Research Associate of the Humanities Institute at University College Dublin.

Jack Callan is a Human Geography PhD student working on reproductive rights in the Department of Geography at Maynooth University.

Linda Connolly is a Professor of Sociology at Maynooth University.

Noëlle Cotter completed a PhD on the topic of assisted human reproduction in Trinity College Dublin's School of Social Work and Social Policy.

Fiona de Londras is Professor of Global Legal Studies at the University of Birmingham.

Elżbieta Drążkiewicz-Grodzicka is a Lecturer in Anthropology at Maynooth University.

Máiréad Enright is a Reader in Feminist Legal Studies at the University of Birmingham.

Gerry Kearns is a Professor in Geography at Maynooth University.

Niamh McDonald is a working-class mother, socialist, feminist and activist who believes in the power of grassroots organising to create change.

Mary McGill is a researcher and writer based in the west of Ireland.

Catherine Jean Nash is a Professor in Geography at Brock University.

Máire Ní Mhórdha is a Lecturer in the Centre for Teaching and Learning at Maynooth University.

Lisa Nic an Bhreithimh is a campaigner and social activist from Dublin who served as the Communications Officer of *Gaeil ar son Rogha*, the Irish language branch of the Repeal campaign.

Lorna O'Hara is a PhD Candidate in Geography at Maynooth University.

Eric Olund is a Lecturer in Geography at the University of Sheffield.

Theresa Reidy is a Senior Lecturer in the Department of Government and Politics at University College Cork.

Richard Scriven is a Lecturer in Geography at University College Cork.

Lisa Smyth is a Senior Lecturer in Sociology at Queen's University Belfast.

Dorota Szelewa is a Lecturer in the School of Social Policy, Social Work and Social Justice at University College Dublin.

Karen E. Till is a Professor in Geography at Maynooth University.

Acknowledgements

This book emerged from a workshop at Maynooth University in November 2018. In the wake of the May 2018 repeal vote, we wanted to bring together scholars from across the social sciences and humanities who could shed light on the campaign, the vote, and the possibilities for the future after the 8th Amendment. The workshop was an intensive one-day discussion where authors presented their work, gave each other feedback and took advice on how to improve the chapters published here. This book has therefore been a collective process. Several people who participated in the workshop do not have chapters in the volume, but we are sincerely grateful for their feedback and engagement, which strengthened the work as a whole. Each chapter in the book has been shaped by its authors and feedback from numerous other readers.

At Maynooth, we are especially grateful for the support of Linda Connolly, Gerry Kearns and Mary Gilmartin who supported this workshop and encouraged us to pursue the book project. Additional thanks go to Sinéad Kennedy, Claire McGing, Fiona Murphy, Louise Maguire and Aileen O'Carroll for their participation in the workshop and its organizing stages. We thank the Maynooth University Social Sciences Institute (MUSSI) who hosted and funded the workshop and Maynooth University Geography Department who provided additional funding for the day; their support made the workshop and subsequent collaboration possible. We also wish to thank Anne Hamilton Black, Una Horton and Neasa Hogan for their assistance.

At Durham, our thanks go to Cynthia Kamwengo for her excellent work preparing this manuscript for publication. The Durham University Geography Department Research Development Fund provided funding for the preparation of this manuscript. Sydney Calkin would like to acknowledge the funding of the Leverhulme Trust, who supported several research trips to Ireland that made this collaboration possible.

We are grateful for the support of Kim Walker at Zed Books, Gayle Green, Melanie Scagliarini, Ger Hanley, and several anonymous reviewers.

We thank Anna Cosgrave of the Repeal Project for allowing her iconic Repeal design to be used on the cover of this book. As Mary McGill writes in this book, the Repeal jumpers created by Anna helped break the silence that had stifled debate on abortion in Ireland and, in doing so, gave visibility and vitality to the pro-repeal movement. We are grateful for permission to reproduce her design.

Introduction: research

Sydney Calkin and Kath Browne

On 25 May 2018, Irish voters passed a referendum to 'repeal the 8th', removing the Republic's constitutional obstacle to legal abortion. In the months that followed, abortion legislation was debated and passed in the legislature and legal abortion services were introduced in Ireland in January 2019. Abortion politics are a perennial site of 'culture war' conflict and polarisation, so the Irish result has specific national and international resonances. In investigating the future *After Repeal* across disciplines and nations, this book provides insights into both the campaign and the reverberations of the result, nationally and internationally, in the immediate aftermath of the vote.

This book offers academic considerations of the repeal of the 8th Amendment. The chapters were written in the autumn and winter of 2018 and take a broad view of the referendum, with a view to exploring its long-lasting effects within and beyond Ireland. The book is structured to address three dimensions of the referendum to repeal the 8th Amendment: First, an analysis of the political and legal context for the Irish abortion debate and the vote itself. Second, an exploration of the work of the referendum campaign through accounts of scholar-activists who mobilised for reform. Third, a consideration of the future of Ireland after the 8th Amendment and the implications of the repeal vote for abortion politics in other places.

Although this book is a work of academic scholarship on the referendum, it is not politically neutral as to the outcome.

The authors come from a pro-choice position, although some chapters discuss the arguments and campaign tactics of those who opposed the removal of the 8th Amendment. The purpose here is not to replay the arguments along pro-choice/anti-abortion lines, but instead to offer critical insights into the national and international implications of repeal. Although *After Repeal* contains chapters by activists and scholar-activists, the content is predominantly formed of academic analyses of the referendum and not reflections on the experience of activism per se. As academics, we offer an analysis that contextualises and complements, but does not substitute for, activist work on the subject. The following chapters are based on data collected by authors: some draw on personal experience of campaigning in the referendum, and where they do this is made explicit, but the majority of this book is based on the analysis of other data such as interviews, legal texts, media reports, legislative debates, campaigning documents and secondary literature. Our personal positions as UK-based academics (for Kath until December 2017) involved in gender and sexual research, and not as activists in Irish sexual and gender politics, have informed this rationale. We sought to facilitate the conference from which this book arose (along with Claire McGing, Gerry Kearns and Linda Connolly) and the collection itself, because we felt that this was important, but it is also limited. Thus, alongside these scholarly considerations, we recognise a pressing need for an activist/community/historical-focused collection that addresses themes that emerge in this volume. This would ensure that key activist voices and reflections are gathered to retain the knowledges built through the campaign and beyond.

In framing this book within broader academic discussions, this introduction begins by offering a short insight into key debates in abortion research. It then focuses on a historical overview of the legal and political developments that shaped Ireland's 8th Amendment and the 2018 referendum. Finally, it outlines the structure of the volume and briefly summarises each chapter.

Key debates in abortion research

After Repeal considers the past, present and future of abortion in Ireland. It does so in the broader context of feminist debates about how we should understand and advocate for greater reproductive autonomy. We are inspired here by the Reproductive Justice movement that asks us to see abortion within a broader range of reproductive activities and who caution us against over-emphasis on legal or political victories that do not translate into freedom for most women (Roberts 1999). As such, this book understands abortion as one key way in which women's bodies, but also their practices, are regulated and where female sexual deviance, in the form of promiscuity, is punished. It is an important touchstone for politics surrounding other reproductive rights, including access to fertility treatments, surrogacy and same-sex parenting (Woliver 2010; Briggs 2018). Abortion access transgresses these traditional family norms, not least because it offers women some level of autonomy over their fertility decisions and can disrupt patriarchal power over family formation (see Luker 1985; Petchesky 1984).

As with any work on feminism, we acknowledge the differences, debates and compromises that are inherent in the editorial choices we have made here. This is particularly important in relation to the question of reproductive freedom: we acknowledge here that the group of people who can become pregnant is not limited to women. Trans and non-binary people who can become pregnant are also implicated by laws that restrict the rights of pregnant people, although they are very often overlooked in legislative and political debates on the subject. In this edited volume, authors have chosen their own terminology and some authors refer to 'women' and others to 'pregnant people'. Many people who can get pregnant do not identify as women, just as many cis gender women cannot or choose not to become pregnant. Nonetheless we retain the category of 'women' in places throughout the introduction and the book as a political choice, because we follow the feminist argument that the laws intended to restrict reproductive freedoms target women as a social group and as a means of sexual control (Briggs 2018). These same forces work to oppress and marginalise lesbian, gay, bi, trans (LGBT) and non-binary people on the basis of their perceived deviance from a hetero-patriarchal gender order.

In the repeal campaign itself, the position of trans people was contested and generated tension within pro-choice campaigns. Some feminists in the Irish pro-choice movement lamented the exclusion of trans people, migrant women, women of colour, Travellers and other marginalised groups from the dominant campaigning narratives of the official repeal campaign (see Enright 2018; Fletcher 2018). There was an unease with a perceived "acquiescence to conservatism" that may have impacted their message and demands (Campbell 2018). Despite advocacy by feminist lawyers and LGBTQ+ activists after repeal, the language of Ireland's new abortion is not trans inclusive and may create barriers and stigma for trans men and non-binary people who seek access to abortion care (see Enright et al. 2018). This volume does not contain in-depth analysis of the implications of the 8th Amendment and new abortion law for trans and non-binary communities; we acknowledge this as a silence in our own editorial work and invite more scholarship on these questions.

Social and legal sanctions against abortion are tied up with a greater variety of policies that restrict sexual and reproductive freedom: restrictions on abortion access travel alongside restrictions on contraception, reproductive technology and modes of assisted reproduction (see for example Takeshita 2012). The social movements committed to the restriction of abortion access often situate it on a 'family' platform that is opposed to what is termed 'death culture' including LGBT rights, euthanasia, same-sex marriage and supportive of 'traditional family' policies (see Browne and Nash, this volume; Browne et al. 2018). The governance of reproduction represents a key mechanism through which broader political economy governance agendas are enacted – pertaining to migration, population and health, among others – across a range of international, state and non-governmental actors (Morgan and Roberts 2012). The study of abortion therefore offers a window into the relationship between the lived experiences of gendered subjects and the broader ideological and political structures that operate around them.

Abortion is almost universally governed by states (and substate entities) through their criminal codes. Although activists have pushed for decriminalisation, with some recent successes, the legal regulation of abortion remains a primary site of contention. Across the world, we see a general trend towards more permissive abortion laws with a few notable sites of retrenchment (Szelewa, this volume). The political processes through which this change occurs are highly place-specific and depend on the political, cultural and institutional contexts (see Nebel and Hurka 2015; Grzymała-Busse 2015). In Northern Ireland, for example, abortion and same-sex marriage have emerged as cultural issues where sectarian divisions can be bridged by conservative politicians who share an opposition to liberalisation (Thomson 2016). By contrast, in the rest of the UK, politicians have generally sought to avoid the politicisation of the abortion issue by framing it as a technical matter for the medical profession (Sheldon 1997). Legal change on abortion can be a slow, and halting, process which results in limited gains. Across the world, pro-choice activists are engaging in alternative forms of resistance that work for abortion reform outside of formal political institutions, or without the traditional process of lobbying for legislative action. This takes place through efforts to spread legal knowledge among lay activists (see González Vélez and Jaramillo 2017; Fletcher 2018; Enright and Cloatre 2018) and the establishment of activist networks who facilitate access to knowledge and medicine for self-managed abortion (see Singer 2018; Drovetta 2015; Calkin 2019a). These modes of pro-choice action reinforce each other. Abortion policy reform often emerges from widespread mobilisation against and violation of existing laws, so social movements that look beyond legal reform to widen access create the political context for policy change (Knill et al. 2015).

The practical availability of abortion depends on many factors beyond the legality of abortion in principle. Multi-day waiting periods, requirements for multiple clinic visits, restrictions on medical personnel, conscientious objection provision, and high costs are all factors that substantially curtail the availability of abortion without rising to the level of a ban (see Statz and Pruitt 2018; de Zordo et al. 2016). Noting these extra-legal restrictions, it is clear that access to abortion depends on more than the legal status of abortion in a person's home jurisdiction; it also implicates socio-economic inequalities and their intersection with place-based, racial, sexual and related inequalities. The lived effect of these inequalities is especially apparent in patterns of abortion travel, where women cross large distances and political borders in search of legal (or *less* criminalised) abortion (see Sethna and Doull 2012; MacQuarrie et al. 2018; Freeman 2017; Calkin and Freeman 2018; de Zordo et al. 2016). As such, abortion travel can be especially difficult for poorer people, and all but impossible for people whose mobility is restricted by their immigration status (see Side 2016; Gilmartin and Kennedy 2018). A growing body of research on abortion travel has also noted the ways that feminist and pro-choice activist groups facilitate this travel by establishing social and financial infrastructures; the Irish diaspora in England exemplifies this cross-border solidarity work (Rossiter 2009; Fletcher 2016). Beyond the travelling of people, the mobilities of the 'abortion pill' have opened new lines of enquiry into access and the effectiveness of state restrictions (Calkin, this volume).

Because abortion is a highly politicised issue, and because it is implicated in broader public debates about gender, sex and the regulation of family life, many scholars have explored its function as a discourse. How do we talk about abortion and how does that talk shape our understanding of what it is, what it means, and how it should be governed? The development and widespread use of ultrasound technologies, for example, dramatically changed public understandings of pregnancy and shaped political debates about the termination of pregnancy (Morgan and Michaels 1999). The emergence of a foetal rights discourse – which envisioned a clash of rights between foetus and pregnant person – gave rise to a legal movement that treats the foetus as a right-bearing individual who needs legal protections (Roth 2003; Sanger 2017). Pro-choice discourses also have political implications for access to abortion: medicalising abortion treats it as a technical matter for doctors, not pregnant people, to decide (Sheldon 1997), while narratives of sadness, shame and regret over abortion decisions can reinforce stereotypes about responsible and irresponsible women, and good vs. bad abortions (Millar 2017). These debates even divide the pro-choice movement, whose factions strongly dispute the political discourses that suit the end goal, be it legalisation, decriminalisation, or de-stigmatisation (Pollitt 2014).

This broad and, necessarily brief, overview of some of the key debates in abortion research indicates the political and cultural import of the area. It is clear that abortion is a fraught and contentious area, with abortion politics key to contemporary cultural wars that are coming to define the second decade of the 21st century. While this volume is limited in scope and cannot adequately explore the breadth of reproductive politics, its detailed exploration of Ireland's 8th referendum undoubtedly offers insights into the power relations that structure lives, cultures and politics.

Abortion and Ireland

Abortion laws, whether restrictive or permissive, reflect broader social and political debates about gender, sex and community. In Ireland, this means the issue of abortion should be understood in the broader context of the Irish "sexual and gender order with its associated cultural, ethnic and racial logics" tied to nation- and state-building (Luibhéid 2013: 37). This sexual and gender order was characterized from the state's foundation by a "sexual puritanism" that was enacted through a ban on divorce, a ban on married women working in the public sector, a ban on contraceptives and a set of patriarchal norms that consigned women to lives of domestic labour and subordination to men (Smyth 2005: 7). This sexual and gender order was largely influenced by the political and social power commanded by the Catholic Church which, although greatly diminished in recent decades, has historically exerted enormous influence over politics, society and family life (Inglis 1998; Scriven, this volume). The institutional power of the Catholic Church to control and discipline sexuality is evident in the legacies of mother and baby homes, Magdalene Laundries, institutional and reformatory schools and international adoption schemes, among others (Fischer 2016). The violation of Catholic sexual norms often met with incarceration in these institutions; other sexual transgressions were 'solved' through emigration to the UK, whether by same-sex couples or women pregnant out of wedlock (Luibhéid 2013; Gilmartin and Kennedy 2018).

The enforcement of a conservative Catholic sexual and gender order has been closely tied to nationalist narratives about the cultural, religious and racial distinctiveness of the Irish. Feminist scholarship has long argued for the need to understand nationalist politics as enacted through claims about reproduction and gender; in nationalist narratives, women and their sexual purity are the symbolic borders of the nation, while their role in childbearing literally populates the nation (Yuval-Davis 1997; Hill-Collins 2009). In Ireland, abortion has been contested as a site for nationalist claim-making where 'pro-life' Catholic Ireland is contrasted with 'pro-abortion' Protestant Britain (Smyth 2005; Fischer 2016). This nationalist orientation to abortion is explicitly evident in the persistent anti-abortion narratives that equate British abortion clinics with British colonial violence, seen in 1983 (Fletcher 2001), as well as 2018. By extension, efforts to restrict abortion in Ireland have worked to uphold an idealised ethnic account of Irishness (Fletcher 2005; Smyth 2005). The social and political norms governing abortion clearly map onto existing hierarchies and inequalities within society; while some women face social and political pressure on their fertility in the form of forced pregnancies, others face social, political and legal interventions to prevent them bearing and raising children as they choose (King 2002). The 8th Amendment played a significant role not only in defining the nation, but in also reconstituting the place of women in 'Catholic Ireland' beyond access to terminations.

A brief history of the 8th Amendment

The 8th Amendment to the Irish constitution was inserted by a referendum passed by 66.9% in 1983. The Amendment's text read:

> The State acknowledges the right to life of the unborn and, with due regard to the equal right to life of the mother, guarantees in its laws to respect and as far as practicable by its laws to defend and vindicate that right.

Famously referred to as the "second partitioning of Ireland", the 1983 referendum was a bitter political struggle with substantial involvement by the Catholic Church (Fletcher 2001). The 8th Amendment had far-reaching consequences for everything from maternity care to immigration to in vitro fertilisation (Luibhéid 2013; de Londras 2015; Cotter, this volume). However, abortion was already illegal in Ireland at the time and had been illegal since the foundation of the state in 1922 (see de Londras and Enright 2018). The 8th Amendment cemented this ban in the constitution, a move which was motivated partly by the fear that the courts could legalise abortion, as recent judicial decisions had liberalised access to contraception.

The 8th Amendment of the constitution created an extremely difficult process for reforming Ireland's abortion law. The Amendment was interpreted in restrictive ways, and was so broad in scope, that even the most conservative abortion legislation would be rendered unconstitutional. For this reason, changes to abortion law in Ireland came through the courts and referendums, rather than through the legislature, from 1983 to 2013 (see de Londras 2015). Despite the extremely restrictive confines of the 8th Amendment, all subsequent referendums on abortion showed the voting public favoured reform rather than further restrictions (see also Reidy, this volume). Three referendums were held in 1992 in the wake of the X case,[1] in which the Supreme Court interpreted the 8th Amendment as permitting abortion only where there was a "real and substantial risk" to the life, as distinct from the health, of the pregnant woman. In 1992, voters approved two measures – to permit women to travel for abortion abroad without being prosecuted when they return and to obtain information about abortion access abroad – and they rejected one measure which would have excluded suicide from the grounds for life-saving abortion (see Smyth 2005). A further referendum was held in 2002 in which voters again rejected a proposal to exclude suicide from the grounds for life-saving abortion.

From 2010 onwards, a series of events brought abortion to the centre of the political conversation and a growing pro-choice movement mobilised for reform, located within a longer history of Irish feminist activism (see Connolly, this volume). In 2010, the European Court of Human Rights ruled that Ireland's laws violated the European Convention on Human Rights because it failed to provide a clear and accessible mechanism by which a woman could determine if she qualified for a legal abortion. In 2012, Savita Halappanavar died in a Galway hospital after being denied an abortion (Holland 2013). Her death triggered widespread protests, vigils and demands for reform. In 2013, the government introduced the Protection of Life During Pregnancy Act (PLDPA) to respond to the European Court judgement: the PLDPA established extremely limited circumstances under which women could access life-saving abortion (see de Londras 2015; Murray 2016). In 2016 and again in 2017, the UN Human Rights Committee ruled that Ireland had violated the human rights of a pregnant woman and subjected her to discrimination and cruel, inhuman or degrading treatment by forcing her to travel to England to terminate a pregnancy with fatal foetal anomalies. This sequence of events galvanised the Irish pro-choice movement who mobilised in growing numbers: in 2012, 20,000 marched in Dublin chanting "Never Again" after the death of Savita Halappanavar. By 2017, the Abortion Rights Campaign March for Choice drew an estimated 40,000 to the city's streets (see Quilty et al. 2015). By 2016, the 8th Amendment was the subject of intense political debate during the election campaign, mainly as a result of activist mobilisation and increased public awareness of fatalities caused by the abortion ban (de Londras and Markicevic 2018).

After the 2016 election, the government called a Citizens Assembly on the 8th Amendment (see Field 2018). At the time, many activists saw this as a stalling tactic by a reluctant political establishment (Darążkiewicz-Grodzicka and Ní Mhórdha, this volume). At its conclusion, however, the Citizens Assembly recommended a progressive list of reforms that began with the repeal of the 8th Amendment and moved well beyond it, including a period of unrestricted access in early pregnancy (see Laffoy 2017). This report was considered by the Joint Oireachtas Committee on the 8th Amendment who invited expert witnesses to testify and released their own report, also recommending the repeal of the 8th Amendment (see Joint Oireachtas Committee 2017b). In March 2018, the government introduced the referendum bill which passed the Dáil and triggered the referendum for 25 May 2018. The Health Minister introduced draft legislation on abortion to signal the kind of law that would follow from the repeal of the 8th Amendment. As such, the referendum on the 8th Amendment dealt with the constitutional provision and the wider campaign involved a discussion of proposed post-repeal legislation.

The referendum to repeal the 8th Amendment passed by 66.4% to 33.6%; voter turnout was 64.1% of the electorate, exit poll data indicated that voters had decided some years in advance of the referendum to vote for repeal (Reidy, this volume). After several court challenges to the result, the 8th Amendment was formally removed from the constitution in September 2018. In December 2018, the Regulation of Termination of Pregnancy bill was passed by the legislature and signed into law; it came into force on 1 January 2019. This law provides for on-request abortion access up to 12 weeks, with further provision for abortion in the case of medical emergencies and fatal foetal anomalies. This legislation marks a momentous change in Ireland's abortion regime, although pro-choice advocates have highlighted the gaps in provision that the new legislation will maintain, including concerns about the mandatory 3-day waiting period, the implementation of conscientious objection provisions, the certification of harm and risk to pregnant people, the certification of fatal foetal anomalies, lack of provision in certain parts of the country and the likelihood that significant numbers of women will still be forced to travel to England for terminations (see Enright 2018; Enright et al. 2018; Enright and de Londras, this volume; Fletcher et al. 2018).

After the 8th: overview

In engaging with key abortion debates and engaging with both the Irish context and the broader symbolism and import of the 8th Amendment, we have structured the book through three sections. These are: The Politics of Repeal, Campaigns and Campaigning and Futures: Ireland and Beyond.

In Part I, *The politics of repeal*, authors examine the political movements, trends, institutions and discourses that shaped the referendum and wider context. The politics of the referendum, including the political institutions and discourses that shaped it, offer critical insights because it is relatively rare for a country to hold a referendum directly on the issue of abortion. Linda Connolly's chapter explores the work of repealing the 8th Amendment that began long before May 2018. The first step in understanding this context is to grapple with the history of Irish feminisms. The feminist mobilisation for the repeal of the 8th is situated in the much longer history of Irish feminist activism in Connolly's chapter. The activist work of campaigning for reproductive rights has, from the 1960s, mobilised around contraception and abortion, although this feminist activism has long negotiated fundamental political and tactical differences within the movement. This account of the longitudinal nature of Irish feminisms works against some of the presentism of the referendum discourse, for example, the oft-repeated idea that repeal was a recent 'quiet revolution' or an electoral shock. Indeed, as Theresa Reidy shows using poll data, including the exit poll on 25

May, the outcome of the referendum was not surprising given the opinion poll trends of the previous decade. Irish voters had consistently signalled their dissatisfaction with the 8th Amendment and expressed their intention to overturn it, if offered the chance to do so. Reidy and Connolly's analyses thus require a consideration of the result that includes, as well as moves beyond the Yes campaign or more recent Repeal politics.

The politics of the referendum were shaped by the unique political, cultural and geographical context of Ireland and its 8th Amendment abortion regime, but also formed through transnational connections. Long before the referendum and the new legislation, as Mairead Enright and Fiona de Londras demonstrate, anti-choice legal arguments have framed the debate about abortion in Ireland. They show that opponents of abortion reform used legal claims and narratives during the campaign, to advance a secular anti-repeal case, as well as in the debates about the new abortion law in which they sought to introduce measures which would curtail access going forward. These tactics indicate the transnational ways in which campaigns are formed in and through specific contexts. The issue of abortion pills also unsettled state-based understandings of abortion control and because of this significantly shaped political and legal arguments made by campaigners and politicians. In the months before the referendum, as Sydney Calkin shows, abortion pills became a focus of legislative debate because their availability undermined the enforcement of the 8th Amendment regime. She argues that abortion pills became a central feature of a pro-repeal political discourse that stressed the importance of safe but limited access and medical control over terminations. After a Citizen's Assembly that ostensibly trusted citizens, these narratives show that mainstream political elites still saw abortion as a medical procedure entrusted to doctors. Elżbieta Drążkiewicz-Grodzicka and Máire Ní Mhórdha build on this engagement with trust to demonstrate the complexities of political trust in their chapter. They show that the democratic process leading up to the referendum and the vote itself provoked debates about the state's trust in women, the public's trust in politicians and the political tool of the referendum itself.

Part II, *Campaigns and campaigning*, deals directly with the campaign to repeal the 8th, foregrounding the voices of activist-scholars who participated in the repeal campaign as canvassers, organisers, spokespeople and public advocates. This campaign sought a constitutional change in the narrowest sense, but also signalled a much broader cultural shift in Irish society, building on the Irish feminist activisms of previous decades. The chapters in this section show that the campaign raised taboo issues, broke long-held silences and elevated the voices of women whose reproductive and sexual lives had historically been regarded as shameful and deviant. In Eric Olund's chapter, public discussion about the 8th Amendment triggered broader debates. He demonstrates how this process took place in the media, where increasing coverage of abortion travel abroad and testimonies from abortion travellers themselves worked to contest traditional ideas about shame, secrecy and sexuality. Breaking the silence on abortion also took place in public spaces through artworks, like Maser's Repeal mural. Lorna O'Hara shows that Maser's mural, its removal and public struggles over that artwork speak to broader debates about speech, silence and political action in Ireland.

Pro-choice messages in the media and public spaces signalled a sea change in Ireland. As the next three chapters in this section show, this change was both created and supported by the face-to-face work of breaking taboos and silences around abortion by the campaign groups who knocked on doors and canvassed Ireland, from central Dublin to the most rural areas of Donegal. The chapters recognise that canvassing work was inspired by the history of Irish feminisms and a feminist ethos of solidarity and sharing.

Niamh McDonald and her co-authors, all members of the Dublin Bay North repeal group, demonstrate that their group's canvassing strategies sought to mobilise votes for repeal, but also to politically activate members of the community who were not seasoned campaigners. Far from urban Dublin, rural Ireland was assumed to hold anti-repeal and conservative views that could sink the repeal vote. Mary McGill shows that these perceptions were, and are, inaccurate. She emphasises the breaking of silence and shame that she encountered through her campaigning experiences, and the importance of recognising that the 8th also had devastating effects for women in rural Ireland. Whereas McGill contests the stereotypes of rural Ireland, creating new narratives and analyses that reject the association of rural Ireland with preventing sexual and gender progress, Lisa Nic an Bhreithimh takes on presumptions of Irish language voters that associated them with conservative, rural and anti-repeal views. The Irish language campaign to repeal mobilised against such assumptions and sought to reach Irish language speakers on their own terms. In doing so, Nic an Bhreithimh contends that they saw the repeal campaign galvanise a wider enthusiasm for the Irish language, mutually (re)creating the language and broader Irish culture in ways that reflect a more open and liberal modern Ireland. This Irishness beyond silence and shame, as McGill argues, still has much to do.

Part III, *Futures: Ireland and beyond*, shows that Ireland's vote to repeal the 8th Amendment has implications that are broader and longer lasting than the specific moment of repeal and they go well beyond the national boundaries of the Republic of Ireland. Richard Scriven begins this section by reflecting on the Irish Catholic Church. In the writings on the historical, social and political power of the Catholic Church in Ireland and its role in the 1983 referendum, the position of the Catholic Church in Ireland is often taken to be uniform and uncontested. In contrast, Scriven argues, the Irish Catholic Church is not as monolithic on social issues, nor are all Irish Catholics as orthodox in their beliefs as has been previously assumed. He contends that the Irish Catholic Church must negotiate its place in an increasingly pluralistic and diverse cultural context. The removal of the 8th Amendment and the waning of Catholic institutional and doctrinal power in Ireland also has implications for other forms of reproduction. Noëlle Cotter shows that the 8th amendment did not fully halt reproductive technologies like in vitro fertilisation, but it did restrict their use and research in this field. Cotter explores the overlaps and intersections and indicates that the removal of the 8th Amendment has the potential to transform regulation and practice in assisted reproduction.

Beyond the shores of Ireland, the result of the 8th Amendment referendum created ripples and impacted ongoing cultural wars that revolve around abortion politics. This section finishes the book by showing some of the transnational ways that the repeal of the 8th galvanised pro-choice activists and provoked anxieties among those who oppose abortion. Lisa Symth's chapter focuses on Northern Ireland, where immediately after the result on 25 May 2018, activists in Ireland and beyond who had campaigned for repeal set their sights. The new goal: "The North is Next" rallied activities to push for abortion reform in Northern Ireland. The momentum and mobilisation from the 8th referendum has generated renewed attention to Northern Ireland's abortion ban, but as Smyth shows, the institutional and political context there is distinct in ways that make a similar process of reform unlikely. Similarly, Dorota Szelewa examines the problems of reform in Poland that could be read as 'following' reform in Ireland. She shows that Poland remains an outlier in Europe where an extremely restrictive abortion law is in force and a conservative political resurgence is engaged in persistent efforts to tighten its already restrictive law. The Irish result resonated in Poland, both among pro- and anti-choice activists who sought to learn lessons from the referendum and Szelewa considers the potential for progressive reforms there, as well as the obstacles that remain. Within the supposed 'liberal West' Kath Browne and Catherine Nash highlight heteroactivists – those who campaign against progressive gender and sexual reforms in order to reinstate specific forms of heteronormativities. They explore the reactions of British and Canadian heteroactivists to the events in Ireland, especially how these activist discourses are both transnationally created and geographically situated. It is clear from this chapter and others (for example Enright and de Londras) that these oppositions will not disappear and for those opposed to abortion the 'battle' is beginning. Overall, then, these chapters show that the national and international futures after the repeal of the 8th Amendment remain contentious and uncertain.

Note

1 In the X case, a teenager, pregnant from rape, was prohibited initially from travelling to the UK for an abortion.

PART I | The politics of repeal

ONE | The 2018 abortion referendum: over before it began!

Theresa Reidy

Introduction

Ireland was a mostly conservative outpost of Western Europe until the 1990s and the conservative values and policy positions contained in the constitution rested easily with a large majority of voters until at least the 1960s (Lee 1989; Ferriter 2010). Economic expansion and social modernisation in the decades that followed led to the emergence of a new and deep-seated conservative-liberal cleavage in politics (Sinnott 1995). Contraception, divorce and abortion were the main issues on this political fault line and debates became increasingly divisive in the ensuing decades and were widely known as the 'culture wars' by the 1980s. Undoubtedly, abortion was the most controversial and enduring of these issues. A process of six referendum questions on four separate polling days began with the passing of the Pro-Life (Anti-Abortion) Amendment in 1983.

Referendums in Ireland have been classified into three categories: international treaties, legal and political reforms and moral-social questions. Abortion falls into the category of moral-social questions (Sinnott 2002). These referendums draw from the fundamental values that citizens have about how society should be organised and campaigns on these questions have tended to be politically charged and divisive. Paddy O'Carroll described the 1983 abortion referendum as having delivered a campaign of "unparalleled divisiveness, bitterness and rancour" (O'Carroll 1991: 57). Abortion was never far from the political agenda in the following decades, but the first referendum, which sought to liberalise abortion provision, was not put before the people until 2018.

This chapter will provide a brief overview of the six abortion votes outlining the evolution of the issue in public debate, the role of campaign actors and the pathway to the 2018 referendum in section one. Section two will present evidence from a series of opinion polls and exit polls which indicate shifting attitudes towards abortion provision. It will use data from the RTÉ-Universities exit poll at the 2018 referendum to demonstrate that Irish attitudes to abortion had liberalised considerably in the previous decade and that the referendum campaign, while important for the mobilisation of voters, was instrumental in changing the views of only a small proportion of voters. In large part, this accounts for the stability in preferences recorded in polls in the lead up to and throughout the campaign. Some reflections on abortion referendums are included in the final section.

The abortion votes

Conservative groups in Ireland became concerned in the early 1980s that efforts might be made to use the Supreme Court to deliver a legal route to abortion, as had happened in the US in the *Roe v Wade* case. A complete ban on abortion was included in the statute books but the pro-life groups initiated a campaign to include an absolute ban in the constitution as the only way to guarantee that there would be no liberalisation of abortion provision. Following some years of political manoeuvring, a referendum was delivered and passed by a two thirds majority and the abortion ban (known as the Pro-Life Amendment) was included in the text of the constitution. Gallagher (2018) has noted that the fact the referendum proposal was known in public discourse as the Pro-Life Amendment points to the political dominance of the pro-life campaign and the extent to which it controlled debates on abortion.

The 1983 campaign was acrimonious, and contemporaneous accounts document how conservatives framed the debate in absolutist terms with all other views treated as anathema to social norms (O'Carroll 1991). Turnout was low at just over 50%, but the Amendment passed comfortably. The black and white campaign claims of 'abortion is murder' and the decrying of any medical need for abortion were to come unstuck in the subsequent decades when multiple cases were to demonstrate with clarity the grave implications of the 8th Amendment for the medical treatment of women during pregnancy.

The first case to come to public prominence took place in 1992. The parents of a pregnant child rape victim (who became known as X in the legal proceedings) sought advice from police authorities about whether medical evidence obtained during an abortion conducted in the UK could be used in the prosecution of the criminal rape case. In response, the authorities sought and were granted an injunction to prevent the child and her parents from travelling to the UK for the abortion. The decision was overturned by the Supreme Court. In its judgment, the court declared that abortion was legal when the life of the woman was at risk and that this risk included the threat of suicide. The X case prompted national debate and the government responded by posing three separate referendum questions to clarify the constitutional position on abortion. The referendum questions were co-scheduled with a general election which meant that the referendums took on a different dynamic to other votes on abortion. Political parties had remained somewhat on the margins in 1983 and the main campaign protagonists were drawn from civil society groups. But in 1992, the government had a more significant role in deciding the wording of the questions and defining the parameters of the debate (Girvin 1993; 1994).

Voters endorsed proposals which provided a right to travel outside the state for abortion services and a right to access information on abortion. The third question, which was labelled the substantive issue in debates, asked voters to undo the Supreme Court decision and remove suicide as a ground for abortion. This proposal was rejected by voters. The 1992 referendums emerge as an important moment in the debate on abortion in Ireland. The restrictive proposition was defeated, but the two other proposals, which were minimally liberalising propositions, were passed. Girvin (1993) provided data from the European Values Surveys of 1981 and 1990 which showed a significant movement in the views of voters, most especially where the life of the woman was at risk due to the pregnancy. While less than 50% of men and women supported abortion in this circumstance in 1981, the figures had jumped to 63% for women and 67% for men by 1990.

Through the 1990s, domestic party politics and the ongoing political power of the pro-life lobby kept the abortion question live. In 1997, the minority coalition government required the support of a small number of non-party TDs (MPs). One of the conditions for their support was a referendum to again attempt to roll back the 1992 court decision on the threat of suicide as a ground for legal abortion. This referendum eventually took place in 2002. As Kennedy outlines, by this stage, abortion had moved from being an issue on which voters had absolute and defined positions to a 'series of moral conundrums' (Kennedy 2002). The dominance of conservative groups was still evident. The proposal put forward was designed to restrict abortion and there was much debate about whether abortion could be a remedy for suicidal ideation. Indeed, the very phrasing of this proposition, which dominated public discourse during the campaign, displayed a specific conservative disposition. The referendum was defeated with the consensus in the aftermath of the vote indicating that a coalition of extreme conservatives and liberals had delivered the narrow defeat (Kennedy 2002).

The tenor of the abortion debate shifted markedly in the early 21st century as the consequences of the Anti-Abortion Constitutional Amendment were detailed in a series of court cases and medical episodes. No legislation was enacted to give legal effect to the 1992 ruling and this led to significant criticism of successive governments. In 2010, the European Court of Human Rights ruled that failure to provide information on the circumstances in which abortion was legal in Ireland was an infringement of human rights. The coalition government elected in 2011 agreed to take action and established an expert group to review the legal position. Its report coincided with the public disclosure of the death of Savita Halappanavar, a Galway-based dentist, due to mismanagement of a miscarriage which was linked to legal uncertainties surrounding the circumstances when a legal abortion was allowable (Health Services Executive 2013). Her death prompted domestic outrage and international condemnation of Ireland's restrictive abortion regime (Quilty et al. 2015; de Londras 2015) The case was instrumental in pushing the government to act on the recommendations of the expert group.

The Protection of Life in Pregnancy Act (2013) was a restrictive piece of legislation which finally gave effect to the 1992 court decision. Introduced by the Fine Gael and Labour coalition, it did little to substantively alter abortion provision, but it was fiercely resisted by a small number of extreme conservatives during its passage through the Dáil. The conservatives were grouped in Fine Gael, Fianna Fáil and among non-party TDs, however, only Fine Gael experienced significant political fall-out from the legislation when several TDs and senators were expelled from the party for failing to support the legislation. The incident reinforced the enduring political divisiveness of abortion.

In parallel with the process of legislative change, civil society groups on the pro-choice side became especially active in public debates and pressure to deliver progressive reform built up within the political system. Terminations for Medical Reasons – a group campaigning for the provision of abortion in cases of fatal foetal abnormality – were especially to the fore in debates and their contribution is notable most especially for highlighting the transformation in the presentation of abortion as an issue (Field 2018). The contrast between the lead-in to the 1983 referendum and the 2018 referendums could not have been starker: by 2018 it was widely accepted that termination of pregnancy was a medical procedure, sometimes necessary on health grounds. This basic point had been widely disputed in the 1983 campaign.

A number of non-party and left wing TDs also engaged in significant parliamentary agitation on the liberal side. When the new minority government took up office in 2016, it agreed quickly that action would have to be taken on abortion provision. On this occasion, the presence of a liberal non-party TD, Katherine Zappone, in the cabinet is highlighted for advancing the referendum proposal (Doyle 2016). The government moved quickly to establish a deliberative forum, the Citizens' Assembly, to discuss abortion provision. Following several weeks of deliberation, the Assembly recommended that a referendum be held to remove the 1983 Amendment and that this should be accompanied by a significant liberalisation of abortion provision (Field 2018). The outcome of the Citizens' Assembly was greeted by some surprise at the time. In a report in *The Irish Times*, the outcome was described as having created "shockwaves by recommending extensive liberalisation" (Minihan 2017). There were also concerns that the liberal proposals were unlikely to find favour with the wider electorate with Minihan reporting that "the consensus in the Oireachtas is that the assembly's recommendations were an overly-liberal interpretation of the current thinking of middle Ireland on the issue" (Minihan 2017). The report of the Assembly was sent to an Oireachtas Committee to consider the details and it too endorsed a repeal referendum and subsequent legislative liberalisation (Elkink et al. 2019). The referendum was held on 25 May 2018.

There are a couple of points which can be distilled from this overview of abortion referendums. No referendum proposal, which sought to make abortion provision more restrictive, was passed after 1983. Abortion moved from being a one-dimensional issue of 'right versus wrong' to a complex and multi-dimensional social problem over the period from 1983–2018. Complex cases involving acute and chronic medical problems came to define the debate in its later stages, wresting it away from the absolutist political framing so evident in 1983 (Reidy 2018). Finally, civil society groups have always been at the forefront of the abortion debates. In the early 1980s, the Pro-Life Amendment Campaign led demands for the Anti-Abortion Amendment and, equally, demand for the 2018 repeal referendum was also driven by a coalition of liberal groups whose strength often lay outside parliamentary politics.

Changing attitudes to abortion

Abortion referendums have always generated intense discussion and often heated and intemperate exchanges on the airwaves and doorsteps, but this intensity is not always reflected in voting patterns. In 1983, turnout stood at 53.7% which was below the average rate of participation for referendums at that time. The 1992 votes were co-scheduled with a general election so there is little to be inferred from turnout on that date, but the 2002 vote yielded a turnout of 42.9%. Figure 1.1 presents an area map of the electorate at each of the six votes with the dark grey shaded area at the top of the figure reflecting the proportion of the electorate that abstained at each of the votes and it clearly shows the sharp drop in engagement with the abortion issue in 2002 and the pointed increase which occurred in 2018.

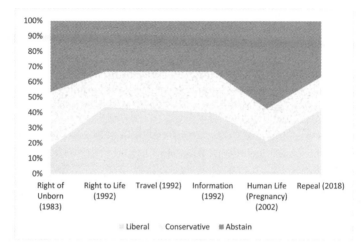

Figure 1.1   Abstainers and voters at abortion referendums

Source: Department of Housing, Planning and Local Government Referendum Results

The second point of note which emerges from Figure 1.1 is that the conservative vote, captured by the middle light greyscale band, is at its widest in 1983. It changed very little from 2002 to 2018, but the liberal position (captured by the mid grey band at the bottom of the figure) jumped sharply from 2002 to 2018. There is no panel data available from this period so some caution is needed when making inferences, but given the size of the jump in the liberal vote from 2002 to 2018, it is reasonable to hypothesise that abstainers became significantly more liberal and more motivated to vote in the intervening period.

LeDuc (2002) provides a useful schema for conceptualising referendum types. In his framework, referendums which ask moral or social questions tend to have voting patterns which are very stable. Essentially, he argues that the positions of political parties and campaign groups and referendum campaign activities may have only a limited impact on the final vote. Indeed, he points out that it would not be unusual for campaign polls to record little opinion movement at these types of referendums. This is largely because these types of questions draw from the fundamental values that voters have about how society should be organised and individuals should be treated. And these types of values change very slowly over long periods of time. Specifically, abortion is an issue which draws from the fundamental values that voters have about individual rights, women's rights and autonomy. Factors which contribute to change on this value dimension include urbanisation, increasing education levels and secularisation. In relation to abortion in Ireland, public disclosure of complex legal and medial cases may also have contributed to value change, in part by crystallising the issues involved. This leads to two important questions: When did attitudes towards abortion begin to change and what influenced the opinion change?

Data availability somewhat limits the ability to deliver precise answers to these questions but there are some valuable insights in the information which does exist. Polling data collected in the five months up to the referendum campaign point to reasonable stability in voting preferences. Figure 1.2 presents the percentage

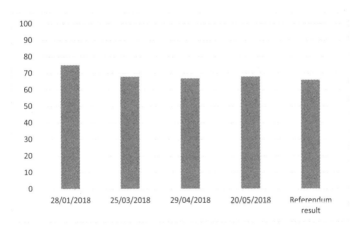

Figure 1.2 Percentage Yes vote in Red C polls and final referendum Yes vote

Source: Red C Research, 2018 (www.redcresearch.ie/battle-repeal-8th/)

Yes vote in Red C[1] polls and records the Yes vote at 75% in January 2018 which points to a decline of less than ten points in the months leading up to polling day. This is a relatively small opinion change (see Suiter and Reidy 2013).

Voters leaving polling stations at the 2016 general election were asked a series of questions for an RTÉ-Universities exit poll (RTÉ-Universities 2016). Included in the survey was an abortion attitudinal scale which was replicated again at the abortion referendum for the RTÉ-Universities exit poll on that date. The question asked of voters was:

> On a scale from 0 to 10 where 0 means you strongly believe that there should be a total ban on abortion in Ireland, and 10 means that you strongly believe that Abortion should be freely available in Ireland to any woman who wants to have one, where would you place your view? (RTÉ-Universities 2018)

Table 1.1 presents the results from the two exit polls and the striking point is how little movement there was in opinions overall in the two years between the general election and the abortion referendum. We can see that the mean position is above six in both which is on the liberal side of the spectrum. This suggests that much of the opinion change on abortion had occurred prior to 2016. This is an interesting observation as it suggests that the Citizens' Assembly and the Oireachtas Committee examination of the abortion issue did not fundamentally drive opinion change on this issue and that the liberal position advocated by the members of the Citizens' Assembly may have been more in line with the majority consensus than had been thought at the time of its vote. There are also a number of clear demographic patterns on display in Table 1.1: younger age cohorts exhibit more liberal views on abortion and women are more liberal than men. The gender point is an interesting one and reflects an important shift as women had been more conservative at earlier referendum

Table 1.1 Mean position on abortion attitudinal scale

	TOTAL	Gender		Age					Social Class		F
		Male	Female	18–24	25–34	35–49	50–64	65+	ABC1	C2DE	
Mean Score 2016	6.07	6.0	6.2	6.8	7.9	6.4	5.8	4.7	6.5	5.8	4.0
Mean Score 2018	6.10	5.8	6.3	7.6	7.1	6.3	5.7	4.1	6.5	5.8	4.6

Source: RTÉ-Universities General Election Exit Poll and RTE-Universities Abortion Referendum Exit Poll

votes (Sinnott 1995; Gallagher 2018). From a social class perspective, the most conservative value position is held by farmers with ABC1 voters displaying more liberal views.

Data from the RTÉ-Universities exit poll are used to investigate patterns at the referendum in more detail. The exit poll was carried out by the Behaviour and Attitudes polling company and 3,779 voters were surveyed at polling stations in a nationally representative sample. Three versions of the survey were used to maximise the information collection and the questions on the timing of vote choice were included in version two. To begin, voters were asked if they had changed their minds on abortion over the last five years. Twenty two percent reported that they had, while 76% said they had not (Don't Know (DK) = 2). Timing of vote questions pose reliability issues as voters may not always accurately recall when they arrived at their decision. As a consequence, a second version of the question was also asked which allowed voters to give more precise information on when they arrived at their voting decision and this information is presented in Table 1.2.

Three quarters of voters had already decided how they would vote before the referendum was called. The Citizens' Assembly

Table 1.2   When did you make up your mind about how you would vote in this referendum?

I always knew how I would vote	75.2
Following public disclosure of the Savita Halappanavar case	8.4
Following the recommendations of the Citizens' Assembly	1.3
Following the recommendations of the Oireachtas committee on the Eighth Amendment	0.7
During the referendum campaign	11.7
Don't recall	2.7
Total	100

Source: RTÉ-Universities Abortion Referendum Exit Poll

and the Oireachtas committee were important for only a very small number of voters, but the death of Savita Halappanavar was much more consequential with 8.4% of voters identifying this as a critical point when they made their vote decision. The data are consistent with the LeDuc (2002) schema for opinion change on fundamental value questions. Attitudes on the abortion issue had been changing for some time in Ireland with a majority of voters having made up their minds many years before the referendum was called.

The exit poll data also allows us to look at whether it was Yes or No voters that changed their minds and the data from Table 1.2 are tabulated by vote choice and presented in Table 1.3. No voters are somewhat more steadfast in their decision making with 80% always knowing how they would vote. The corresponding figure for Yes voters is 73%. The Savita Halappanavar case, the Citizens' Assembly and the Oireachtas committee moved more Yes voters than No voters, but in percentage terms, marginally more No voters made up their minds during the campaign.

Finally, Table 1.4 presents the data on the information that was influential for voters in making their decisions. Again this is tabulated by vote choice. The "experiences of people I know" and "Peoples' personal stories as covered in the media" are especially influential for Yes voters; they matter for No voters as well but on a much lesser scale. We know from earlier research that religious values were very important for No voters (Elkink et al. 2019) and this

Table 1.3 Timing of vote tabulated by vote choice

	Voted Yes	Voted No
I always knew how I would vote	73.3	79.6
Following public disclosure of the Savita Halappanavar case	10.7	2.9
Following the recommendations of the Citizens' Assembly	1.5	1.1
Following the recommendations of the Oireachtas committee on the Eighth Amendment	0.8	0.5
During the referendum campaign	11.2	12.9
Don't recall	2.6	2.9
TOTAL	100	100

Source: RTÉ-Universities Abortion Referendum Exit Poll

likely explains the very high percentage of No voters who indicated that "Other" reasons were influential in their decision making.

Campaigns have many functions, often summarised as priming, persuasion and mobilisation (Norris 2006). Priming refers to the ways in which some issues are given public airing during a campaign, while others are not: in effect, the agenda-setting power of a campaign. Mobilisation is focused on getting out the vote and focuses on how effective a campaign is in convincing voters that the issue being decided is important. The evidence presented in this section has focused on persuasion. It explored the timing of voter decision making. The evidence from the exit

Table 1.4 Factors influencing vote choice tabulated by vote choice

	Yes	No
Campaign posters	10	9
Direct contact with campaigners	7	6
The experiences of people I know	37	24
Peoples' personal stories as covered in the media	50	24
Other	18	38

Source: RTÉ-Universities Abortion Referendum Exit Poll

Note: Row percentages are for those who answered Yes on each item poll is clear: the vast majority of voters had arrived at their voting decision before the referendum campaign began. However, this should not be taken to imply that the campaign was irrelevant or marginal. Voter mobilisation was very strong in 2018, turnout was at its highest for a referendum in nearly 25 years and priming has not been considered.

Conclusion

The availability of abortion services has been a divisive political issue in Ireland for more than four decades. Civil society groups have dominated the politics of abortion while political parties and parliament have always been followers on the issue. The insertion of the pro-life clause in the constitution in 1983, far from settling the issue, precipitated an enduring political cleavage among conservatives and liberals, the balance of which had shifted significantly towards the liberal side by the early 21st century.

The changing value disposition of voters was given decisive airing in the result of the 2018 referendum. The scale of the Yes vote, on a high turnout, underscored the extent of the value change which had taken place between the first abortion vote in 1983 and the decision to repeal that anti-abortion clause in 2018. The analysis presented in this chapter highlights that political leaders lagged voters by some distance in relation to abortion. Three quarters of voters had made up their minds many years before the referendum and close to 10% made a decision on the abortion issue following public disclosure of the Halappanavar case in 2012. No conservative proposition on abortion achieved a majority vote after 1983 which suggests that the liberalising tendency has deep roots. Personal experiences and the testimony of those affected by abortion restrictions in Ireland were especially influential for Yes voters, while campaign activities were seen as persuasive by a very small proportion of voters.

Acknowledgements

Funding for the 2016 Irish National Election Study was provided by the School of Politics and International Relations at University College Dublin; the Department of Political Science at Trinity College Dublin; the Department of Government at University College Cork; the School of Politics, International Studies and Philosophy at Queen's University Belfast; the School of Law and Government at Dublin City University; the Oireachtas (Irish parliament); the Department of Justice and Equality; and Radio Teilifís Éireann.

Funding for the 2018 abortion referendum exit poll was provided by Radio Teilifís Éireann; the School of Politics and International Relations at University College Dublin; the College of Arts, Celtic Studies and Social Sciences at University College Cork; and the School of Communications at Dublin City University.

Note

1 Red C polls are published in the *Sunday Business Post* and are preferred in academic research because data is collected at monthly intervals throughout the year and the poll series had four data points for abortion. Data is also collected using random digit dialling of mobile phones and landlines.

TWO | Explaining repeal: a long-term view

Linda Connolly

Two thirds of the Irish electorate voted in 2018 to repeal the 8th Amendment to the constitution – a century after women first achieved the right to vote. The process of democratisation that began in 1918, extending rights to women in the arena of parliamentary representation, preceded democratisation in the arena of Irish women's reproductive rights and bodily integrity by 100 years. As feminist activists themselves recognised in 1918, the vote was a critical step for women in society but for many feminists at the time it also underlined the fact that the revolution was incomplete in key areas. The women's movement did not begin and end in 1918 with votes for women, it continued to demand change thereafter for many years after.

The campaign for reproductive autonomy emerged in Ireland after abortion was legalised in Britain in 1967 but it began with the clear need to legalise contraception first. In keeping with the theme of this collection, this chapter focuses on the tension that has long existed between feminism that works to progress reproductive rights from within the Irish State and institutional politics – alongside feminism that perceived a need for an autonomous and radical social movement that could bring a different kind of pressure to bear in a society. The achievement of repeal in 2018 is interconnected with a longer and broader history of feminist activism, in both these political spaces, that is multifaceted and premised on *difference* (Connolly 2003; Connolly and O'Toole

2005; Quilty et al. 2015). Feminism is one of the most important social movements that has mobilised in different forms since at least the 1860s in Ireland. It is a movement that is local, national and global, inherently complex and comprised of different positions on the emancipation of women in society that do not always gel and *nor should they*. Difference is the driving force and core energy of the women's movement – combined with the capacity to put *our* differences aside as needed in concerted campaigns – which was evident both in the campaign for suffrage in 1918 and in the recent campaign to repeal the 8th Amendment, a century later (Smyth 1992; Quilty et al. 2015). This chapter will trace the origins and development of the campaign to repeal the 8th Amendment to the Irish constitution. The central role of feminist activism will be connected to critical developments in the arena of Irish reproductive rights, including landmark court cases and controversies, from the 1970s to the present. It first traces the emergence of the contemporary Irish feminist movement in the 1970s and its activism on the issue of contraception. Next, it explores the history of Irish feminist activism on the issue of abortion from 1983 to the present day. It concludes by considering some of the tensions *within* the Irish feminist movement that shaped the repeal movement in 2018 and beyond.

1970s: the second wave and contraceptive activism

Feminist scholars in Ireland have demonstrated how, from at least the second half of the 19th century, numerous feminist organisations and individuals have maintained an active and diverse women's movement in the Irish context – even in periods when it was assumed feminism had 'disappeared' (Connolly 2003). The emergence of a 'second wave' of feminism in Ireland is generally connected to the emergence of several new women's organisations and networks on a national scale, throughout the 1970s, in particular. During the second wave, the Council for the Status of Women, now the National Women's Council, became the chief liberal feminist organisation in Ireland after an ad hoc coalition of established organisations successfully campaigned the government to set up a National Commission on the Status of Women. However, two other Dublin-based organisations also became particularly prominent in the public arena of Irish feminist politics in the 1970s, providing a forum for the development of a radical feminist perspective in Ireland, particularly in the arena of reproductive rights: the Irish Women's Liberation Movement (IWLM) which was formed in 1970 primarily by a small group of journalists, left wing and professional women; and the more radical Irishwomen United (IWU) which emerged in 1975 for a period of about 18 months (Connolly and O'Toole 2005). Alongside these prominent groups, several organisations, frequently in the form of small consciousness-raising groups, single issue campaigns or with the function of providing services for women also emerged. Many of these groups were formed by women who had left prominent radical organisations in the 1970s while others emerged more autonomously. IWU, for example, was the main catalyst for the formation of the Contraceptive Action Programme in 1976, the first Rape Crisis Centre in 1977 and the first Women's Right to Choose group in 1979.

The IWLM tended to engage in more expressive and spontaneous action than the corresponding ad hoc committee on women's rights. A matrix of informal radical feminist groups, some in the universities or the new suburban housing estates in Ireland, emerged throughout the country in the early 1970s quite independently of the more established women's groups, who were concentrating on lobbying for the First Commission on the Status of Women.

The original group of activists who formed the IWLM were considered extremely radical and aroused widespread interest.

In particular, their methods of protest were highly controversial. The distinctive character of the IWLM was related to the particular social composition of the founding group and the kind of strategies and ideologies employed. The IWLM was clearly influenced by the radical style of protest internationally in the new social movements of the 1960s (including the student, peace and civil rights movements). Radical feminist tactics in America had an influence on some of the founding members, some of whom were working there as journalists when second wave feminism emerged (Connolly 2003).

The IWLM incorporated diverse activists and ideas, including left wing and Republican women, women in the media (many of the founding group were journalists) and professional/ university-educated women. Some of the group encouraged a distinctive confrontational style of organisation and encouraged 'direct action'. The development of the civil rights movement in Northern Ireland in 1968 and the flowering of Republican, student and left-wing politics encouraged a new social movement network across Irish society in this period. The women from the left in the IWLM tended to be involved in other movements and politics (such as the occupation of the Hume Street Houses in 1969–70, the anti-Vietnam war demonstration of 1971, the People's Democracy organisation and the Civil Rights Movement). As a consequence, the IWLM knew how to organise radically and strategically. The IWLM's strategies included meeting weekly with a view to producing a set of demands which resulted in the manifesto *Chains or Change* (see for example, IWLM 1971). Other activities included consciousness-raising and the planning of confrontational direct-action tactics which resulted in the staging of a 'Contraceptive Train' to Belfast. In particular, a close relationship with the media was fostered.

The methods, writings and ideas of Anglo-American feminism were adapted to the particular circumstances of Irish women's lives in the early 1970s. In particular, consciousness-raising brought about shared knowledge of the reality of women's lived experience, still 'invisible' and unexplored in Irish public discourse at this time. 'Private' subjects such as fertility control and female sexuality entered the political arena and public debate in this period primarily through the writings of feminists in the newspapers and consciousness-raising groups. Consciousness-raising was introduced by activists in the IWLM who had experienced the American women's movement, in particular. Over time, it became a popular activity in radical women's groups nationally, including in small local groups that formed in suburban/urban areas and in universities. So far, we know little about the activities and impact of consciousness-raising groups outside of the prominent Dublin-based organisations like the IWLM in Ireland. In the US, for example, there was a consciousness-raising group in almost every area and it was extremely fashionable. It was out of these groups that many of the major English-speaking writings on radical feminism emerged.

A number of events propelled the IWLM into the public arena in a dramatic manner. The IWLM was invited to manage an entire programme of Ireland's most popular television chat show (The Late Late Show) in 1971. The appearance was intended to mark the official launch of the movement. The event generated widespread public reaction and the group's demands (outlined in *Chains or Change*) were fully reviewed in the media, as a result. The core demands of the IWLM included one family one house, removal of the marriage bar, equal pay, equal access to education, legal rights and, crucially, the availability of contraception.

The IWLM staged a mass meeting in response to the widespread coverage and subsequent attention received. A public meeting was held in the Mansion House, Dublin in April 1971. This event became another major turning point. Over 1,000 women attended, which was far in excess of the numbers expected. The demands of the movement were outlined and discussed. On the surface, there was overall consensus between the large audience of women that night. Following the meeting at the Mansion House, a plethora of women's liberation groups formed. Women's liberation was capturing the attention and energy of young educated women. It was also creating a new forum for consciousness-raising and debate among women in Ireland.

A consensus was reached in the IWLM that contraception was a crucial issue for Irish women's liberation (Connolly and O'Toole 2005). In the absence of contraceptives being legalised, any campaign for abortion on demand had to be delayed. The 'Contraceptive Train' was subsequently staged in May 1971. IWLM members, and many other women on the day, travelled to Belfast and brought contraceptives (of which the sale, import and advertisement was banned in the Irish Republic since the 1935 Censorship of Publications Act until partial legislation was introduced in 1979 to legalise contraception for married couples only) illegally and in a confrontational manner marched them through customs at Connolly Station, Dublin. After half an hour of chaos, the women were let through customs without being stopped, chanting and waving banners. The protest created huge international media attention and publicity. Negative reactions (both within the IWLM, other women's organisations and across the whole social spectrum of Irish society as a whole) were numerous. The 'Contraceptive Train' was a method of protest duplicated in later years, including in the 'Abortion Pill Train' in 2014. Different reproductive rights regimes north and south of the Irish border continue to shape feminist political strategies.

The radical women's movement expanded well beyond the original concerns of the IWLM founding group in this period. While a number of women's organisations had highlighted not dissimilar issues from the 1920s to the 1960s, the reaction created by the IWLM managed to alert Irish women to new international feminist demands in the 1970s. Some women's groups distanced themselves from what were extremely radical tactics in the context of Irish society in the 1970s. The 'undignified' nature of events like the 'Contraceptive Train' led a divergent constituency of activists to call for the IWLM to moderate its tone. The prominence of the IWLM, combined with the consolidation of the Council for the Status of Women in the early 1970s, provided a basis for the formation of several organisations. New groups formed and networked between 1970–1975, including: Action, Information, Motivation (1972), Adapt (1973), Women's Aid (1974), the Women's Progressive Association (subsequently the Women's Political Association, 1970), Ally (1971), Family Planning Services (1972), the Cork Federation of Women's Organisations (1972, representing seventeen local associations and responsible for opening the first Citizens Advice Bureau) and Cherish (1972). Feminist organisations developed into effective political lobby groups and provided practical women's services which were in increasing demand by Irish women throughout this period. Irish women who were not active in any feminist organisation in this period were also, therefore, 'silently' expressing their own liberation by availing of the range of services (many still illegal or else unrecognised by the State) established by pioneering feminists in the 1970s. In addition, over time the Council for the Status of Women took on board many of the campaigns and issues instigated by early radical feminists in Ireland, including contraception. After the breakup of the IWLM, it was not until 1975 that a women's liberation group comparable in impact to the IWLM emerged – Irishwomen United (IWU).

Irishwomen United (IWU) was formed by activists with a background in radical and socialist politics. IWU's membership encompassed a diverse grouping of left-wing philosophies, including, for instance, the Movement for a Socialist Republic, the Communist Party of Ireland, the Socialist Workers Movement, the Irish Republican Socialist Party and the International Lesbian

Caucus. The Working Women's Charter, drawn up by the Irish Transport and General Workers' Union, provided an organisational focus. In addition to the key demands of the IWLM, IWU added free contraception, self-determined sexuality, equal pay based on a national minimum wage and the establishment of women's centres. Although some activists in IWU were former members of the IWLM, IWU was, in many respects, a different type of organisation and recruited a new constituency of feminist activists to the radical Irish women's movement.

Irishwomen United held their first public conference in Liberty Hall on 8 June 1975. At that meeting, the principles of internal democracy and a communal approach to the administrative work of the group were explicitly adopted. *Banshee*, the group's magazine, had a rotating editorial committee. IWU's stated aims were focused on the need for an autonomous women's movement. While IWU used a similar repertoire of tactics and group-centred activities to the IWLM, this group was further politicised by events in the international women's movement. Inter-organisational documents, including discussion papers, position papers, workshop proceedings, letters and minutes of meetings provide evidence of vibrant ideological debate within the organisation. The group's agenda was a mixture of participatory democracy, direct action, consciousness-raising and political campaigns.

Organisational publications show that the demands of the group included state financed, community run, birth control clinics throughout the country, staffed by those trained to advise on all aspects of birth control. The group advocated that contraceptives of all types and attendant services should be provided free with full, free, sex education programmes in these clinics, in maternity hospitals and in schools. More fundamentally, the legal right to advocate contraception through literature, meetings and discussion was demanded, challenging the culture of censorship which had developed in Ireland since the Censorship of Publications Act (1935) was introduced. Between 1975 and 1977 the work of IWU was intense (see Cloatre and Enright 2017). For instance, the Contraceptive Action Programme was initiated by members of IWU in 1976 and became an important mobilising issue. Members of IWU were later involved with the setting up of the group that preceded the abortion referral/ information organisation, Open Line Counselling, in 1979, and also in setting up the first Rape Crisis Centre in 1977.

The radical aims of the Contraceptive Action Programme included:

1. Legislation of contraception and the end of restrictive legislation;
2. Availability of all methods to all who wish to use them;
3. Provision of contraception advice and counselling in all maternity and child welfare clinics;
4. Introduction of education programmes on sex, birth, contraception and personal relationships in schools and colleges;
5. Inclusion of methods of birth control in the training of doctors, nurses, health visitors, social workers and lay counsellors; and
6. Distribution of contraceptives free through Health Service Clinics and at a controlled minimum cost through general practitioners, pharmacies and specialised voluntary clinics (see Wicca 1977 quoted in Connolly 2003: 143).

While the activism of prominent radical organisations, notably the IWLM and IWU, had scaled down by the end of the 1970s, feminism had clearly not disappeared. Feminism had, however, diffused more widely as a political discourse and as a network of organisations mainstreaming in Irish society. While radical feminist organising became less prominent, at the same time, a range of issues, nurtured in the radical women's movement, had entered the public sphere and policy arena by the 1980s. The 'lid had been lifted' on a whole range of issues which had never been discussed in an open manner in the public sphere, including self-determined sexuality and reproductive rights, which could not be reversed despite the patriarchal response of the Church and State to these demands. The women's movement maintained activism in several areas despite the retreat of the general social movements of the sixties in this period and, in some sectors, grew in strength and impact by developing professional structures and formal leadership. The Council for the Status of Women expanded significantly in this period and the efforts of its affiliate organisations, such as the Women's Political Association, was gaining acceptance among Irish women. By the 1980s, greater co-operation between liberal and radical feminists also became possible in the face of organised opposition to the extending of laws on contraception and 'new right' politics – notably in the run up to and aftermath of an abortion referendum in 1983 that inserted a pro-life clause in the constitution. Contraception was fully legalised in the interim in 1985 in the aftermath of AIDS emerging as a new STI (see Enright and Cloatre 2018). Co-operation across the women's movement in the arena of reproductive rights was now concentrating on repealing the 8th.

1980s–1990s: repeal the 8th and its antecedents

In May 2018, a referendum to repeal the 8th Amendment was held. In November, the Minister for Health introduced the Regulation of the Termination of Pregnancy Bill in the Dáil (Irish parliament) to legalise abortion services in Ireland. This was undoubtedly an historic occasion in a state and society that had demonstrated a deeply troubled relationship with women who fall pregnant outside of marriage by institutionalising or criminalising them (see for example Fischer 2016). "Today we begin the job they have given us, of making the law that follows the repeal of the 8th Amendment and after 35 years in our constitution, in doing so, we are also making history", the Minister said.[1] History was made in the streets, in homes and in ballot boxes across the country by people, including politicians, who had campaigned "steadfastly for years".

History was already being 'made' in the arena of reproductive rights long before the 8th was introduced in 1983, as I have demonstrated above, both in a campaign for reproductive rights that had begun much earlier and through the silent, secretive actions of many thousands of Irish women who got themselves 'into trouble' as it was termed. Abortions were provided illicitly in Ireland, as documented in court prosecutions throughout the 20th century, and infanticide was commonplace (Ryan 1996). Over 100 Irish women were estimated to be dying annually from unsafe backstreet abortions in the 1930s, for instance. 'Extra marital' or unwanted pregnancy remained for decades a matter that was swept under the carpet or exported to be dealt with in Britain (Luibhéid 2013). The legalising of abortion in Britain in 1967 in an effort to abolish risky 'backstreet' procedures combined with the mobilisation of a second wave feminist movement demanding abortion rights in several countries were destined to provoke controversy and activism in Ireland (see Rossiter 2009). Although initial energy in feminist and liberal reproductive rights campaigns in Ireland from the early 1970s went into securing the legalisation of contraception first, the right to free, and safe, legal abortions was already a core stated demand of the feminist group Irishwomen United by 1976.

Although contraception was an initial focus in second wave feminism in Ireland, the political antecedents for legalising abortion in 2018 can be traced back to the 1970s. The principal strategies of the first Women's Right to Choose group, formed in late 1979, were the decriminalisation of abortion and the establishment of a feminist pregnancy counselling service. The first Irish Pregnancy Counselling Centre was set up in June 1980. Early in

1981 a conference on 'Abortion, Contraception and Sterilisation' was organised by activists at Trinity College Dublin. In March of that year, a public meeting was held at Liberty Hall to publicise the demands of the group and recruit members. Counter-pickets were mounted on the Liberty Hall meeting and the audience was antagonistic to the pro-choice platform.

The emergence of an organised right in Ireland, however, dates from before the formation of the Women's Right to Choose group. The Pro-Life Amendment Campaign had its foundations in the 1970s and was generally opposed to changes in the status of women that had occurred in a number of areas in the previous decade. Around the single issue of abortion, the campaign was launched on a rather quiet note in April 1981 and few political activists at the time could have realised the impact it would subsequently generate. Pro-choice activists began to realise the implications of the campaign after the Fianna Fáil wording of the proposed amendment was disputed and the campaign intensified. Gradually, various sections of Irish society became embroiled in a complex political debate, which culminated in a constitutional referendum in September 1983.

The pro-life movement thought it could successfully block pro-choice organisations from providing information and abortion referral services by winning a constitutional referendum. A pro-life clause in the constitution was considered the most successful way to guarantee the 'right to life of the unborn'. Right to choose groups, prominent journalists/media personalities, family planning clinic workers, students unions and other feminist activists tentatively formed an Anti-Amendment Campaign. Opposing the referendum was an extremely difficult task for a disparate group of this scale with a limited constituency and resources to fight a national referendum campaign.

After the 1983 referendum was lost, the campaigning focus of a small group of pro-choice activists within the women's movement shifted and became focused on the right to access information about legal abortion services *in another jurisdiction*. However, a subsequent series of legal cases taken through the courts against pro-choice services in Ireland drove abortion referral and information services *underground*. Sympathetic doctors, family planning practitioners and students' union officials continued to either provide written information on abortion services in other jurisdictions or directly referred women to Irish feminist information/referral services. Gradually, abortion information, in particular, became recognised as an integral feminist mobilising issue in the other sectors of the mainstream women's movement. The campaign was diverted into the right to *procure* information about abortion in another jurisdiction – a more acceptable demand to the wider mainstream constituency in the women's movement and to the general public.

The Women's Information Network was established in November 1987 as an underground, voluntary emergency non-directive helpline service for women with crisis pregnancies (Connolly 2003; Smyth 1992). The helpline was founded by a group of women appalled by the Hamilton ruling, which banned the dissemination of abortion information. It was launched with the support and assistance of the then Defend the Clinics campaign. Contact with British abortion clinics was particularly important, and the helpline volunteer group undertook continuous training in counselling skills and visited and monitored abortion clinics in Britain.

The relative ease of passage to Britain for a legal in-clinic abortion was undoubtedly a game changer for Irish women seeking a safe alternative to illegal abortions, but the dangers to women not in a position to travel became all the more apparent in the 1980s. Numerous reproductive tragedies and abortion have dominated Irish political debate since the 1980s. The death of fourteen-year-old Anne Lovett in childbirth alongside her stillborn baby in a grotto in County Longford in 1984 was a profound event. Joanne Hayes, a single mother, was falsely accused of a double infanticide in a tribunal of inquiry into what became known as the 'Kerry Babies' case in the same year. In a radio interview in 2018, *Irish Times* journalist Michael O'Regan stated on national radio, after the State apology to Joanne Hayes, that Ireland was "riddled with misogyny" in the 1980s (see also O'Regan 2018). Nell McCafferty referred to the divisive referenda on abortion and divorce in the 1980s as "a virtual civil war" (McCafferty 2016). More recently, in 2018, the Scally Report into a cervical smear test scandal in Ireland more recently suggested women's reproductive healthcare is characterised by "institutional misogyny" (see Loughlin et al. 2018).

By 1992, change of opinion was influenced by rulings in favour of abortion information and the right of Irish women to travel by the European Courts of Human Rights and Justice. Following the Hamilton ruling (1986), Open Door Counselling appealed to the European Court of Human Rights, of which Ireland is a signatory to the Human Rights Convention. In October 1992, the Court found that the order of the Irish courts was in breach of the Convention's information rights clause, Article 10:

> Everyone has the right to freedom of expression. This right shall include freedom to hold opinions and to receive and impart information and ideas without interference by public authority and without frontiers.

Open Door Counselling subsequently initiated proceedings to have the restraining order of the Supreme Court lifted in order to restore services. One of the most important turning points in the campaign occurred in 1992 when the Attorney General successfully sought a High Court injunction against 'Miss X', which prevented a fourteen-year-old girl, who had been raped, from travelling to England for a termination (see Smyth 1992).

A subsequent appeal to the Supreme Court lifted this injunction, and in its judgement found that Article 40.3.3 could actually *permit abortion* in certain circumstances:

> if it established as a matter of probability that there is a real and substantial risk to the life as distinct to the health of the mother, which can only be avoided by the termination of the pregnancy, that such a termination is permissible, having regard to the true interpretation of Article 40.3.3 of the constitution. (quoted in Girvin 1996)

The right to life of 'the unborn' was protected by Article 40.3.3 of the constitution introduced in 1983, however, in reality, its existence profoundly impacted women who could not leave Ireland because of stigma, shame, poverty or citizenship status but it also profoundly impacted women whose lives were at risk because no terminations were permissible in Irish maternity hospitals. In short, women died in Irish maternity hospitals because of the 8th Amendment. Individual women impacted by reproductive injustices have also been the subjects of a range of litigation in both Irish and international courts on abortion in Ireland. In the case of *A, B and C v Ireland* in 2010, for instance, the European Court of Human Rights found that Ireland had violated the European Convention on Human Rights by failing to provide an accessible and effective procedure by which a woman can have established whether she qualifies for a legal abortion under Irish law (see de Londras and Enright 2018). A number of cases related to whether an abortion was permissible in cases of fatal foetal abnormalities were taken. The story of P in December 2014 demonstrated the chaos that resulted from the 8th Amendment, which the courts confirmed served to deny women and their families' autonomy, consent and dignity in the case of maternal death prior to childbirth. P was pregnant and kept on a life support machine to deleterious effect and against the wishes of her family because of the 8th Amendment to the constitution; the details of the case are harrowing (Ibid.).

2018 and beyond: conclusion

Irish abortion law received worldwide attention when Savita Halappanavar died in 2012. She requested and was denied an abortion in an Irish maternity hospital while suffering from septicaemia during a miscarriage. Sadly, such a dreadful tragedy was predicted. Savita's death was a key turning point and brought thousands of protestors onto the streets, including a new generation of young women that campaigned extensively during the May 2018 referendum. The focus of the debate had shifted from the rights of mobile women with means forced to discontinue their unwanted pregnancies in Britain to the 8th being a life-threatening risk and danger to pregnant, immobile and incarcerated women in Irish maternity hospitals. Asylum seekers and women in direct provision centres were acutely impacted by the 8th Amendment (Holland 2013).

The 2018 referendum decisively repealed the 8th – a gigantic step in the politics of reproductive rights that first mobilised in the 1970s. But the concealed abortion stories of many thousands of pregnant Irish women will, of course, endure, having been buried, denied and silenced for decades.

In 2018, Ireland witnessed again a mobilisation on the scale of 1970s feminism which repealed the 8th Amendment. Schisms as one would expect emerged in this campaign with some activist groups preferring direct action to collaborating so closely with the Fine Gael-led government, establishment obstetricians and even celebrities. Politicians featured prominently on the stage at Dublin Castle when crowds gathered to quite rightly celebrate the result (see, for example, RTÉ 2018). It is clear, however, that an activist coalition, characterised by a tension between autonomous mobilisation outside the State whilst working within the

State, *ultimately* produced the end result. As Ireland moves into the implementation stage of legal abortion services in Irish institutions, political challenges remain and counter-right tactics are already evident in pro-life pickets staged on Irish hospitals providing services. The movement that emerged over three decades ago to establish reproductive choice and autonomy for Irish women will therefore necessarily *continue* and will remain interconnected with global and Northern Irish campaigns to *repeal* restrictions on abortion.

Note
1   See Health (Regulation of Termination of Pregnancy) Bill 2018: Second Stage debate, 4 October 2018.

THREE

"The only lawyer on the panel":
anti-choice lawfare in the battle for
abortion law reform

Fiona de Londras and Máiréad Enright

Lawyers played a very limited public role in the official civil society campaign for a Yes vote in the Irish constitutional referendum on repeal[1] of the 8th Amendment. However, the No campaign staked a claim to legal expertise and structured much of its advocacy around detailed, if often flawed, arguments rooted in conservative constitutional and statutory interpretation. In this paper, we frame the No side's reliance on law as part of a much longer practice of anti-abortion lawfare in Ireland, and interrogate the recent debates on the Health (Regulation of Termination of Pregnancy) Bill 2018 to reveal the persistence of anti-abortion lawfare post-repeal. We also point to the ways in which the new law on abortion in Ireland reinforces and re-instantiates the violence of the pre-repeal law, albeit in different and slighter forms, demonstrating the deeply embedded nature of anti-abortion and anti-choice rhetoric within our continuing language, law and political discourse of abortion. In doing so, we demonstrate that while repeal and the subsequent legalisation of abortion in Ireland are important breaks with a past abortion law regime, they do not yet reflect the new, emancipatory discourse of reproductive agency that might have been possible in the wake of repeal of the 8th Amendment (de Londras and Enright 2018).

Lawfare: an outline
In this paper, we discuss lawfare by anti-choice civil society actors in Ireland. Having origins in security contexts, 'lawfare' is a

neologism which describes the strategic use of law or law-making processes to achieve a political objective (see further Dunlap 2008). It encompasses both attempts to mobilise existing legal structures to achieve political aims, and attempts to reform law, or resist those reforms (Gloppen and St Clair 2012: 900). Gloppen and St Clair use the term 'social lawfare' to describe the use of law in the service of progressive social change (Ibid.: 907). Here, however, we are concerned with conservative lawfare by Irish anti-abortion activists, i.e. the use of law in the attempt to prevent legal access to abortion or, where legal access seems inevitable, to impose requirements and processes that substantially narrow it.

Law gives access to institutional power, particularly powers of decision and punishment. For Comaroff and Comaroff, 'lawfare' describes the appropriation of law's inherent violence to dominate and discipline colonised populations (2006: 30). Successful anti-choice lawfare subjects women to coercive force; it dominates women and pregnant people in their reproductive lives and punishes deviations from prescribed reproductive behaviour. It obstructs access to abortion care and proceduralises abortion in a way that continues its exceptionalisation as part of healthcare and reinforces stigma and shame. However, as Comaroff and Comaroff write, lawfare obscures violence (2009: 37). Law can clothe violence in state legitimacy; in "duly enacted penal codes . . . charters and mandates and warrants . . . norms of engagement" which "impose a sense of order . . . by means of violence rendered legible, legal and legitimate by [the state's] own sovereign word" (Comaroff and Comaroff 2006: 30). In anti-abortion lawfare, law obscures violence by presenting it as 'mere' process or procedure or even as legal protection for 'vulnerable' women and pregnant people.

Lawfare strategies are diverse, but always intentional. As we will show in the remainder of this paper, in the last 35 years anti-choice legal mobilisation in Ireland has encompassed referendum campaigns, litigation and participation in legislative debates.

While we mainly focus here on anti-choice lawfare in and after the May 2018 referendum on the 8th Amendment, we will start by outlining the history of anti-abortion lawfare in Ireland.

The Irish anti-choice movement: a short history of lawfare
The 8th Amendment was itself the product of anti-choice lawfare. In recent work, John L. Comaroff has used the term "theo-legality" to describe conservative religious actors' engagement with state law. In an argument which is useful for our understanding of conservative Catholic anti-choice attachment to Irish law, he notes how religious groups interpolate themselves into law in order to extend the reach of their own teachings across the wider community (2009: 53). The 1983 referendum to place the 8th Amendment into the Constitution is an excellent illustration of this phenomenon.

The Pro-Life Amendment Campaign (PLAC) was founded in 1981 and quickly became what Ursula Barry has called "the most powerful campaigning group in recent Irish history" (1998: 57–8). An umbrella group of fourteen organisations including the Society for the Protection of the Unborn Child (SPUC), Family Solidarity, the Knights of Columbanus and Opus Dei, it led the campaign for the insertion of the 8th Amendment. Exercising a degree of influence no longer held by 'religious' stakeholders in Ireland, PLAC took advantage of considerable political instability in Ireland to extract promises from Fine Gael and Fianna Fáil that the proposition would be put before the people.[2] Its campaigning was famously based on a potent mixture of theocratic anti-contraception and anti-abortion dogma and post-colonial natalist nationalism (see Fletcher 1998; 2001; Smyth 2005). Having extracted political promises to hold a referendum on a 'pro-life' amendment, it designed the amendment to guard against future legalisation of abortion, either through judicial activism or political will (see Fitzgerald 2014). PLAC was undoubtedly influenced by

American anti-choice lawfare. From 1979, for example, Americans United for Life conducted a public engagement campaign in Ireland in support of anti-choice law.[3] Although abortion had been illegal in Ireland since 1861,[4] the demand for further action was framed in legal terms. William Binchy famously argued that the Irish Supreme Court's discovery of an entitlement to access contraception within marriage[5] would lead in time to an Irish *Roe v Wade* (Hug 1998; Binchy 1977: 333–5). In the USA, anti-choice campaigners had unsuccessfully sought to undo *Roe* with a constitutional 'Human Life Amendment' (Lynch 1974: 303). Ireland had the opportunity to pre-emptively obstruct any *Roe*-like judicial activism by inserting an amendment prohibiting abortion. While other legal arguments about the possible impact of the amendment emerged during the referendum,[6] this imperative towards 'protecting' against the discovery of a right to access abortion was presented as the primary legal argument in favour of inserting the 8th.[7] The campaign itself was underpinned by a deep religiosity and Catholic conservatism, all forming part of a larger set of conservative representations "about woman's role and woman's place" in Ireland in which "we were shown clearly what that was. It was to be invisible" (McCafferty 1984).

Inaugurating a theme of "legal certainty" which remains important to this day, the Attorney General Peter Sutherland had warned against the wording eventually put to the people, noting its vagueness and likely incompatibility with women's internationally protected human rights. In the process of legislating to have a referendum, a confusing and ineffective debate about alternative constitutional texts ensued. Fine Gael's attempt to change the wording (to read 'Nothing in this Constitution shall be invoked invalidating a provision of a law on the grounds that it prohibits abortion') failed (Fitzgerald 2014). Instead, the wording proposed by Fianna Fáil, but effectively written by PLAC, was put before the people. In the end, it was passed by a two-to-one majority, on a turn-out of 53%.

As the then-Taoiseach put it "[t]he campaign for the amendment was conducted on emotional lines and almost completely without regard to the actual issues at stake . . . The ambiguities of the . . . wording were either ignored or were rejected without serious discussion by its supporters" (Ibid.; see also Connolly 2001).

The 8th Amendment was the first and most significant exercise of lawfare by anti-abortion campaigners in Ireland, but it was not the last. Not satisfied with the insertion of the 8th, anti-abortion campaigners organised to take a series of important cases in which they persuaded the courts to place the most restrictive interpretation possible on the 8th (see Jackson 1992; de Londras 2015) This was achieved through two extremely important strategic lawfare moves. The first was to establish that, given its vulnerability and its constitutional position, the foetus required constitutional protection. However, because the foetus could not itself take a case, and because its 'parent' might well be the person who posed the risk to the maintenance of its constitutional rights, persons unconnected with the foetus could litigate on its behalf in order to vindicate its rights. This was established in *SPUC v Coogan*,[8] a case taken by a central player in the Pro-Life Amendment Campaign: the Society for the Protection of the Unborn Child. As a result of this case, interested third parties could bring strategic cases to limit pregnant people's rights and autonomy in the name of foetal rights.

The same was not true, incidentally, of attempts to vindicate the constitutional rights of pregnant people: cases of this kind required individual litigants and as might be expected, few women were willing or able to step into this breach. Where pregnant women needed abortion care, they were usually too focused on making the necessary arrangements to raise funds and travel to the UK, or (understandably) anxious about adverse publicity and the maintenance of their privacy, to try to enforce their rights in the High Court. Although some cases did arise, these were largely where pregnant people were in state care or incapacitated by extreme ill-health, or were cases taken to international forums subsequent to accessing abortion care abroad.[9]

SPUC v Coogan meant that activities by agencies or organisations (such as women's health clinics) that worked to mitigate the worst effects of the 8th Amendment could be targeted with litigation. As a result, the provision of information about abortion (including abortion clinics in the UK) was prohibited and pro-choice activists – from students unions to women's health counselling services – were dragged through national and European courts.[10] Within a decade of the 8th Amendment's insertion into the Irish Constitution, the mixture of the provision and the associated litigation had succeeded in making pregnancy a constitutional state of exception from which a pregnant person could not escape without illegality, expense, travel and isolation. Abortion was highly stigmatised even though thousands of women based in Ireland actually accessed abortion care in England and Wales every year.[11] Later in the life of the amendment, anti-abortion activists used more minor lawfare tactics, such as 'stings', to test pro-choice organisations' compliance with the strict abortion law (see Duffy et al. 2018).

Some constitutional softening did come from 1992 onward, in particular, as a result of *Attorney General v X*, which exposed some of the brutalities of the 8th Amendment.[12] In *X*, the Supreme Court confirmed that the 8th Amendment allowed for abortion access where there was a "real and substantial risk to the life" of the pregnant person. Controversially, the court held that this could include a risk of suicide. While the first of these propositions was quite in line with what PLAC and anti-abortion activists understood the 8th Amendment to mean,[13] the latter was attacked as an unjustified and unjustifiable judicial adjustment of the 8th and perversion of the will of the people. The views of William Binchy are illustrative. Writing in the *Irish Times*, he said:

The Supreme Court . . . has introduced an abortion regime
of wide-ranging dimensions, beyond any effective control
or practical limitation . . . In practice, no prosecution of an
abortionist will have any real prospect of success if the woman
seeking an abortion has threatened suicide. (Binchy 1992: 13)

Shortly after that, the campaign to have the *X Case* reversed by
an express exclusion of suicide took shape, and referenda were
twice proposed (and twice rejected) to this end: in 1992 and again
in 2002. In the 2002 referendum, not only was there an attempt to
reverse *X* but also to have a piece of legislation 'embedded' in the
Constitution so that not only the constitutional position but the
statutory provisions giving effect to it would be set in constitutional
stone (see de Londras 2015). Indeed, the Bill proposed to (and
rejected by) the people in 2002 had a zombie-like existence, reap-
pearing in large part as the Protection of Life During Pregnancy
Act 2013. Lawfare about 'suicide' continued in the debates on that
2013 Act, which finally gave statutory effect to the finding in *X*.
In the debates on that Act, making abortion available where there
was a real and substantial risk of suicide was deeply controversial,
and anti-abortion advocates argued that it fundamentally undermined the constitutional protection of foetal life. For example,
Brian Walsh TD claimed that the suicide provision would "defile
the Statute Book with the absurd premise that the suicidality of
one human being can be abated by the destruction and killing
of another", while others argued that it would "open the floodgates to widespread abortion" (Eamon O'Cuiv) and "normalise
suicidal ideation" (Lucinda Creighton). In the Act itself, suicide
was treated differently to other risks to life, and pregnant people
had to undergo far more extensive, intrusive and traumatising
'procedures' to provide entitlement to abortion in such cases (see
Murray 2016). Although lawfare had not succeeded in undoing *X*,
it had succeeded in infecting parliamentary discourse and legislative provisions with a deep suspicion of suicidality and thus

continued to ensure that the 8th Amendment exercised as tight a grip on women's reproductive agency as could be imagined, even in situations of severe mental ill-health.

After *X*, new constitutional provisions were inserted to ensure that pregnant people had a right to information (thus undoing in part some of the post-1983 lawfare litigation) and that the 8th did not undermine the general right to travel to access services lawfully available elsewhere, including abortion. However, information about abortion remained highly regulated: legislation required it to be non-directive, doctors could not in any way assist their patients, for example, by making referrals for care in another country (even in very complex cases such as fatal foetal anomalies)[14] and the state did nothing to assist women who travelled for abortion. Indeed, in the important case of *Amanda Mellet v Ireland*, the UN Human Rights Committee recognised that the burdens of travel and the lack of assistance from the state, including the unavailability of bereavement counselling for people who 'travelled' in cases of fatal foetal anomaly, was such as to violate the right to be free from torture, inhuman and degrading treatment and punishment under the International Covenant on Civil and Political Rights.[15]

Anti-choice actors and lawfare in the 2018 No campaign

These patterns, and the 'theo-legality' of the anti-abortion lobby in Ireland, continued in the 2018 referendum campaign. The main organisational actors in the No campaign were Love Both (founded 2016) and Save the 8th (founded 2017). Love Both has close associations with the Pro-Life Campaign, which inherited the mantle of the Pro-Life Amendment Campaign in 1992. This organisation thus had a long history and within its predecessor organisation had developed a substantial group of lawyers engaged in anti-abortion activity. Although founded in 2007, Save the 8th also had impeccable anti-abortion credentials. It was closely associated with the Life

Institute, an offshoot of the militant pro-life organisation Youth Defence, which has been prominent in Irish abortion politics since the 1990s. Beyond these actors, members of the Iona Institute, a Catholic think-tank founded in 2007, were also prominent on the No side. Although overseas pro-life activism had an undoubted role in the campaign to retain the amendment, particularly at the stage of the Citizens' Assembly,[16] this was less visible in public activities by the time of the main referendum campaign.

Many of the key advocates for a No vote, most of whom were women, such as Cora Sherlock (Love Both), Caroline Simons (Love Both), Maria Steen (Iona Institute) and Senator Ronán Mullen were qualified, if not practicing, lawyers. They often identified as such in the public domain, making much of their legal knowledge to claim a kind of expertise that substantiated their arguments. For example, in the first main television debate of the referendum on the Claire Byrne show on RTÉ, Maria Steen repeatedly reinforced her arguments with the phrase we use in the title of this chapter, reminding viewers that she was "the only lawyer on the panel". William Binchy was also involved as an advisor to Love Both, although he participated less publicly in the formal referendum campaign than Simons, Steen and Sherlock. Instead, he mostly limited his public engagement to a series of letters to the *Irish Times*, often focused on technical claims about the alleged implications of the proposed post-repeal legislation for foetal life.[17]

In the latter half of the referendum campaign, barrister and Love Both activist Ben O'Floinn founded Lawyers for Retain. Its job appeared to be to echo, and confer legal gloss on, arguments already established by the No campaign rather than to develop a new one, and to reinforce the construction of the 8th Amendment as a guardian, rather than a violator, of rights. It established a website (www.rights.ie) providing a brief guide to the referendum. It issued two statements, both of which were signed by senior lawyers in the anti-abortion movement and former High Court judges including Aindrias O'Caoimh, Iarfhlaith O'Neill (formerly a member of the Pro-Life Amendment Campaign) and Bryan McMahon. These 'monumental' interventions were used by Save the 8th to warn that "the public had a choice: to trust Simon Harris, or to trust experienced lawyers and judges".[18]

The prominence of lawyers on the No side perhaps necessarily meant that much of the core argumentation advanced against repeal was couched in legal or *quasi*-legal terms. However, as we have already shown, the No side's parent organisations have a long history of anti-abortion lawfare, much of which was remarkably successful in keeping abortion stigmatised, shameful and hidden in Ireland for three and a half decades. No wonder, then, that the anti-reform campaign retained a focus on law in its arguments around repeal: law had proven itself a powerful and effective weapon in its hands. Even though it had not prevented abortion entirely, it was perceived positively to have 'saved hundreds of thousands of lives', notwithstanding (or, rather, as a result of) the excessive burdens it placed on women.[19]

Importantly, law was also an avenue for the secularisation of anti-abortion arguments and narratives. In the 2010s, the anti-abortion campaign could not rely on arguments of religion, religiosity or sanctity to persuade the electorate of the moral superiority of the 8th Amendment over alternative approaches. This was clear from polling done by Amnesty International Ireland, which suggested that only a small percentage of the electorate was influenced by religion in its approach to abortion (see RED C 2015; Reidy, this volume). Similarly, a large sample analysis of the public submissions to the Citizens' Assembly shows that religion played an extremely limited explicit role in anti-abortion narratives progressed by members of the general public (de Londras and Markicevic 2018). Although many of those involved in the No campaign did have publicly declared connections with Catholicism (e.g. Steen, whose association with the Iona Institute indicated such), their arguments were not rooted in religiosity. Rather, well-documented secularising moves from the international anti-abortion movement were in evidence (see Brown 2009). Rather than God, they talked about the security from (imagined) pro-abortion political whim offered by a constitutional protection of foetal life; rather than the sanctity of unborn life they focused on the dignity of 'preborn disabled children' which only a near-absolute ban on abortion could protect.[20]

During the referendum, the No campaign advanced some key lawfare arguments: (1) repeal would open the floodgates to 'unlimited abortion'; (2) the post-repeal law would be 'among the most liberal' in the world; (3) the foetus would be left with no legal protection whatsoever; (4) there would be no protection for 'unborn disabled children'; and (5) medical practitioners would be forced to participate in the provision of abortion against their consciences and their human rights. Advocates would dramatically hold the proposed General Scheme of the Health (Regulation of Termination of Pregnancy) Bill up in front of Yes campaigners in television debates and ask them to identify where exactly in the Scheme it said that abortion on the basis of disability was 'banned'. They would quote the definition of termination of pregnancy from the Scheme as if it were somehow shocking that abortion was being defined as a medical or surgical procedure intended to end foetal life. Misleading analogies to the Abortion Act 1967 were used to suggest that Ireland would become 'as bad if not worse' than 'England' when it came to rates of abortion, especially in cases of diagnosis of foetal anomaly. Bringing a heavily highlighted and marked-up copy of the General Scheme to public debates, radio and TV studios became a dramatic set piece of the No campaign's lawyers; they were determined to make this campaign about law and legality, presumably relying on their well-worn pattern of construing reproductive agency as being about law rather than about life. All of these claims were misleading, often in what seemed to be calculated ways (see About the 8th).[21] Nevertheless, they were proposed by people who had already made claims to legal authority through their professional and educational backgrounds (see Fletcher 2018 and Enright 2018).

Ultimately, these techniques were unsuccessful; the referendum passed with an overwhelming majority and the exit polls suggested that the campaign itself had had only a marginal impact on voter intention (RTÉ-Universities 2018). However, if anti-choice advocates were seeking to play a 'long game', then the debates on the Health (Regulation of Termination of Pregnancy) Bill 2018 suggest they may well have been as successful as could be imagined in the face of such a strong level of support for repeal. As we will show in the next section, those debates were influenced by lawfare. The No side's technique of focusing on the General Scheme during the referendum seems to have had the effect of identifying (or at least to have added to the political inclination to treat) that Scheme as almost unmovable. In other words, it was treated as a text on which voters had effectively cast their ballots in the referendum so that its core elements could not be revisited during the legislative debates that followed repeal. In the Second Stage speeches, for example, many politicians who campaigned against repeal, as well as some of those who campaigned in favour, stressed the importance of delivering on, and not substantially deviating from, the General Scheme as put before the people in the final legislation.[22] This was so even in respect of elements of the Scheme (such as the mandatory waiting period, for example) that clearly ran against the very strong pro-choice sentiment reflected in the referendum result.[23]

Lawfare in the debates on the Health (Regulation of Termination of Pregnancy) Act 2018

Anti-choice TDs and senators proposed amendments to the Bill at all stages of the process, ensuring the persistence of the ideologies that underpinned the 8th and which operated like "a weed, which threatens to pop up all over the place in the new garden that we have worked so hard to clean up" (Fletcher 2018). The amendments were essentially the same across the Dáil and the Seanad and across all stages of the Bill's passage, albeit some minor (mostly technical) changes that were made here and there. In short, these amendments (many of which seem to have been substantially influenced by techniques developed by Americans United for Life, see Enright 2018b) related to the 'protection of infants born alive'; the amelioration of 'foetal pain'; the 'dignified disposal of foetal remains'; mandatory ultrasounds that a pregnant person must be given an opportunity to view; express prohibitions on abortion 'sought because of' sex, race or disability; so-called information and informed consent amendments; extensive data-gathering obligations including on the ethnicity, marital status and pregnancy history of people seeking abortion; parental notification requirements; a provision that only abortions undertaken where there is a risk to the pregnant person's life would be paid from public monies; and substantial extensions to the conscientious objection provision.[24] The discourse around these amendments in both Houses of the Oireachtas was saturated in abortion mythology, patronising and patriarchal language and sometimes deeply offensive statements about women, reproductive autonomy and reproductive life.[25]

None of these amendments were successful; all were rejected and in many cases they provoked hurt and sometimes angry responses from other parliamentarians who considered that their proposers were attempting to 'rerun the referendum', to shame and punish women, and to impose unjustifiable burdens to accessing care. Anti-choice engagement in legislative debates was not only motivated by this communicative impulse, but was highly instrumentalist. By seeking to demonstrate alleged discursive inequities in rights discourse, anti-choice filibustering to delay the passage of abortion legislation, for example, is as much a part of anti-choice lawfare as is anti-choice constitutional meaning-making (McIvor 2018). Although they denied filibustering, that was precisely the effect of anti-choice politicians' engagement with the Bill. In large part, it does not seem that their amendments were proposed in any reasonable expectation of success; this was sometimes expressly acknowledged by proposers, and even where voice votes were overwhelming against the amendments, or where technical errors with the amendments had been identified, meaning that they could not be supported,[26] it was standard practice to call for a full vote (which takes anything from 2 to more than 10 minutes of parliamentary time, depending on the House and the type of 'votáil' in question) and amendments were almost always pressed.

It is hard to avoid the sense that the proposal, debate and pressing of these amendments were intended to inscribe shaming and stigmatising narratives into the debate, to re-take control of the narrative of abortion law reform in Ireland, particularly with a view to future attempts to amend the law, and to use up time and energy in the parliamentary debates. The amendments sent a clear signal that, as Senator Rónán Mullen put it at the eventual passage of the law: "Today is not the end of the pro-life movement. Today is the beginning of a new phase in its work."[27] The signal that these amendments sent out was very clear: "Having lost the referendum battle, they [were] scrambling for legislative means to retain a fetocentric abortion law in Ireland, and to ensure continued state interference in pregnant people's medical care, often through hyper-medicalisation, or corrupted medicalisation of abortion care" (Enright 2018a). There is little to suggest that this will change in the future. Furthermore, anti-choice politicians' imposed delays heaped pressure on pro-choice politicians to withdraw their own amendments, and to support the minister in getting his legislation through the Oireachtas.

Siri Gloppen distinguishes between lawfare (formal engagement with law-making institutions, particularly courts) and 'rights talk' (discursive use of legal concepts and production of legal knowledge and meaning outside of those institutional spaces, including in the media) (Gloppen and St. Clair 2012). However, anti-choice participation in recent legislative debates demonstrates that the two are tightly entwined. Following the referendum, as anti-choice actors lost political influence, much of their engagement in the debates was reduced to 'rights talk'. This did not mean that it was useless; although they could no longer bring about legal change directly, anti-choice legislators used their platform to continue to shape wider public discourse, on the law itself and on their own place as legal actors, through those amendments repeatedly proposed, debated and pressed throughout almost all stages of the legislative process. As Méadhbh McIvor writes, by engaging with pro-choice legal discourse, and losing, anti-choice activists solidify their identity as underdogs to a political elite (McIvor 2018). This is very clearly in evidence in the parliamentary debates on the 2018 Act, and well demonstrated by this response by anti-choice TD Mattie McGrath in a debate on a 'parental notification' amendment:

> I will not be lectured here about being anti-choice. We are not one bit anti-choice. We are pro-life and proud of it . . . We have been accused of filibustering. The records will show we did not, do not and will not. We are moving amendments that we tabled with good intentions . . . It is our right. Do we want it to be totally anti-democratic? We are supposed to be anti-choice. What about the anti-democratic Deputies who want to silence us? They want to silence the more than 730,000 people and the many thousands who have stated in polls since that they have concerns.[28]

Conclusion: the impact of anti-choice lawfare on liberal legal discourse

Anti-choice TDs' engagements in the debates on the Health (Regulation of Termination of Pregnancy) Bill 2018 demonstrate well-worn techniques of anti-abortion lawfare and have a firm provenance in the almost-four decades of abortion lawfare that preceded them in Ireland. These legislative engagements stretched across jurisdictions, reaching for techniques and tactics employed elsewhere. In spite of the enormous vote for change in how reproductive agency is understood and enabled by law, these anti-abortion interventions managed to shape the 2018 legal and political discourses on abortion law reform, continuing to exceptionalise abortion as something distinct from healthcare, uniquely or particularly morally difficult, and requiring wholly new and more burdensome regulatory frameworks than other healthcare procedures. In doing so, they laid the groundwork for future lawfare. The amendments, ideas, language and discursive turns evident in the almost-three months of debate on the Bill will, we expect, reappear and recur repeatedly, maybe even as early as 2020 when we expect legislation to create safe access or buffer zones around locations where abortion care is provided to be introduced.

As well as this, they removed the space – in temporal terms, but also in political terms – to critique the new abortion legislation. That legislation falls substantially short of best medical and legal practice, of human rights standards and arguably of the expectations and sentiments of the overwhelming pro-choice vote that removed the 8th Amendment. It exceptionalises abortion through the mandatory waiting period. It over-medicalises abortion, so that only GPs can prescribe medical abortion, even in very early pregnancy, although nurse practitioners or midwives could easily be trained to do so. It imposes an unjustifiably high threshold for access to abortion after 12 weeks. It asserts an extensive and seemingly meaningful criminalisation of abortion, including assisting someone to access abortion pills outside of the law. These provisions, all in their own ways, reinscribe the exceptionalism and stigma of the 8th Amendment, even in this post-repeal reality (see Enright et al. 2018; Fletcher et al. 2018; de Londras et al. 2018).

Continuing pre-repeal patterns of marginalising women and pregnant people, during the parliamentary debates on the abortion legislation, no attention was given to the constitutional rights of pregnant people (see also de Londras and Enright 2018). Nobody asked whether the Bill actually vindicated women's rights to privacy, bodily integrity and freedom from torture, inhuman and degrading treatment or punishment. All space for emancipatory discourses on abortion and reproductive agency disappeared into a potent mixture of political inertia by the main parties, which seemed determined simply to pass something very close to the draft legislation published during the referendum and thus 'deliver' on the mandate given in the referendum, and abortion lawfare, which swallowed the time and space for meaningful debate and put pressure on pro-choice politicians to get the law enacted in order to make abortion available, rather than continue to press for improvements. Anti-abortion politicians may not have written the provisions of the law, but they set the frame within which it was passed.

Notes

1 We say 'repeal' here, but it is more accurate to say 'repeal and replace', since the 8th Amendment was replaced with the 36th Amendment.

2 Article 46 of the Constitution provides that amendment is permissible by referendum only, and no popular initiative is permitted; rather a referendum must be initiated by government.

3 See e.g. https://aulaction.org.

4 Offences Against the Person Act 1861.

5 *McGee v Attorney General* [1974] IR 284.

6 See, for example, the debate between William Binchy and Mary Robinson on the *Today Tonight* programme on the day of the 8th

Amendment referendum for a neat summary of these arguments about legal impact. Available on YouTube https://youtu.be/GLWnoQjTNiw.

7 See, for example, the lecture of leading campaigner John O'Reilly to the Protect Life in All nations (PLAN) conference of Rome in September 1983, quoted in Hesketh 1990 and O'Reilly 1992.

8 [1989] I.R. 734.

9 *Attorney General v X* [1992] 1 I.R. 1; *PP v HSE* [2014] IEHC 622; *A. and B. v EHB and C* [1997] IEHC 176; *D v HSE* Unreported High Court May 2007, McKechnie J; *A, B and C v Ireland* [2011] 53 E.H.R.R; *Mellet v Ireland* [9 June 2016] UN Human Rights Committee Decision CCPR/C/116/D/2324/2013; *Whelan v Ireland* [12 June 2017] UN Doc CCPR/C/119/D/2425/2014.

10 See, for example, *Attorney General (SPUC) v Open Door Counselling & Well Woman Centre Ltd* [1988] I.R. 93; *SPUC v Grogan* [1989] I.R. 753.

11 This was also true prior to the insertion of the 8th Amendment; around 35,000 women were estimated to have accessed abortion in England and Wales between 1970 and 1983 (see Whitty 1993).

12 [1992] 1 IR 1.

13 In this it aligned with the application of the Catholic principle of double effect to the 'abortion' context, according to which the death of a foetus as an unintended consequence of medical treatment undertaken to save the life of a pregnant woman is not considered abortion (see McIntyre 2014; Whitty 1993).

14 See generally Access to Information (Services outside the State for Termination of Pregnancy) Act 1995.

15 *Mellet v Ireland* [9 June 2016] UN Human Rights Committee Decision CCPR/C/116/D/2324/2013.

16 For example, Women Hurt was invited to present to the Citizens' Assembly and on 5 March 2017 was represented by Dr Anthiny Levatino, a prominent anti-abortion physician based in New Mexico, USA.

17 See, for example, letters from William Binchy published on 5 May 2018, 1 May 2018, 26 April 2018, 24 March 2018.

18 Save the 8th. 2018. *Intervention by Judges "monumental"* [Press release]. 11 May 2018. www.save8.ie/intervention-by-judges-monumental-save-the-8th/.

19 See, for example, the exchange between Ruth Coppinger TD and William Binchy in the Joint Oireachtas Committee on the 8th Amendment in which Binchy maintained that in his eyes the 8th Amendment had been a success as it had prevented abortion in Ireland. Joint Oireachtas Committee on the 8th Amendment of the Constitution. 2017. *Debate, Wednesday, 4 October 2017.* Available at: www.oireachtas.ie/ga/debates/debate/joint_committee_on_the_eighth_amendment_of_the_constitution/2017-10-04/2/.

20 See, for example, Binchy 2018 and his further letters to the editor of that same newspaper published on 25 January 2018, 26 April 2018, 1 May 2018, 5 May 2018, stressing that even the General Scheme of

the proposed post-repeal law – which did not include non-fatal foetal diagnosis as a ground for permissible abortion – would "authorize the intentional ending of the lives of disabled babies" (5 May 2018).

21 de Londras, F. and Enright, M. 2018. Questions and Answers., *About the 8th*. www.aboutthe8th.com.

22 Second stage debates took place on 4, 16, 17, 18, and 23 October 2018. All debates on the Bill are gathered together and can be accessed here: www.oireachtas.ie/en/bills/bill/2018/105/?tab=debates.

23 For comprehensive critiques of these elements of the Bill see the position papers developed by a sub-group of Lawyers for Choice (Enright et al. 2018; Fletcher et al. 2018; de Londras et al. 2018).

24 Amendment No 98 at Committee Stage (Dáil Éireann); Amendment No 38 at Report Stage (Dáil Éireann); Amendment No 35 at Committee Stage (Seanad Éireann); Amendment No 99 at Committee Stage (Dáil Éireann); Amendment No 37 at Report Stage (Dáil Éireann); Amendment No 36 at Committee Stage (Seanad Éireann); Amendment No 101 at Committee Stage (Dáil Éireann); Amendment No 59 at Report Stage (Dáil Éireann); Amendment No 53 at Committee Stage (Seanad Éireann); Amendment No 33 at Report Stage (Seanad Éireann); Amendment No 100 at Committee Stage (Dáil Éireann); Amendment No 44 at Report Stage (Dáil Éireann); Amendment No 46 at Committee Stage (Seanad Éireann); Amendment No 27 at Report Stage (Seanad Éireann); Amendment No 81 at Committee Stage (Dáil Éireann); Amendment No 28 at Report Stage (Dáil Éireann); Amendment No 24 at Committee Stage (Seanad Éireann); Amendment No 146 at Committee Stage (Dáil Éireann); Amendments No 46, 46a at Report Stage (Dáil Éireann); Amendment No 44 at Committee Stage (Seanad Éireann); Amendments No 141, 142, 144 at Committee Stage (Dáil Éireann); Amendments No 43a, 43b at Report Stage (Dáil Éireann); Amendments No, 43 42 at Committee Stage (Seanad Éireann); Amendment No 25 at Report Stage (Seanad Éireann); Amendment No 145 at Committee Stage (Dáil Éireann); Amendment No 45 at Report Stage (Dáil Éireann); Amendment No 45 at Committee Stage (Seanad Éireann); Amendment No 26 at Report Stage (Seanad Éireann); Amendment No 13 at Committee Stage (Dáil Éireann); Amendments No 61, 62, 64, 65 at Report Stage (Dáil Éireann); Amendment No 1 at Report Stage (Seanad Éireann); Amendments No 147, 148, 149, 152, 158, 159, 160, 163 at Committee Stage; Amendments No 47, 48, 51, 55 at Report Stage (Dáil Éireann); Amendments No 47, 48, 49, 50, 52 at Committee Stage (Seanad Éireann); and Amendments No 28, 30, 31, 32 at Report Stage (Seanad Éireann).

25 Lawyers4Choice catalogued the debates on the Bill through its Twitter account where a substantial account of the debates is to be found: https://twitter.com/Lawyers4Choice.

26 See, for example, the debate on Amendment No 45 at Report Stage in
    Dáil Éireann, 4 December 2018.
27 Report and Final Stages, Seanad Eireann, 13 December 2018.
28 Debate on Amendment No 45 at Report Stage in Dáil Éireann, 4
    December 2018.

FOUR | Abortion pills in Ireland and beyond: what can the 8th Amendment referendum tell us about the future of self-managed abortion?

Sydney Calkin

Introduction

For women living under Ireland's abortion ban, the practical availability of abortion was generally a factor of financial resources, social networks and the ability to travel abroad to England. Over the past ten years, the abortion access strategies of Irish women have been transformed by access to medication abortion pills ordered online and shipped (indirectly) to their homes. Whereas 'backstreet abortion' is historically associated with illicit surgery carried out by unlicensed practitioners resulting in high rates of complication and death, contemporary access to abortion with pills has increased the safety of illegal abortion and dramatically lowered global maternal mortality figures associated with it (Guttmacher 2018). In Ireland, where the relative availability of abortion abroad meant that there were very few dangerous 'backstreet' abortions, abortion pills have had a major impact on the geography and politics of abortion.

This chapter explores the role of abortion pills on the Irish abortion debate and 8th Amendment referendum. The first half of the chapter traces the movement of pills into Ireland in the years between 2006 and 2016. As abortion pills became more widely available in Ireland, they destabilised established patterns of abortion travel and challenged official state narratives about abortion *inside* Ireland. The second half of the chapter examines the role of abortion pills in Irish political discourse from 2016–2018, focused especially on the Oireachtas debates surrounding the decision to hold a referendum on the 8th Amendment. The chapter argues that abortion pills provided a powerful political script for reluctant pro-repeal politicians by allowing them to simultaneously advocate for the protection of abortion-seeking women and the increased regulation of abortions inside Ireland after the repeal of the 8th Amendment. These scripts remain significant after the repeal of the 8th and the passage of new abortion legislation because they reveal a great deal about the political, medical and moral meanings attached to abortion in Ireland today. The end of the 8th Amendment regime is a welcome development and substantial feminist success, but the treatment of abortion pills in the 2018 political debates signals that the politics of abortion in Ireland will continue to be focused around the principles of restriction, control and medical authority.

By plane or pill: changing patterns of abortion access

Ireland presents an interesting site to study the changes brought about by abortion pills. On the one hand, it has enforced a near-total abortion ban since 1983 (and indeed before).[1] Reproductive health data have decisively shown that abortion restrictions do not lead to fewer abortions but to more unsafe abortions and more maternal deaths (Guttmacher 2018). For the most part, Ireland had been able to avoid this maternal health crisis because of the 'escape valve' of abortion travel to England, where abortion is accessible for non-resident patients who can pay. Irish women who could afford to travel to England did so, assisted by a changing group of feminist supporters and information networks from the Irish Women's Abortion Support Group in the 1980s to the Abortion Support Network today (see Rossiter 2009; Fletcher 2015). An estimated 170,000 women from Ireland have accessed abortion by travelling since 1983 (Irish Family Planning

Association 2018). Access to abortion in another country is, of course, dependent on a woman's financial resources, immigration status and general mobility: poor women, migrant women, undocumented women and women in controlling or abusive relationships have been disproportionately harmed by Ireland's policy of banning abortion at home while permitting it abroad (Gilmartin and Kennedy 2018).

The policy decision to outsource abortion abroad helped to sustain the political myth that Ireland was "abortion free" (Calkin 2018b); however, this narrative became increasingly unsustainable during the first decade of the 2000s, when new modes of abortion mobility created pathways to access that did not involve international travel. Self-managed abortion with pills offered new ways to access abortion in Ireland. In Latin America, where highly restrictive abortion laws are the norm, medication abortion pills (misoprostol only) have been used since the late 1980s for clandestine self-managed abortion when lay activists discovered they could buy the abortifacient misoprostol[2] in pharmacies because it was sold for other uses (de Zordo 2016). Medication abortion (combination of mifepristone and misoprostol) was introduced in the late 1980s by a French pharmaceutical company and came into use across Europe during the 1990s. Medication abortion rates quickly matched or exceeded surgical abortion rates in several European countries (Jones and Henshaw 2002). These abortion pills were first used in Ireland around 2006 when the Dutch telemedicine service Women on Web was established (Sheldon 2016). After 2006, abortion pills slowly became accessible to women in Ireland through this service and wider clandestine distribution networks organised by pro-choice activists there, although the general lack of public knowledge about the pills kept demand very low in the early years.[3]

Access to abortion pills online appears to have had a significant impact on abortion travel from Ireland. At the highest point in 2001, eighteen women per day travelled from Ireland to England for abortion; by 2016, this number had fallen to nine (Irish Family Planning Association 2018). Abortion travel numbers began to fall between 2002 and 2006, when abortion pills were not yet accessible in Ireland, but after the establishment of pill networks between 2006 and 2007, numbers of abortion-travellers declined more sharply (Aiken 2017). Requests for abortion pills from women in Ireland and Northern Ireland tripled between 2010 and 2016, according to one telemedicine provider (Aiken et al. 2017).[4] A few years after Women on Web began sending abortion pills to Ireland by post, the state began to intercept them. The Irish customs and medicines agency first announced that they had seized shipments of abortion pills in 2008; over the next two years, seizures of pills increased steeply and between twenty-five and sixty shipments of pills have been intercepted every year since 2009 (HSE quoted in Power 2017). In response, pro-choice networks that distributed pills changed their strategy to avoid sending pills directly into the Republic of Ireland.[5] Instead, they routed pills to Northern Ireland from where pills could be re-packaged and sent to the south or collected by individuals in physical trips across the border (Sheldon 2018). Although they are different legal jurisdictions and their customs agencies took different approaches to seizing pills – customs in the Republic of Ireland seized all pills, while UK customs generally did not[6] – the open border between the two presented an opportunity for activists.

In the Republic of Ireland, the inflow of abortion pills into the country has been generally met with what Sally Sheldon calls a "choreographed official ignorance" (2018: 16) on behalf of the state's criminal justice wing. This was sustained by the government's refusal to collect its own numbers on the use of abortion pills and its refusal to prosecute individual women for procuring pills (Ibid.). By contrast, the government agency tasked with providing information on crisis pregnancies dealt with the increased use of pills by releasing official statements to advise women that they should seek medical care after taking abortion pills (see, for example, AbortionAftercare.ie). The Irish government's "choreographed" ignorance around pills during this period is all the more notable because the 2013 Protection of Life During Pregnancy Act put in place a 14-year prison penalty for the use of abortion pills and all other forms of clandestine abortion (de Londras and Enright 2018). Despite the harsh criminal penalty available for those who used abortion pills, the Irish government showed no appetite for arresting or prosecuting individual women who self-managed abortion. By contrast, in Northern Ireland four people have been prosecuted for crimes relating to obtaining and using abortion pills.

Abortion pills and the 8th Amendment referendum
It was in this context that calls for a referendum on the 8th Amendment entered the mainstream political agenda. Intense and sustained pressure for abortion reform meant that political parties in the 2016 general election were forced to contend with the issue: Fine Gael was able to form a minority government in part through its commitment to hold a Citizens Assembly on the 8th Amendment (see Field 2018; Farrell et al. 2018). The Citizens Assembly sat from November 2016 until April 2017, after which its recommendations were considered by a Joint Oireachtas Committee who sat from September to December 2017. In January 2018, the government introduced a bill to hold a referendum on the repeal of the 8th Amendment, which was debated and passed by the Oireachtas in March 2018. The period between the end of the Citizens Assembly and the passage of the referendum bill is a crucial one for understanding the role of abortion pills in Irish political discourse. During this time period, politicians confronted and debated the issue of abortion as a moral proposition

and as a practical feature of Irish women's lives. From the Joint Oireachtas Committee onwards, politicians pointed to newfound knowledge about abortion pills as a rationale for engaging with the process and pushing for a more progressive abortion law than had been expected (see Conlon 2017; Murray 2017). The abortion pill loomed large in the political conversation about the 8th Amendment, because it destabilised the dominant understandings of abortion abroad and presented legislators with an alternative geography of clandestine abortion.

The remainder of this chapter explores the political narratives that were used to understand the abortion pill and considers the implications of these narratives for Irish abortion politics and provision. The data for this analysis was collected by studying transcripts of the debates in the Dáil and Seanad on the report of the Joint Oireachtas Committee on the 8th Amendment and subsequent referendum bill. The data was analysed with the assistance of qualitative coding software, which I used to code all transcripts and identify all instances where abortion pills were discussed. The issue of abortion pills was almost exclusively raised by pro-repeal legislators and, as such, the dominant political scripts for abortion pills that are explored below reflect pro-repeal narratives used by politicians across party lines (because legislators were given a conscience vote, rather than whipped for a party-line vote). Through coding and analysis of the data, I identified three discursive 'scripts' that were used most often to discuss abortion pills in Oireachtas debates; these 'scripts' are not mutually exclusive and were often used in combination by legislators. Their main arguments can be paraphrased as follows:

(i) The pragmatic script: *Although they are illegal, abortion pills are being widely used in Ireland today. The law is therefore unenforceable and the legislature should take pragmatic action to regularise the use of abortion pills;*

(ii) The medical script: *Because they are illegal, abortion pills are used in secret without any medical supervision. Women fear criminal penalties for using the pills and therefore avoid seeking the necessary medical care*;

(iii) The danger script: *When they are used without medical supervision, the pills are very dangerous and women who take them put themselves at serious risk. These girls and women are especially vulnerable and need the state's protection.*

The pragmatic script

When members of the Oireachtas discussed abortion pills during debates, a pragmatic narrative was by far the most popular approach. Such pragmatic appeals for abortion reform drew a distinction between the Ireland of the past, when abortion could be ignored and exported abroad, with the Ireland of the present where abortion pills are being used *inside the state*. They stressed the simultaneity of the demand for abortion with the legislature's debate on the issue and the location of abortion pills inside Irish territory:

> This evening, three girls or women will take abortion pills. They will put a towel down, lie on a bathroom floor and induce a miscarriage. That will happen in houses throughout this country tonight. Nobody can deny that it is happening. Terminations are taking place. They are unlawful in this country, but they are taking place in bathrooms by way of abortion pills. (Bill Kelleher *Dáil Debates* 966, 6)

Proponents of the pragmatic narrative drew on the ideas of honesty, reality, practicality and legislative duty to stress the urgency of the matter. As such, this narrative emphasised that the legislature's decision on abortion was a pragmatic policy decision rather than a moral question that should be influenced by personal beliefs. Proponents of this pragmatic narrative implored their colleagues to acknowledge the reality they face: "It is not about whether one is for or against the abortion pills because it is already being used in Ireland" (Simon Harris *Seanad Debates* 257, 1). Abortion happens in Ireland "and the question is not whether we personally agree with it but whether we want to ensure Irish women's healthcare is safe" (Frances Black *Seanad Debates* 255, 5). The pragmatic script on abortion pills provided political cover for self-identified 'pro-life' politicians to endorse reform, like TD Hildegarde Naughton, who changed her position on the abortion ban after learning about abortion pills as a member of the Joint Oireachtas Committee. She told journalists: "We can either close our eyes to this, as usual, or actually deal with the dangers of unsupervised access to abortion pills. I choose the latter" (quoted in Murray 2017).

The pragmatic narrative was the most commonly used among TDs and Senators to advocate for repeal of the 8th Amendment, but different strands of this narrative emerged across the course of the debates. For some, the failure to take action on abortion law was a shameful sign that the legislature had deliberately chosen to ignore the issue or accept the status quo of abortion travel. The Health Minister Simon Harris, for example, compared the Oireachtas to "an ostrich" with its "head in the sand" (*Seanad Debates* 257, 1). For others, it was a sign that the legislature must act because technological change had recently made Ireland's laws obsolete. Abortion can no longer be ignored and exported abroad, explained Fine Gael Senator Jerry Buttimer: "In the modern world that we all live in, we have the abortion pill" (*Seanad Debates* 255, 5). If the 8th Amendment was ever effective, its relevance has been challenged by pills: "[O]nce the possibility of pharmaceutical termination of pregnancy came about, a totally different situation was created. The state cannot, in fact, prevent it and cannot realistically put people on trial" for self-administering the abortion pill (Michael McDowell *Seanad Debates* 257, 1).

If technological change has transformed the way that abortion occurs, so this narrative goes, it has also seriously eroded the state's ability to control where and when abortion occurs.

Calls for a realistic, pragmatic look at abortion in Ireland sometimes asked for compassion for women who are accessing illegal terminations. But they also contained an implicit critique of the legislature's failure, arguing that the current laws were unenforceable and demonstrated that the state has lost control of a dangerous issue. Under the 8th Amendment, the legislature cannot properly regulate abortion pills, Fine Gael's Alan Farrell argued: "If we could remove the ban we could facilitate a proper medical and diagnostic analysis of those pills and we could make a decision to ban them, regulate them, or limit their availability to medical practitioners" (*Dáil Debates* 963, 7). The pragmatic case is not just about recognising the reality of abortion in Ireland, but re-asserting the Irish government's control over abortion as an issue which must be supervised, regulated and limited:

> We do not suggest one should be able to walk into one's local
> convenience store and purchase an abortion pill as one would a
> box of Panadol. What is being proposed is highly restricted and
> regulated and will be carried out in conjunction with the medical
> profession. Women buy abortion pills online and self-administer
> them without medical supervision. That is unrestricted. (Lisa
> Chambers *Dáil Debates* 966, 7)

It is notable that many proponents of the pragmatic case for repeal couched their support in a desire to impose formal, democratic and enforceable restrictions on abortion pills. Access to illegal abortion pills, these politicians argued, effectively permits unlimited abortion and liberalisation of the laws would allow for greater controls to be imposed. In the Oireachtas debates, pragmatism on abortion pills underpinned a popular political position that endorses repeal of the 8th and restrictive limits on abortion access.

The medical script

In Oireachtas debates on the Joint Oireachtas Committee report and referendum bill, pro-repeal advocates frequently argued that the 8th Amendment harmed women by forcing them to take abortion pills without medical supervision and obstructed the doctor-patient relationship because both parties feared criminal penalties. This medical script for abortion pills is closely entwined with the pragmatic script, because a concern to medically regulate and control abortion provision underpins the pragmatist's case for reform: as Lisa Chambers' statement above suggests, many pragmatists framed the status quo as one of dangerously unregulated abortion inside Ireland. The call to regulate abortion pills, and to offer abortion within clear limitations, is indicative of a strong deference to medical authority in the Oireachtas debates as well as the growing influence of medical practitioners in debates about abortion law since the passage of the Protection of Life During Pregnancy Act (Henchion 2018; Field 2018; see Enright and de Londras, this volume). Medical testimony heavily influenced the Joint Oireachtas Committee's proceedings and its final report; of its twenty-four invited witnesses, eleven were medical doctors, nine of whom were obstetricians, gynaecologists, or reproductive health specialists (Joint Oireachtas Committee 2017b).

In the Oireachtas debates on the 8th Amendment, the medical script allowed reluctant pro-repeal figures to make a conservative endorsement of reform, because it emphasised the need to reintroduce medical authority over the abortion decision. Micheál Martin, the leader of Fianna Fáil, led his party's campaign in 2002 for a referendum to remove suicide as grounds for life-saving abortion; in January 2018 he surprised colleagues by endorsing the repeal of the 8th Amendment and the proposal to abortion to 12 weeks. Martin argued for the importance of legal, but limited, abortion access under medical supervision:

[I]t is clear that the reality of the abortion pill means we are no longer talking about a procedure that involves the broader medical system during the early stages of pregnancy. We must have a system which actively encourages women to seek support from medical professionals as soon as possible. (*Dáil Debates* 963, 7)

The use of a medical frame for abortion also signals an effort to move the abortion issue out of moral or religious domains and into the domain of healthcare (Lowe 2016). The medical script employed by politicians in Oireachtas debates tended to frame abortion as a serious but potentially appropriate decision, provided it is decided in the right clinical circumstances and with the approval of designated medical professionals:

Mothers and fathers must ask themselves if that was their daughter, would they want her to be supported by a doctor and to know the medication she is accessing is safe. The Institute of Obstetricians and Gynaecologists, the people who run our maternity services, deliver our babies and mind our mothers and wives when they give birth, have clear views on the danger and risk to women as a result of abortion pills. (Simon Harris *Seanad Debates* 257, 1)

This reflects a commonplace political narrative in pro-choice politics today: because abortion decisions are regarded as deviant or tragic by default, legal frameworks for the medical control of abortion tend to frame women as irrational victims and doctors as rational authority figures (Sheldon 1997; Millar 2017). Medical narratives in the Irish 8th Amendment debates employed this same logic to stress the uncontrolled and unregulated nature of abortion pills, for which there was no formal medical supervision before or after the abortion. The principle of medical supervision as a check on abortion-seeking women is evident in the 72-hour waiting period in the 2018 Regulation of Termination of Pregnancy law. The Health Minister posed the choice as such:

> Would one want one's daughter, wife, sister or mother to
> access such medicines through a doctor and go through a *very
> deliberative process* involving a 72-hour waiting period, *all
> options* being outlined in a *proper consultation* and knowing
> the quality of the medication or to order them on the Internet?
> (Simon Harris *Seanad Debates* 257, 1, emphasis added)

Arguments in favour of medical supervision of abortion often highlighted the adverse effect of the criminal penalties on women and their doctors imposed by the Protection of Life During Pregnancy Act. Numerous legislators argued for the need to remove criminal penalties from the use of abortion pills, because women deliberately avoided medical supervision and advice under fear of prosecution. When women are forced to obtain clandestine abortions, a Fine Gael Senator explained: "they use these tablets without any medical supervision or support and when they develop complications, they feel concerned about approaching their doctors lest they be accused of breaking the law and bringing more trouble upon themselves" (James Reilly *Seanad Debates* 257, 1). The tenor of this debate marks a sea change: while 5 years previously, the legislature introduced criminal sanctions for self-managed abortion, by 2018, legislators across parties harshly denounced the criminalisation of self-managed abortion and repeatedly highlighted its negative impact on women's access to healthcare. Medical supervision stands in for state authority here, where legislators call for pro-choice reforms that would impose clear professional boundaries on the provision of abortion, rather than restrict its use through the threat of criminal penalties.

The danger script

The third key narrative about abortion pills that emerged from the Oireachtas debates sought to draw parallels between 'backstreet' surgical abortion and self-managed abortion with pills. The notion that self-managed abortion with pills is highly dangerous proved a persuasive and popular rationale for legislators to advocate repeal, often employed as part of a broader paternalistic account of Irish abortions that emphasised the youth and vulnerability of abortion-seeking women. Legislators frequently repeated the idea that reform was urgently needed before a woman died from the secret use of abortion pills: "If we do nothing, some woman in the not-too-distant future will rupture her uterus and die. It has happened elsewhere and will happen here" (Hildegarde Naughton *Dáil Debates* 963, 6). Testimony from doctors in the Joint Oireachtas Committee and media was frequently referenced in this regard, recounting the "harrowing stories" from obstetricians who had seen "women with ruptured uteruses as a result of taking these pills unsupervised" (Simon Harris *Seanad Debates* 257, 1). Pills were repeatedly associated with danger because they were used in self-managed abortion without a doctor's prescription, taken without medical advice in the event of complications and obtained through the internet from unregulated providers.

That girls and women would put their health at risk by purchasing pills from the internet was used to demonstrate their desperation and vulnerability. Legislators spoke of women's "anguish and torture", their feelings of "fear", "desperation", their loneliness and their "extreme" vulnerability when they ordered pills online to terminate a pregnancy. References to danger and health risk evoked compassion for the circumstances of women with crisis pregnancies who sought abortion pills, but it also allowed legislators to frame their plight in strongly paternalistic terms:

> I am an Irishman, so I struggle to imagine the anguish and torture in a young woman's mind as she handles an abortion pill she ordered online as she sits alone in her room, consumed with the reality that she cannot tell anyone, not a friend, a doctor, not even a soulmate. These women are of Ireland, as much as our music, sport and dance. They are to be trusted to

be empowered. The Constitution must protect them in every
single way as much as it protects Irishmen. (Aodhán Ó Ríordáin
Seanad Debates 255, 5)

Among legislators in the Oireachtas, a danger narrative that
placed emphasis on the vulnerability, youth and psychological
fragility of abortion-seekers was a popular and salient script for
advocating reform. In particular, numerous legislators conjured
an emotive picture of the vulnerable abortion-seeker by describing her physical location. Legislators' speeches were filled with
references to abortion pills taken in "bedrooms", in "bathrooms",
in "public restrooms", in "toilets in colleges", in "sheds dotted
around the country" and "behind closed doors". A Fine Gael
senator argued that "we are allowing back-street abortions to take
place through the use of abortion pills" (Jerry Buttimer *Seanad
Debates* 257, 2). The image of young girls buying pills from their
bedrooms became a dominant rhetorical theme throughout the
8th referendum campaign, appearing frequently in speeches by
the Taoiseach, cabinet members and high-profile surrogates of
the Yes side, although it was strongly contested by other pro-
choice activists (see McDonald et al., this volume).

The emphasis on the vulnerability of the abortion-seeker
frames abortion reform as a matter of compassion and paternalistic
protection for women who put themselves at risk. The tropes of
the abortion-seeking woman as a "helpless victim" with "culturally potent" reasons for abortion – like youth, poverty, or family
pressure – have long been used to attract support for legal
abortion in other contexts, because they frame women's reasons
for seeking abortion in ways that comport with gendered expectations and moralism about female sexuality (Condit 1990: 25).
In Ireland, these tropes proved similarly resonant with legislators
and politicians who led the campaign. They called for compassion, pragmatism and urgent reform to bring abortion care into
line with other forms of medical care, but they also served to

recuperate pro-choice narratives within conservative notions about proper femininities and sexualities.

Conclusion

By the time the Irish government and Oireachtas began to seriously investigate and debate abortion pills as part of wider abortion reform, the use of abortion pills inside Ireland was well-established and provided a source of abortion access for around three women per day. As the chairman of the Irish Institute of Obstetricians and Gynaecologists told Joint Oireachtas Committee members: on the issue of abortion pills, "the genie is out of the bottle" (Boylan quoted in Joint Oireachtas Committee 2017a). The Oireachtas debates on abortion reform demonstrate the impact of abortion pills on legislators' understanding of the issue and the eventual recognition that pills had made restrictions obsolete or unenforceable, undermining the totality of the 8th Amendment legal regime. These narratives would prove popular in the referendum campaign, particularly in their reliance on medical expertise and authority by the pro-repeal campaign (Field 2018; Henchion 2018). However, studies of voter behaviour in the 8th referendum suggest that information about abortion pills was the deciding factor for a very small portion of the electorate (see Reidy, this volume). Nonetheless, evidence from the legislative proceedings demonstrates that information about abortion pills, and growing awareness of their use among policymakers, were decisive factors in the political process that led to the May 2018 referendum.

Ireland's experience with abortion pills is clearly the result of unique political, geographical and cultural circumstances. Its lessons cannot be neatly translated into other contexts. Nonetheless, what might we learn from the case of abortion pills in Ireland for reform elsewhere? First, the medical technology of the abortion pill has substantial political power. The abortion pill is small, mobile and discrete, so it can be moved across jurisdictions in ways that states find difficult to control. State infrastructure can limit its movement, to some extent, although operationalising a full block on abortion pills is extremely difficult (see Calkin 2019b). Second, as public health research has shown, self-managed abortion with pills is safe and acceptable to women, meaning it cannot be understood as analogous to surgical 'back street' abortions (Aiken et al. 2017). Dire warnings about the danger of illegal use of abortion pills will likely fail to dissuade women from using them, especially as information about their safe use spreads and telemedical services expand their geographical reach. Third, and by extension, in contexts where the abortion pill is relatively easy to access and being safely used by women for self-managed abortion, the state has few incentives to enforce a ban on such pills through criminal prosecutions. The role that the abortion pill played in persuading reluctant legislators in Ireland to support repeal suggests that clandestine access to self-managed abortion has the potential to prompt a pragmatic, rather than punitive, state response. This is not to say that these political forces inevitably lead to emancipatory outcomes or that this rule applies across all contexts: legislative efforts to regularise access to the abortion pill, decriminalise its use and institutionalise its medical control can impose new barriers to access and enforce new modes of control over abortion. Some states still do pursue prosecutions against women who use abortion pills, as is the case in Northern Ireland where, ironically, most of the abortion pills used in Ireland first enter the island. Nonetheless, the role abortion pills played in Ireland, before and during the 8th Amendment referendum, demonstrates the political power of self-managed abortion to challenge abortion restrictions and advocate for progressive reforms.

Notes

1 Abortion was already illegal before the 8th Amendment, as it was a criminal offence under a 1861 law inherited from British rule (de Londras and Enright 2018: 25).
2 Misoprostol, licensed in many countries under the name Cytotec, is used to treat stomach ulcers and post-partum haemorrhage, among other things (see de Zordo 2016). Mifepristone, by contrast, is much more tightly restricted because it is used primarily for abortion (see Gynuity 2017).
3 Interview with Dublin-based activist, 2018.
4 Data on abortion-travellers and abortion pills requests are both estimates, drawn from incomplete data. Abortion-travellers are counted based on women who gave Irish home addresses in English and Dutch clinics. Abortion pill numbers are based on reported data from the two main telemedicine services, Women on Web and Women Help Women.
5 Interview with Women on Web, 2018.
6 Interview with Derry-based activist, 2018.

Legislative debates cited

Full transcripts of the debates listed below are available at www.oireachtas.ie.
Seanad Debates Vol. 255, No. 5. Report of the Joint Committee on the Eighth Amendment of the Constitution: Statements. 17 January 2018.
Seanad Debates Vol. 257, No. 1. Thirty-sixth Amendment of the Constitution Bill 2018. 27 March 2018.
Seanad Debates Vol. 257, No. 2. Thirty-sixth Amendment of the Constitution Bill 2018. 28 March 2018.
Dáil Debates Vol. 963, No. 6. Report of the Joint Committee on the Eighth Amendment of the Constitution: Statements. 17 January 2018.
Dáil Debates Vol. 963, No. 7. Report of the Joint Committee on the Eighth Amendment of the Constitution: Statements. 18 January 2018.
Dáil Debates Vol. 966, No. 6. Thirty-sixth Amendment of the Constitution Bill 2018. 9 March 2018.
Dáil Debates Vol. 966, No. 7. Thirty-sixth Amendment of the Constitution Bill 2018. 20 March 2018.

FIVE | Of trust and mistrust: the politics of repeal

Elżbieta Drążkiewicz-Grodzicka and Máire Ní Mhórdha

Introduction

Referendums are often seen as the epitome of democracy, as an opportunity for the public to have their voices heard on issues of the utmost importance (Qvortrup 2014, 2018). Such was the 2018 referendum to repeal the 8th Amendment to the Constitution in Ireland. Indeed, the repeal process appeared to be a veritable carnival of democracy, preceded as it was by the Citizens' Assembly and touted by many as a unique example of direct democracy. Belgian political commentator David Van Reybrouck proclaimed that the latter experiment in deliberative democracy was "a model for Europe", showing that Ireland "trusts its citizens, instead of fearing them" (Humphreys 2016). The subsequent two-to-one landslide vote in the 25 May 2018 referendum to legalise abortion was reported by domestic and international commentators as a historic victory for women's rights (Provost and Rebollo 2018), but also evidence of a uniquely Irish political culture of innovation (Farrell et al. 2018), based on trust and consensus: "The reverberations of what is first and foremost an Irish victory for women's reproductive rights will be felt across the world", declared the *Observer* (2018), offering "hope to the 1.25 billion women globally who have no access to safe abortion".

As people living in Ireland who can become pregnant, parents and activists within the repeal campaign, we naturally share in the joy and relief of this hard-won and far-reaching victory.

However, as anthropologists living through and observing this significant historical moment, our aim in this chapter is to move beyond the hype surrounding the process to critically examine the meaning of the movement for democracy in Ireland. Like Van Reybrouck, we are specifically concerned with the issue of trust and its role in the repeal movement and the democratic process that enabled the change.

The importance of political trust (usually understood as citizens' confidence in political institutions and systems of governance) has been long recognised as a fundamental precondition for stable societies (Sztompka 1997; Uslaner 2002; Dyck 2009; Freitag and Ackermann 2016). A primary assumption of these studies is that trust provides an essential foundation for social cohesion, working as a social glue that enables societies to flourish and providing political actors and institutions with support and legitimacy. Often focusing on measuring degrees of social and political trust around the world, these studies[1] tend to correlate high degrees of trust with modern democracies and Western states, while simultaneously attributing a low level of trust to non-Western states. In much of this work, "cultures of trust" are seen as an ideal type, while "cultures of mistrust" are understood as anomalous and attributive of failed or developing states. Mistrust is thus seen as a source of social chaos, a "social acid", whose power lies in the destruction and corrosion of human bonds (Carey 2017: 2).

In this chapter, we move beyond this overly dualistic and deterministic understanding of political trust, drawing on the anthropological literature that highlights how social and political trust are more a luxury than a norm across cultures, and key to the cultivation of social change and political action (Evans-Pritchard and Gillies 1976; Carey 2017; Douglas 2013; Liisberg et al. 2015). Focusing on the repeal movement in Ireland, we demonstrate that political trust is not necessarily a prerequisite of modern democracies; instead, we contend that both political trust and *mistrust* are essential, complementary and productive elements of political life. Furthermore, given the relational nature of trust in general and political trust in particular, we argue that in order to really understand the way modern democracies work, it is important to understand not only the relationship that citizens have with the state, but also how the relationship between politicians and their constituents is circumscribed and negotiated. In this, we argue, the struggle in Ireland for abortion rights contradicts prevailing narratives about the decline in public trust in political institutions across European societies (see, for example, Abrams and Travaglino 2018). Instead, we contend that while notions of trust were central to the successful message of the referendum campaign itself (e.g. Taoiseach Leo Varadkar's exhortation to "trust women and trust doctors", McMahon 2018), a key influence on the trajectory of the repeal movement was actually *mistrust* on the part of professional politicians vis-à-vis their constituents. At the same time, for the Yes campaigners, harnessing public *trust* in state institutions was essential to the functioning of their movement. Here, we follow Jiménez's (2011: 178–9) observation that "the question today is not what trust is, but what kind of work the notion does", and explore how trust (or the lack thereof) shaped the trajectory and processes of the repeal campaign. Below, we briefly lay out the key literature on trust and political culture in Ireland that informs our analysis of the Citizens' Assembly and the Yes campaign.

Political trust and the Irish context

Niklas Luhman argues that one of the most important characteristics of trust is that it involves "telescoping" the present and the future. The act of trust takes place in the present, but concerns the future – a future that is probable, possible and potentially achievable. In this sense, trust differs from hope, which concerns a radically different future (1979: 10). As Liisberg and Pedersen (2015: 1) put it: "[I]f I hope for events and phenomena that lie closer to my immediate life-world, my hope seems to be backed up by some kind of trust in these things being possible to realize". As such, relations of trust are closely connected to the act of *knowing* (Carey 2017). People have the capacity to trust each other because they assume that they know what to expect from one another. By the same logic, people also actively mistrust each other when they are unable to predict the views or behaviours of others, when the latter's motives seem unclear. Both trusting and mistrusting are thus often vulnerable to error. This is especially the case when it comes to building trust relationships between certain groups based on stereotypes and presumptions. Consequently, trust contains an element of *risk*: "knowing" is assumed, but not guaranteed, it always depends on our relationships with and perception of others on both the individual and group level (see Sztompka 1997).

As we will demonstrate, this relational characteristic of trust was essential to the political trajectory of the repeal campaign, which relied not only on relationships of trust/mistrust between Irish citizens and politicians but also on politicians' trust in their constituents. Yet, despite the fact that the relational and transactional nature of trust is crucial for professional relationships, including professional politicians (Grimen 2009), the reciprocal nature of trust is often neglected in analysis of political trust, even though it is fundamental for governance; the act of trusting another person involves "exchang[ing] a piece of our freedom with another person" (Liisberg and Pedersen 2015: 5). This is highlighted in the transactional nature of voting itself: as voters, we engage in relationships with politicians wherein we trade our trust for our vote. The act of voting for political candidates implies trust on the part of the electorate that the former will represent their interests. Voters thus transfer discretionary powers to professional politicians. Once elected, politicians can decide how the lives of their electorate should be governed in the absence of any guarantee that they will fulfil their electoral promises. Trust may therefore be understood as a central social and political technology, strongly connected to issues of dependency and control (Carey 2017).

The relational and reciprocal nature of political trust is particularly important in the Irish political context, which is locally-oriented and clientelist in nature. There is long scholarship on the political system in Ireland and how it is characterised by relationships of patronage and clientelism, in which even high rank politicians are willing to exchange favours and engage in individual or local matters in exchange for support (Bax 1970; Komito 1984; Gibbon and Higgins 1974; Coakley 2006). The latest findings from Thomsen and Suiter (2016) confirm this, clearly showing that the Irish democratic model differs from other European democracies. In the latter, support for parties and party leaders is generally more important than support for local candidates, while Irish political culture is characterised by close relationships of patronage and clientelism between voters and local politicians. The Irish variant of political clientelism, like relationships of trust, relies heavily on reciprocity; as we will show, this characteristic proved an essential factor in influencing politicians to support or work against the repeal movement.

Political (mis)trust: the Citizens' Assembly

The 2018 referendum was the outcome of a long process. While the 1983 referendum, which inscribed the ban on abortion into the Constitution, promised to "solve" the controversial issue once and for all, it in fact generated decades of legal, political, social and medical controversies. As a result, the abortion question would repeatedly return to the Oireachtas (parliament), national courts and international tribunals, including the European Court of Justice and the European Court of Human Rights. While women and their families were contesting their rights through legal actions and mass demonstrations, politicians, once eager to control reproductive rights, were now generally loathe to deal with the particularities of abortion prohibition by creating clear legislation on issues such as the right to abortion information, the right to travel for abortion, the protection of pregnant women's lives and so on.[2] By the turn of the century, a topic that had been a central issue for all political parties in 1983 was now a hot potato, avoided by most members of the Oireachtas. Yet, as politicians grew increasingly reticent on the issue, the streets were becoming louder, with the cases of Ms X, Ms Y and the tragic death of Savita Halappanavar in 2012 driving thousands of people out onto the streets to demand change. From 2011, the March for Choice had become an annual fixture on the streets of Dublin. It was clear that more and more people wanted change (Quilty et al. 2015).

However, most politicians remained reluctant to engage directly with these public debates. It was only in the run up to the 2016 general election, following massive protests focusing on the death of Savita Halappanavar and reports on the case of 'Ms P',[3] that some politicians began to express support for changes to the Irish abortion law.[4] As a result of this popular outcry and the negotiations that led to the formation of a government, then-Taoiseach Enda Kenny established a Citizens' Assembly in late 2016 to consider the repeal of the 8th Amendment, as well as other issues including fixed term parliaments and climate change (Farrell et al. 2018). The Assembly consisted of ninety-nine randomly chosen citizens, working with an advisory group of five experts (a medical lawyer, two constitutional lawyers and two obstetricians) to consider expert testimony from both sides of the debate, as well as submissions from members of the public. In relation to abortion, the Assembly was tasked with voting in favour of or against repealing the 8th

Amendment, as well as producing non-binding recommendations for envisaged Oireachtas legislation.[5]

The Citizens' Assembly was ostensibly inspired by the 2012–14 Constitutional Convention, set up under the government programme agreed by the 2011 Fine Gael-Labour coalition. This Convention comprised ninety-nine members (thirty-three representatives chosen by political parties and sixty-six randomly chosen citizens), tasked with considering proposed amendments to the Constitution of Ireland. The establishment of this body was influenced by We the Citizens,[6] an experimental project led by academics, advocating for a shift in Irish politics towards a more participatory model. The 2016 Citizens' Assembly was one of the first initiatives of its kind in modern democracies. Examining such institutions in Canada, Iceland and Ireland, Lang (2007), Farrell et al. (2013), Farrell (2014) and Suiter et al. (2016) almost unanimously agree that such forms of participatory governance are a response to political crises and failings and decreasing public engagement in formal electoral and party-driven politics. In this view, such bodies are seen as a positive remedy to a decrease in political trust and a way to advance citizen participation in political life (Ibid.).

However, questions remain about the relationships that politicians have with such citizen bodies and the situations in which political elites are willing to cede power and decision-making capacities to citizens. Such questions are particularly important to consider in any assessment of the effectiveness of these assemblies, as it is ultimately political leaders who both initiate these processes and have the power to decide whether and how their recommendations should be implemented. What is at stake here is not people's trust in state institutions, but rather politicians' trust in citizens.

We argue that the Citizens' Assembly and the Constitutional Convention were designed in such a way that they never had the capacity to meaningfully challenge the existing power structure of Ireland's political system. Both were limited in terms of their agenda to items that, while socially important, did not strike at the heart of Ireland's deep-seated institutional problems. Furthermore, both were confined to the role of inputting ideas to an Oireachtas that was obliged only to "consider" and "respond" to recommendations that if necessary, could easily be side-lined. These deliberative bodies were designed to operate simply as well-resourced focus groups on potentially tricky referendum campaigns for Ireland's (doubting) political leaders, allowing voters to experience the various arguments and framings in a concentrated format and politicians to gain an insight into public perceptions and reactions.

Nonetheless, the Citizens' Assembly is widely considered to be a breakthrough element of the repeal process, not least because its recommendations (free, safe and legal abortion) were so radically beyond the parameters of hitherto acceptable public debate on the issue of abortion in Ireland. The Assembly's political origins show however, that for the government of the day, it had not necessarily been set up with a view to facilitating a major shift in Irish democratic culture at large, nor as part of a specific plan to introduce reform of the abortion laws, but rather as a stalling technique, aimed at "kick[ing] the can [of responsibility] down the road", as one newspaper commentator put it (Clifford 2016). Despite domestic and international pressure (see de Londras 2015), instead of simply exercising their power to call a referendum straightaway and then legislate for abortion, the Fine Gael government delayed dealing for as long as possible with an issue they clearly viewed as divisive and politically hazardous:

> The suspicion was that the Citizens' Assembly was nothing more than a delaying tactic that would put abortion law reform on the long finger of a government that it was broadly anticipated would be unstable due to its minority status and unorthodox composition. (de Londras and Markicevic 2018: 89)

The establishment of the Citizens' Assembly was thus initially critiqued by both supporters and opponents of repeal. For example, pro-choice TD Ruth Coppinger derided it in 2016 as a "charade that the Government felt they had to come up with", declaring in the Dáil that "the Government is struggling to find a formula to not deal with what has essentially become the key civil rights issue for this generation" (Loughlin 2016). Ironically, it was exactly at this point that direct and participatory democracy presented itself as an ideal solution for politicians, happy to shift responsibility for a controversial topic onto this experimental new body. Despite the enthusiastic predictions emerging from the previous We the Citizens initiative, that the political elite in Ireland is open to the idea of greater citizen involvement (Farrell et al. 2013), the political context of the Citizens' Assembly shows that its instigation was little more than a convenient solution to an awkward problem.

In public debates, particularly in the mainstream media in Ireland, the Assembly was viewed as a way of reaching consensus on a divisive issue. However, as the subsequent referendum result revealed, the core of the problem was not the fact that abortion *was* a divisive topic and politicians rightly feared engaging with it, but rather that it was *perceived* as such. Conflict avoidance and fear of social disharmony (Scheper-Hughes 1979; Donnan and Wilson 2006), combined with the memory of the bitterness of the abortion debate in the 1980s (sometimes referred to as the "second partitioning" of Ireland (Hesketh 1990), contributed to political inaction on the subject in Ireland for decades.

By early 2018, it was clear that many mainstream politicians in Ireland were still wary of actively engaging with the topic of abortion and faced difficulties in gauging public opinion in relation to it. The careful and reserved language (particularly avoidance of terms such as 'abortion', and an emphasis on the 'sensitive' nature of the topic) used by those politicians who were personally in favour of repeal revealed their lack of trust that their view was shared by the wider public. Notably, this approach was the strategy of Tánaiste Frances Fitzgerald throughout 2016, who, by late 2017, was considered likely to lead Fine Gael's referendum campaign on abortion (see O'Regan 2017). Because reform of abortion law in Ireland could not simply be enacted by law-makers alone, instead requiring a change to the Constitution and thus a referendum and public vote, politicians needed to trust that a majority of citizens were actually in favour of reforming access to abortion.

Ireland's highly centralised, locally rooted political system means that the future of politicians depends strongly on their ability to discern and anticipate the views of their local constituencies (Thomsen and Suiter 2016). Political careers depend strongly on clear and nuanced understandings of local needs, values and expectations. The repeal process clearly demonstrated that many politicians are not only out of sync with their electorate, but that they have a distorted image of broader society in Ireland. Despite clear signals from the streets, courtrooms and social media that society was desperate for reform of the abortion regime, politicians feared to trust that their constituents would actually support repealing the notorious 8th Amendment, which is why (paradoxically) they preferred to give voice to the people (through the Citizens' Assembly) than to risk speaking up themselves, thereby miscalculating actual public support for those issues, which poll data had shown had long been in favour of change. Hence, even following the emphatic recommendation of the Assembly to repeal the 8th, and its resounding agreement with longstanding demands by activists for "Free, Safe and Legal" abortion in Ireland, many politicians (including the Taoiseach himself) remained hesitant to call a referendum[7], and when they eventually did, were slow to express their own voting preferences on the record.

The 2018 Yes vote was, at two-to-one, an exact reversal of the 1983 majority vote that introduced the 8th Amendment. The day after the referendum, the deputy political editor of the *Irish Times*, Fiach Kelly, proclaimed: "The Yes vote shows an overwhelming desire for change that *nobody foresaw*" (emphasis added), mirroring the evident surprise of many within the media and political establishment at this result (Kelly 2018). Despite signals from society for decades that demand for abortion access and reform of maternity care were desperately sought (de Londras 2018; de Londras and Markicevic 2018; Quilty et al. 2015) and the difficulties that the abortion regime caused, not only in regard to the specific issue of termination of pregnancy but also general maternal care, politicians' reluctance to act was an indication of their lack of trust that "Middle Ireland" was "ready" for the change (McGee 2018). Indeed, this dynamic is evident in a promise made by government in the run-up to the vote to appease the so-called 'middle ground': despite the lack of any medical rationale or general political demand, beyond that of the extreme 'pro-life' minority, the government refused to abandon a 3-day waiting period in the new abortion legislation.

There is clear evidence to suggest that at least until the referendum phase of the repeal campaign, politicians in Ireland lacked trust in their electorate. Indeed, a significant turning point in the campaign was the announcement in January 2018 by Fianna Fáil leader, Micheál Martin, that, following a "long period of reflection", he supported removing the 8th Amendment and legalising abortion up to 12 weeks of pregnancy (Brennan 2018). This major U-turn in opinion by Martin, whose landmark speech noted that he had hitherto "been on the record as being against a significant change in our abortion laws", was significant too in the language he used, that echoed the narratives of choice and compassion that underpinned pro-choice campaigning on abortion:

> If we are sincere in our compassion for women and if we are sincere in respecting their choices, we must act, because the Eighth Amendment has been shown to cause real damage to Irish women. (Ibid.)

Both the content and form of Martin's announcement contrasted with the views of many in his historically conservative opposition party, but were an important indicator of increasing awareness by key political leaders that by 2018, a major shift in public opinion on abortion had occurred; it was clearly now essential for political leaders to be on the right side of history in this regard.

This historic lack of trust by politicians vis-à-vis their electorate is a characteristic of Irish political culture that is rarely considered by analysts; paradoxically, the focus tends to be on the perceived decline in public trust in State institutions (Loscher 2017). This is despite the fact that in Ireland people *do* have a basic level of trust in the State and its institutions; as we have shown, for at least the last decade, Irish citizens and residents tenaciously expressed their dissatisfaction with existing laws through the available democratic means, including demonstrations, debates and self-organisation (de Londras 2018).

This indicates the lack of balance and reciprocity in the trust relationship connecting politicians and citizens. While State representatives demonstrated a problem with trusting that voters would support repeal, conversely, we argue, in this process Irish citizens demonstrated a leap of trust in the Irish political apparatus that change could be achieved through democratic means. Regarding the 25 May vote itself, people knew that they were voting simply to remove or retain the 8th Amendment to the Constitution. The referendum did not give the voters the opportunity to comment on or control what the new legislation following repeal of the 8th would look like. Although the government had published the Heads of Bill of the proposed replacement legislation, there was no guarantee that this document would be accepted by the Dáil (and indeed when the document reached the Dáil's Health Committee, no fewer than 180 amendments were tabled for discussion). Voters did not know any detail in advance of the referendum about the policies and practicalities of implementing new laws on abortion.

Yet, despite this lack of this knowledge, voters *trusted* that once they expressed the wish to repeal the 8th, their TDs, when passing the bill, would, through will and deed, "do the right thing".

Significantly, the No campaign attempted to harness the argument that politicians could not be trusted when it came to abortion regulation. In a debate with Máire (representing the Meath Together for Yes group) on local radio in April 2018, Pro-Life campaign representative Cora Sherlock stated disparagingly that removal of the 8th would leave decisions about pregnancy "in the hands of politicians in Leinster House" (and not, as would in fact be the case, in the hands of women themselves). The idea that politicians could not be trusted was a reoccurring theme of the No campaign, with anti-abortion activist Declan Ganley stating that people should vote against repeal because "otherwise we would be putting our trust in politicians" (Byrne 2018). However, significantly, this view failed to gain traction. The specific dynamic of the referendum and the lead up to it are a clear indication of the relative amount of trust among the Irish public vis-à-vis their political representatives and institutions, in contrast to prevailing narratives to the contrary.

Conclusion

The success of the repeal movement was a momentous leap forward for women's rights in Ireland. It also exposed an important characteristic of Irish political culture, and social dynamics in the country more broadly, revealing that one of the major problems with Irish democracy is not a lack of public trust in politicians and state institutions, but rather a historic lack of trust on the part of politicians vis-à-vis their constituents, shaped by a political system wherein politicians view their political existence as reliant on their ability to leverage patronage politics at the local level.

The history of repeal revealed the weakness of Irish parliamentary democracy. The clientelist, (local) vote-chasing nature of formal Irish politics, coupled with politicians' lack of knowledge of wider social views on abortion, paralysed government politicians and prevented them from becoming leaders of the repeal movement until they perceived that it was politically safe for them to do so: when they could increase rather than jeopardise their political capital. Instead, they resorted to the Citizens' Assembly, a decision that was not the outcome of *trust* on the part of politicians in the public, but rather *mistrust*. The public was given the power to participate in this decision-making process not because political representatives trusted in citizens' ability to make good decisions, but because they were fearful of taking responsibility for and facing the potentially negative consequences of a firm stance on repeal, this a product of their disconnect from the wider public. As Sztompka (1997: 10) argues, in politics, mistrust always works against innovation and non-conformity. In the case of abortion, the mistrust of mainstream Irish politicians made them reluctant actors in the reform process, until such point as they felt it was politically safe and/or expedient to do so. At the same time, paradoxically, for those few politicians who were hoping for change, their mistrust in citizens became creative. While fearing to be leaders of change themselves they gave a space to the Citizens' Assembly and, consequently, indirectly contributed to the formulation of new innovative mechanism of participatory democracy. In that sense, the mistrust proved to have, to some extent, a creative power.

We argue that our observations from Ireland might have particularly strong implications for our understanding of the parliamentary democracies at large. As we have demonstrated in this study, in order to understand the mechanisms facilitating institutional and social change we need to pay equal attention the creative and disruptive power of *both* political trust and mistrust. We also need to better understand *mutual* relationships linking politicians and citizens and the ways in which locally situated political cultures are influencing them.

Following the referendum, Ms Justice Mary Laffoy, the retired judge who had chaired the Citizens' Assembly, recommended that other countries emulate this clearly successful model for public deliberation on important issues (McGreevy 2018). Like Van Reybrouck, Laffoy was enthused by the emergence and implementation of this new participatory model in Irish politics. However, closer analysis of the context and formation of the Citizens' Assembly, and the formal repeal process more broadly, disrupt such enthusiastic pronouncements about a 'revolution' in Irish political culture, which may be premature. As highlighted throughout our chapter and this volume, the momentous victory for women's rights that was the achievement of repeal owes more to the commitment and bravery of feminist activists holding distrusting politicians' feet to the fire, stoking the flames of public trust in the latter's promises to bring about reproductive justice, than to any inherent democratic quality of the political institutions in Ireland.

Notes

1 See for instance www.worldvaluessurvey.org or https://ourworldindata. org/trust.
2 This is exemplified by the failure of successive governments to legislate for the 1992 Supreme Court judgment in the infamous 1992 'X' case, which allowed for abortion where pregnancy endangers a woman's life, including through a risk of suicide. This refusal by politicians to legislate occurred despite successive referendums in the aftermath of the judgment asking the people of Ireland if the threat of suicide as a ground for abortion should be removed; in each case, the proposal was rejected by the electorate. It was clear that the public wished to have abortion available when the life of the woman was at risk, and yet it was not until 2013 (21 years after the original Supreme Court ruling), that the government enacted this law, through the Protection of Life During Pregnancy Act.
3 This case involved a young, pregnant braindead woman who was maintained on life support against her family's wishes due to the presence of a foetal heartbeat.

4 In June 2016, the online news outlet TheJournal.ie asked all 158 TDs (Members of Parliament) whether they were in favour of repealing the 8th Amendment, of whom only seventy-six responded. Forty-seven of these identified themselves as pro-repeal www.thejournal.ie/varadkar-belfast-dup-3529705-Aug2017.

5 www.citizensassembly.ie/en.

6 www.wethecitizens.ie.

7 Although Leo Varadkar, as Minister for Health, stated in 2016 that he would support repeal of the 8th Amendment, by 2017, as Taoiseach, he suffered from a version of strategic amnesia by postponing the announcement of his voting intentions to a very late stage of the campaign. See www.thejournal.ie/varadkar-belfast-dup-3529705-Aug2017.

PART II | Campaigns and campaigning

SIX | "Enough judgement": reflections on campaigning for repeal in rural Ireland

Mary McGill

Introduction

As a geography and an imaginary, rural Ireland occupies a distinct space in the Irish landscape, one which is often characterised by the region's assumed conservatism. With this point in mind, the following reflection explores how the repeal of the 8th Amendment complicates the longstanding binary of rural versus urban in an Irish context. It is written from the perspective of an Ireland where repeal is now a reality. This reality is regularly depicted as evidence of a 'new' nation. Yet, in the run up to the referendum, rural Ireland was repeatedly defined by its traditional conservatism as a stumbling block for the pro-choice campaign. However, as the referendum results illustrated, rural Ireland proved to be readier for repeal than many had anticipated. This suggests that the frequently invoked divide of rural versus urban in Ireland needs to be carefully recalibrated in the current era. With this in mind, the following reflection will first briefly explore representations of rural Ireland and how progressive social change complicates these narratives. It will then consider the tensions between Catholicism's enduring influence in rural communities and the embrace of progressive norms by such communities. Finally, it will reflect on pro-choice campaigning in rural communities before considering the role of digital technologies in rural Ireland's repeal campaign. Although not an academic exercise, this essay interweaves key insights from select scholarship to explore the themes raised.

Into the west: representations of rural Ireland

Depictions of rural Ireland usually position it within one of two distinct spheres. Romantic interpretations of the rural emphasise its connection to Irish understandings of nationhood as symbolised by land and nature. By contrast, parochial interpretations cast it as existing in a repressive past which the rest of the country – particularly the urban areas – are seen to have long since moved on from. Such contrasts find powerful expression in the Irish media, as Tom Inglis and Carol MacKeogh (2012) explore in their examination of reporting on a notorious 2009 rape trial in Kerry.[1] In this instance, as in others, rural Ireland is depicted as 'embarrassing' the more enlightened, urbane sibling, a simplistic binary which fudges the complications at play. In reality, as Inglis and MacKeogh argue, both versions of Ireland and the Irish media itself are entangled in the complex and dramatic social change which began in the 1970s and accelerated in the 1990s.

Repeal's success should inspire a re-examination of assumptions about rural Ireland's conservatism. However, the impacts of the social change that had grown apace since the 1990s were beginning to show many years before. China Scherz's (2010) study of changing mores in country communities provides a striking example of this. An anthropologist, Scherz examines evolving attitudes to single mothers, focusing on communities in western Ireland in the early 2000s. Using the story of one family as an example, Scherz recounts the differences in reactions to the pregnancies of two sisters who fell pregnant outside of marriage in 1988 and 2001 respectively. The earlier pregnancy was treated with horror, shame and secrecy. Adoption was discussed as an option. The daughter in question ultimately had her baby in England, quietly marrying the father of her child a few months later. In contrast, the pregnancy of the second daughter in 2001 was treated as a 'typical' pregnancy might be with celebration and joy. The daughter in question gave birth in a local hospital where family members visited her and her newborn without censure or shaming. This story, and the numerous other accounts Scherz (2010: 306) gathered during her fieldwork, leads her to conclude that there was a "growing acceptance of unmarried motherhood" in communities where "ten years prior it was not uncommon for unmarried women in the area to spend their pregnancy at a centre for unmarried mothers far away from their homes".

The rapid social change Scherz identifies marks rural Ireland as a key site where narratives of change in Irish society are played out and embodied. These dynamics challenge the traditional "moral geographies" (Crowley and Kitchin 2008) which defined Irish country life for much of the 20th century. The potential for such dynamics to question and reimagine understandings of Irish nationhood should not be understated. After all, the West of Ireland is critical to constructions of Irish nationhood, so much so that Catherine Nash (2002: 121) notes how its representations are central to "conservative versions of Irish identity". It is fair to assert that rural Ireland's support for repeal complicates the kind of idealisation Nash describes.

In Scherz's study, the sites of transformation are not only the west of Ireland as a specific geography but also women and attitudes to them. It is important to stress here that narratives of nationhood find expression not only in storytelling and so on, but through embodiment. Irish women were, and continue to be, impacted by ideas of nationhood which are "projected" as Angela K. Martin (1999: 66) puts it, onto their very person. Martin (1999: 67) rightly notes that this produces a burden whereby "[t]he labor of representation" falls to women, producing "very real material consequences for body, self and nation". Crowley and Kitchin (2008: 364) point out that from the inception of the Irish state, rural women were regarded as "a source of purity in the national narrative". This was the case even when sexually trans-mitted infection (STI) rates in rural communities, for example, complicated any such narrative. As the next section outlines in relation to Catholicism, the contradictions and harms of Ireland's purity culture has – and continues to have – specific effects for rural women.

The urban rural divide was a frequent theme in media coverage of the referendum. In November 2017, pro-life TD Mattie McGrath gave an interview to a farming website in which he claimed that what he termed the "traditional values of rural Ireland" were being "wiped out by a liberal crusade". McGrath made this statement in the aftermath of the Citizens' Assembly which voted by an overwhelming majority to recommend the liberalisation of Ireland's abortion laws, setting the wheels in motion for a referendum. McGrath's remarks here echo Angela K. Martin's (1999) points on how militaristic-style language is used to cast the erosion of Ireland's conservative value system as the undoing of the State itself. Further stories highlighted the urban-rural divide among TDs (*Irish Examiner* January 2018), the supposed slim chance of the referendum passing as evidenced by polls comparing rural and urban voters (*Irish Independent* May 2018), while a piece in *The Guardian* (May 2018) aligned Ireland with other countries in which cities were seen as the 'protectors' of reproductive rights.[2]

On 25 May 2018, thirty-nine out of Ireland's forty constituencies voted to repeal the 8th Amendment. It was a landslide few in the media – nationally or internationally – had predicted, a myopia that was based, at least in part, on expectations regarding rural Ireland's conservatism. "Old assumptions about the urban/rural divide proved to be wrong", reported the *Irish Times* (May 2018) when the result was announced in a piece entitled: "Yes vote shows overwhelming desire for change that nobody foresaw".[3] It is a sentiment I query, asserting that it was less that nobody foresaw rather than few in the national and international media took the time to consider rural Ireland as a site of potential rather than as a foregone conclusion.

Canvassing in Galway East,[4] the Yes votes generally – but not always – topped our tallies. They were usually closely followed by the 'undecideds' while the level of No votes was never so low as to be dismissed. We canvassers were often downhearted at the high rates of 'undecideds', assuming these would ultimately translate into No votes. Nevertheless, it was enough for some of us to dream. Sitting in a friend's car one evening after a canvass, I dared say aloud: "What if it's a landslide? What if we win?" After a few minutes of excited speculation, we stopped ourselves, scared of jinxing it. Ultimately, Galway East was the first constituency declared after the referendum, recording the result we dared hoped for: a majority of 60.2 percent in favour of repeal.

Catholicism: keeping the faith?

As is well-documented, the dominance of Catholicism in Irish society has had profound and deeply harmful implications for Irish women. The "cult of the Virgin Mary" as Nash (2002: 117) terms it, emphasised an ideal femininity for Irish women based on notions of self-sacrifice, chastity outside of marriage with high rates of fertility within marriage, and confinement to the domestic sphere. In the west of Ireland and elsewhere, this idealisation was entangled with the gendering of the land itself as 'female'. As Nash (2002: 120) writes, in Irish cultural traditions, "identity and femininity are eternally tied to the rural – to the land and to the earth".

The continuing power of the church in rural communities, as illustrated by their higher numbers of practicing Catholics, is one reason why such communities are characterised as regressive. However, this aspect of rural life should not elide the possibility of progress, specifically in relation to the evolution of personal attitudes to issues like marriage equality and abortion. Critical to this during the campaign, as the experience of many pro-choice activists can attest, was the necessity for conversation and good faith engagement between pro-choice activists and would-be voters. This was partly borne out of an awareness that the church's dominance of Irish life in rural communities and elsewhere meant that, in the run up to the referendum, many people would be discussing abortion for the first time. This was likely a daunting prospect as, for generations, the issue of abortion had been presented to those who attended Ireland's Catholic educational institutions exclusively in terms of sin, not as a social issue or as healthcare. Conversation provided a critical point of intervention to reframe understandings away from the strictures of Catholic morality.

In reflecting on these points now, I am reminded of Katha Pollitt's (2014) well-asked provocation: "What do abortion opponents really oppose?" Pollitt posits that it is not merely abortion itself but the autonomy it grants women that raises the hackles of the likes of the Catholic Church. In Ireland, problematic forms of femininity were traditionally treated as aberrations to be contained, both in a physical sense by the use of carceral institutions and in a psychological and emotional sense. Communities, families and even women themselves closely monitored each other's behaviour, promoting conformity under the guise of respectability. This legacy had special implications for the issue of abortion, which grants women agency over their own bodies and fertility, a move that runs counter to romantic notions of Irish womanhood. As Pollitt (2014: 33) observes, using same-sex marriage as an example, many progressive movements seek to "bring more people *into* beloved bedrock conservative institutions" [emphasis Pollitt's]. Abortion, on the other hand, represents "a much deeper and more radical social change" (Ibid.).

For rural Ireland, a geography shaped by and burdened by gendered archetypes of nationhood and religion, the repeal movement was undoubtedly an exemplar of the radical social change Pollitt describes. Yet, what the referendum ultimately showed was that while Catholicism remains a feature of rural life, it is far from the totalising force of yore. Rather, the acceptance of repeal by rural Ireland and the country more broadly displays, I would argue, a form of intellectual and emotional maturity whereby one's faith does not preclude one's ability to recognise the autonomy of another, even when that autonomy is 'in tension' with the rules of one's faith. This point is perhaps best articulated by exit polls after the referendum which showed that 84% of those who voted Yes cited a woman's right to choose as their reason for doing so.[5]

Saying 'yes' to repeal in rural Ireland: reflections on a campaign

Recalling the campaign now, I am reminded of how much trepidation I felt setting up my first repeal information stall in the middle of Athenry, a market town in Galway East, one Saturday morning in early March 2018. Much to the relief and surprise of myself and my two colleagues, the afternoon went surprising well. We had been braced for hostility that did not materialise on the day. I should point out that this lack of hostility could never be taken for granted during the campaign. Pro-choice campaigners, wherever they organised, were keenly aware of the possibility of abuse and intimidation.

Standing outside the AIB bank in the heart of a market town like Athenry, our pro-choice banner draped across a table stacked with repeal merchandise, felt like a radical act of self-disclosure. My two colleagues and I were doing the uncomfortable but necessary work of claiming visibility, a move which was characteristic of the repeal campaign more broadly. At that point, while the date for the referendum had not been set, the pro-choice movement was galvanising for what was a once-in-a-generation opportunity to liberalise Irish abortion law. This galvanisation took different forms, many of which were characterised by their visibility. This was a visibility that challenged the silences and polarisation that had previously defined Ireland's abortion debate, centring openness, dialogue and trust. These modes of visibility included the wearing of 'Repeal' sweatshirts in everyday contexts, women sharing their experiences on old and new media and the convening of public meetings and information sessions where citizens could engage with activists and experts.

The risk of pro-choice campaigning was generally regarded as more pronounced in rural communities. While not discounting this risk, as someone who grew up in a rural community in the north-west of the country and now lives in Galway East, a similarly rural area, the result of the 2015 Marriage Equality referendum emphasized to me that progressiveness was not confined to Ireland's cities and towns. Like every constituency bar one, Galway East, for example, had voted in favour of marriage equality (53.3% 'yes' to 46.7% 'no'). However, there was also the sense that abortion was a uniquely divisive issue, one which could potentially serve as a 'push back' against the progressivism Ireland was perceived as shifting towards. In order to win, the pro-choice movement needed to connect with as many people as possible. To do so, we could not afford to overlook communities like the one I had grown up in.

Among the women I worked with on the ground during the campaign, there was a tentative sense that rural Ireland would accept repeal but it was certainly not a foregone conclusion. Here, the characterization of rural Ireland as regressive stood to cause harm in the sense that it foreclosed on the outcome of the referendum without considering the nuances at play. Belittling or writing rural Ireland out of the campaign as some kind of 'lost cause' was not an option. As the results of the referendum showed, any attempt to do so would have been utterly self-defeating. To this end, the work and visibility of regional and rural pro-choice groups around Ireland must be emphasized as a critical contributing factor to the repeal's success.

The African-American poet and activist Audre Lorde (2007) has written movingly and insightfully on what she calls the 'tyrannies of silence'. In her essay, *The Transformation of Silence into Language and Action*, Lorde (2007: 41) cautions: "My silences had not protected me. Your silence will not protect you." Lorde sees the breaking of silences as a site of transformation where the once unsayable takes the form of language which in turn challenges prejudice and erasure. This is, as she acknowledges, no easy task. I was reminded of Lorde's insights regularly during the campaign. Rural Ireland is marked by silence and absence, from the ravages of the Great Famine to mass emigration to scars of industrial schools, county homes and laundries. A mere twenty-minute car drive from Athenry is the town of Tuam, where a mass grave of an estimated almost 800 infants was uncovered a few years ago on the grounds of a Catholic-run former mother and baby 'home'. All of which is to say, the effects of silence on the Irish landscape and psychic are not simply historical; they continue to exert a powerful influence.

It is interesting to note that the referendum itself was partly provoked by a kind of civic silence breaking in the form of the Citizens' Assembly.[6] Although not without issue (see Enright 2018c), what was so useful about the Assembly format was the kinds of dialogue it facilitated. This space was perhaps unique in the history of Ireland's approach to abortion in that it created conditions where citizens could discuss the issue beyond the usual religious dogma or polarized debates. Instead, the Assembly offered a space where a group of citizens had the ability to discuss abortion *as a social issue* not simply a sin, to ask questions, to hear different perspectives, and to do this work in a respectful environment. This process resulted in the Assembly making unprecedented recommendations to the Irish government, not only to change Ireland's abortion law, but to do so in a much more liberal fashion than had been predicted.

What the Citizens' Assembly suggested to me and others was that people were ready to talk about abortion, provided they could do so in the right kind of environment. Hence, the visibility of pro-choice campaigners in rural communities was, to my mind, paramount, signalling to those who wanted to engage that there were others in the community who were willing to listen. It was also proof that support for repeal was not, as some suggested, convened to metropolitan areas or to the upper middle class. The women I campaigned with were recognisable from the local supermarket, the morning train, the playground; in country parlance, you knew us to see. Many came from families who had lived in the area for generations. Visibility in this context was not easy – the prospect of abuse (verbal and physical) not to mention ostracisation and familial conflict were always a major concern – but it proved vital, enabling conversations that otherwise would never have happened.

Visibility can produce unexpected outcomes. What I remember most about our repeal stall that Saturday afternoon in March is the variety of people we spoke to, from young mothers to elderly farmers. We were standing quite close to one of the pubs. There was a rugby match on so the street was busy. At one stage, a middle-aged man came out of the pub and approached us. His face was flushed. I braced myself, expecting vitriol, until I spotted the bank note in his hand – he wanted to donate. "I believe in this", he said in a voice heavy with emotion. "I believe in ye." As so often happened when canvassing, it was a sobering reminder of the hidden impact of the 8th Amendment and how important it is that we never judge a book by its cover. Who knows what experiences that man and so many like him had endured in trying to support a woman or girl he cared about in a country that had turned its back on them.

#Repealthe8th: rural Ireland's digital toolbox

Writing in the aftermath of the Cambridge Analytica[7] scandal, at a time when the fracturing of public discourse is being blamed on the rise of social media, it is interesting to reflect upon how digital technologies served the work of repeal in rural Ireland. My website, for example, is hosted by Wordpress, a popular blogging platform with global reach. Having it gave me the freedom me to produce a blog post during the campaign on canvassing for repeal in rural Ireland which subsequently went somewhat viral (McGill 2018). The architecture of social media facilitated the dissemination of the post across multiple platforms, including Twitter and Facebook. In the month of its publication, the post was viewed more than 1,200 times, receiving hundreds of shares, including shares from social media accounts associated with the repeal campaign on a local and national level. I heard from campaigners across the country who shared my sentiments about the need for pro-choice visibility in rural communities. In this sense, despite being based in rural Ireland (which can be isolating), social media and the internet helped my work connect with other activists and the wider campaign.

A powerful illustration of how social media linked rural campaigners to the wider campaign network is the massively impactful In Her Shoes Facebook page. Founded by Erin Darcy of Galway East for Choice/Galway East Together for Yes, the page was conceived as a way to help people understand "the various and complex reasons why women would seek to terminate a pregnancy".[8] Its creation was inspired by conversations campaigners had with people on the street who were unaware of the complexities and tragedies the 8th Amendment had given rise to. It was particularly aimed at undecided voters, whom the page invited to 'take a walk in her shoes' by reading the real stories of Irish women who had undergone abortions. Each story was accompanied by an image of the shoes of the woman concerned, adding poignancy by underscoring the lived experience being expressed.

This approach proved to be hugely effective, shaping the narrative around abortion at a local and national level. For example, on that afternoon canvassing in Athenry, a woman with a gaggle of children remarked to us: "It's your *body*, like", adding "Have you seen In Her Shoes? Those stories would break your heart." At the time of writing, the In Her Shoes Facebook page has a following of 113,040; it has been liked over 100,000 times. It is a space where the second wave feminist maxim 'the personal is political' finds new expression in the digital age, harnessing the power of both the old and the new to help deliver political change.

One should be cautious about overestimating the ability of digital technologies to preserve and expand democracy (Dean 2005; Morozov 2012); neither should we assume that the digital will function as a substitute for declining public spaces. It should also be noted that concerns about material circulating online in the run up to the referendum prompted companies like Google and YouTube to ban all advertisements relating to the vote.[9] These points underline the potential for technologies to be used in myriad ways, not of all which can be construed as supporting a progressive agenda. Likewise, campaigners faced much abuse on social media for their efforts, a factor which made the already difficult work of repealing the 8th Amendment all the more emotionally demanding. Another important point is the issue of accessibility, given that rural Ireland's internet service can be patchy and unreliable.

While keeping these points in mind, there is no denying that the availability of social media and the internet were significant for those of us campaigning for repeal in rural Ireland. Firstly, these technologies easily connected us with each other, reducing the sense of isolation and instilling confidence in one's position (I was not, as I had feared, the only pro-choice person in the village). Secondly, technology connected rural activists to the wider campaign, making the participation of rural women at a national level all the more feasible and impactful. Thirdly, the practical element of arranging canvassing, meetings and stalls across multiple and disparate sites, along with disseminating campaign information was made easier by the cheap, quick and targeted communication enabled by apps and email. While there are a growing number of examples of how digital technology can undermine democracy, repeal in rural Ireland is one example of how such technologies, where available, can be utilised in service to it, as a tool to help overcome some of the organisational limitations of a particular topography.

Conclusion

For me, a young woman who stopped by the stall in Athenry that Saturday afternoon summed up the repeal movement when she said flatly, "enough judgement". Her words articulated a desire many citizens were shown to have, to break with the silence and shame which haunted Irish life for much of the 20th century. This reflection is by no means a comprehensive retelling or overview of the repeal campaign in rural Ireland – that is a story which demands far more space than this undertaking allows. It is also a story that goes beyond the referendum itself, stretching back through generations of campaigners and through generations of rural women and girls who struggled to travel to access abortion abroad and those who could not. However, I hope it provides some briefly-sketched insights of a changing landscape and a changing people which gently suggest our presumptions about rural Ireland need to be recalibrated. Although repeal has been achieved, more work remains to be done. Access to abortion services, for example, remains a critical issue for rural women, not to mention for all women living in Northern Ireland where abortion is still illegal. There is also the issue of access to abortion and other services for migrant women now living in rural Ireland, particularly those confined to Direct Provision[10] centres, an isolation which compounds the traumas they have suffered. The work of silence-shattering and creating an equal Ireland for all thus continues, buoyed by the knowledge that what was assumed could never happen has, changing not just the law, but who the Irish, as a nation, understand ourselves to be.

Notes

1 When the defendant was found guilty of rape, approximately fifty members of the local community lined up in the courtroom to shake his hand as a sign of solidarity. This was widely reported in the media.

2 Irish Examiner. 2018. Survey finds rural-urban divide among TDs about abortion. *Irish Examiner*, 16 January 2018. Available at: www. irishexaminer.com/breakingnews/ireland/survey-finds-urban-rural-divide-among-tds-over-abortion-823009.html; Corcoran, J. 2018. Young urban women giving Yes side referendum edge – but it is a narrow lead. *Independent.ie*, 6 May 2018. Available at: www.independent.ie/irish-news/abortion-referendum/poll-young-urban-women-giving-yes-side-referendum-edge-but-it-is-a-narrow-lead-36877996.html; Agnew, R. 2018. Urban versus rural: can cities protect reproductive rights? *The Guardian*, 16 May 2018 Available at: www.theguardian.com/cities/2018/may/16/urban-v-rural-can-cities-protect-reproductive-rights-ireland-eighth-amendment.

3 Kelly, F. 2018. Yes vote shows overwhelming desire for change that no one foresaw. *Irish Times*, 25 May 2018. Available at: www.irishtimes.com/news/ireland/irish-news/yes-vote-shows-overwhelming-desire-for-change-that-nobody-foresaw-1.3508879.

4 'Galway East' refers to a constituency in County Galway in the West of Ireland. During the campaign to repeal the 8th Amendment, Galway East for Choice, the local pro-choice campaign group, became Galway East Together for Yes as part of the national Together for Yes campaign co-led by the National Women's Council, the Coalition to Repeal the 8th Amendment and the Abortion Rights Campaign.

5 Ryan, P. 2018. Voters put aside personal opinions to allow women to make their own choices. *Independent.ie*, 25 May 2018. Available at: www.independent.ie/irish-news/abortion-referendum/voters-put-aside-personal-opinions-to-allow-women-make-their-own-choices-36950345. html.

6 The Assembly is a body comprising of the chairperson and ninety-nine citizens, randomly selected to be broadly representative of the Irish electorate, established to consider some of the most important issues facing Ireland's future. From November 2016 to April 2017 the Assembly considered Ireland's then highly restrictive abortion laws. Their findings and recommendations prompted the government to agree to a referendum on the 8th Amendment.

7   Cambridge Analytica was the name of a now defunct data mining company which used nefarious means to harvest huge amounts of user data from Facebook. This data was then used to produce targeted social media advertising for the Trump campaign during the 2016 American Presidential election and for the Leave campaign in the 2016 Brexit referendum.

8   See 'In Her Shoes: Women of the Eighth' on Facebook at: www.facebook.com/InHerIrishShoes.

9   Leahy, P. 2018. Rising number of unregulated online ads in abortion campaign. *Irish Times*, 3 May 2018. Available at: www.irishtimes.com/news/politics/rising-number-of-unregulated-online-ads-in-abortion-campaign-1.3481842.

10 Ireland's Direct Provision Centres are a network of accommodation facilities for asylum seekers which have been heavily criticised by human rights campaigners. Many of these centres are based in rural communities that are ill-equipped to deal with the needs of asylum-seekers.

SEVEN | Campaigning for choice: canvassing as feminist pedagogy in Dublin Bay North

Niamh McDonald, Kate Antosik-Parsons, Karen E. Till, Gerry Kearns and Jack Callan[1]

> The whole group were incredibly supportive and encouraging, especially with beginners. All my fears about talking to strangers on their doorsteps were allayed with one short evening shadowing a more senior member. There was a wonderful sense of unity and egalitarianism, and any ideas that I had were listened to and encouraged. (DBN member survey response, June 2018)

The dramatic and resounding vote for abortion rights in Ireland was won by committed women sharing their personal stories. While some of these stories were circulated in the mass media, many more were shared with family and friends in the privacy of a kitchen or living room. Still more were retailed on doorsteps to complete strangers face-to-face when activists canvassed. This aspect of the Repeal campaign was prepared for and supported by groups who organised locally in their constituencies. This chapter comes from our membership and activism in Dublin Bay North Together For Yes (DBN Repeal) group, a grassroots, women-led group set up to remove the 8th Amendment from the Irish constitution. In this chapter, we draw upon a survey of June 2018 conducted by and of 125 activists from DBN Repeal to describe how this vote was won and the particular place of the canvass in the campaign.[2] After providing an overview of our constituency, group and campaign, we argue that our approach to canvassing may properly be understood as a form of feminist activist pedagogy.

Dublin Bay North

Dublin Bay North (DBN) is the capital's largest constituency, with an electorate of 108,209 at the time of the referendum (Elections Ireland 2018). It had the largest voter turnout in Dublin – 71.6% compared to the Dublin average of 65.7% and a national average of 64.1% – and with its margin for Repeal of 38,181, it contributed the largest net Yes vote to the national total of any constituency.[3] These are striking statistics when considering that DBN is a rather mixed constituency, and in terms of class rather close to the Dublin average.[4] On the one hand, DBN has a noticeably higher proportion of households living in houses or bungalows (82.2%) than the Dublin average (73.1%), which range from the grand villas on Griffith Avenue in the north-west, abutting the early planned suburb of Marino, extending to the stately terraces of Clontarf in the south, which march eastwards towards the architectural jewels of Howth. Between and around these are bedsits and apartments in Kilmore, modest cottages in Raheny and areas of social housing in Darndale, Edenmore and Kilbarrack, the latter of which, when taken together, are slightly below the city average for local authority housing (7.2% compared to 9.3% in Dublin). Unemployment is below the city average (5.9%; Dublin 6.5%; RoI: 7.1%) and health is only a little below the average with 89.1% being reported as in good or very good health (Dublin: 90.5%; RoI: 90.0%). It has a relatively lower share of non-Irish born (14.2%) when compared to Dublin (21.8%) and the Republic (17.3%).

On the other hand, DBN also recorded Dublin's highest share of the electorate voting No (18.1%, compared to the Dublin average of 16.1% and the national average of 21.5%). The one age group that exit polls found to have voted in majority against Repeal was over 64 (RTÉ-Universities 2018: 10), and the percentage of DBN voters in this age range is relatively high, 21.6% compared to 15.8% for Dublin and 17.9% for the Republic. It also has a relatively high proportion of retired persons (18.2%; Dublin: 13.4%; RoI: 14.5%). The share of the population that is elderly may explain the high proportion whose education was finished by the age of 18 (38.6%; Dublin 31.7%; RoI: 35.9%). It may also explain the relatively high proportion of the people reporting themselves as Catholic (75.9%; Dublin: 68.9%; RoI: 78.3%), since nationally the share of the population that is Catholic is 75.0% for the age group 20–64, but 88.1% for those older than 64.[5] These figures indicate the local challenge that existed for the Repeal campaign, and also its success.

If we consider the campaign historically, in the 1983 referendum which established the 8th Amendment, only five of eleven Dublin constituencies voted against it.[6] The area now covered by DBN was then in two constituencies, one of which voted narrowly in favour of the amendment to establish a 'right to life of the unborn', and one narrowly did not. Only 59.7% of the constituency voted in the 1983 turnout for the area now designated DBN, which was significantly below 2018 numbers. In 1983, the proportion of the electorate voting *for* abortion rights (27.6%) was about *half the proportion in 2018* (53.4%).[7] Moreover, the share of the electorate voting *against* the right to abortion in 1983 was *far higher* (31.9%) than the recent poll (18.1%).

Within about one generation, in DBN, as in Dublin generally, a narrow majority against abortion rights has been transformed into a decisive 3:1 margin in favour – far ahead of the national shift, where a 2:1 margin against abortion rights has reversed to a 2:1 margin in favour. This remarkable change in attitudes had many causes but among these must be counted the activism of local grassroots campaigns. Below we describe the history and campaign of DBN Repeal, with a focus on canvassing, which we believe resulted in such a high voter turnout in our constituency.

The campaign in Dublin Bay North

Our paired buddy system built confidence, served to integrate people . . ., established friendships and built in a level of camaraderie . . . It offered new insights into the repeal campaign and enabled people to 'find their voice'. (DBN member survey response, June 2018)

DBN Repeal was a consensus-based and largely female-run grassroots group that included pro-choice groups and activists in our constituency. It was established in August 2017, beginning with twenty members from various backgrounds of activism, political traditions and members new to campaigning. In its first months, the focus was mobilising to the March for Choice; developing our logo, social media and messaging; offering canvasing training; fundraising activities; and lobbying local politicians. The group created its campaign foundations in anticipation of the referendum. In January 2018, officers were elected, a group constitution written, bank accounts opened and canvassing began. After the national Together for Yes (T4Y) campaign was launched in March 2018, DBN had a long discussion about whether to dissolve into the national campaign or not, and decided to affiliate while maintaining its autonomy for strategic decision-making and organisational independence.[8]

DBN Repeal had two levels of organisation: officers led monthly (and later biweekly) meetings open to all members, while 'on the ground' team leaders coordinated specific projects. For monthly group meetings, three elected officers (chair, secretary, treasurer) solicited action items and volunteers to coordinate activities decided upon by the larger group; a closed member Facebook (FB) group and an 'opt in' email listserv was the primary means of communicating amongst members. Geographically-located team leaders coordinated canvassing, leafletting and stalls in their own neighbourhoods and they organised open public meetings, postering and other activities. Other project-leaders were responsible for larger fund raising events and the rally. Team leaders used social media (WhatsApp) and email to organise local members, often at short notice. While some members of DBN were also members of political parties, the group did not want its campaign to be a platform for any party or elected official and rejected top-down organising.

This long and intensive local campaign mobilised between 400 and 500 volunteers; our survey of 125 respondents suggests that about 80% of these were women.[9] Beyond concerns with abortion rights, our members described a variety of causes that impelled their joining. About one-quarter said they joined out of solidarity with women affected by the lack of abortion rights in Ireland. A fear that the referendum might fail motivated about one-sixth of those joining in March and April 2018, and in the final month 22% joined due to their anger at No campaign tactics. A sense of the urgency of the issue is also reflected in the intensive commitment of members in the final month: 61% of the eighteen respondents who joined in May reported working on a daily basis of the campaign, with 28% early joiners (before March 2018), 19% of those joining in March and 23% of those joining in April also sustaining a daily engagement.

Almost half (43%) of the survey respondents reported that this campaign was their first experience of political activism; this was particularly true of women joining during the last three months of the campaign (59%). Fifteen of our 125 respondents came to DBN Repeal from pre-existing Repeal organisations. Work in political parties was a common background for 27% of male and 11% of female respondents. Other issue-based campaigns and movements, including housing and water charges, were supported by 7% of members replying to the survey. The largest cohort among those whose activism antedated the Repeal campaign were the fourteen women and seven men (17% of survey) who had worked to secure passage of the referendum mandating marriage equality.

The central experience of the campaign was canvassing, which, alongside leafleting (89%), was the main form of participation in the group (90%). Door-to-door canvassing, known as 'ground campaign', has long been employed in Irish politics for local and general elections to promote a platform, increase a politician's visibility and gauge the support for different issues in local areas. DBN's goals in canvassing were to gauge the level of support for a Yes vote and to reach undecided voters. Canvassing also helped with visibility, demonstrating that the Repeal campaign was active in our constituency. In general, while canvassing, our members focused on the importance of the right to choose, whilst being prepared to address specific questions on legislation. We also shared and listened to personal stories with strangers while canvassing, an approach that, until the 2015 Marriage Equality Referendum, was not at all common (Healy et al. 2016). Those involved with the 'Yes Equality' civil campaign were asked to share their personal reasons for supporting marriage equality when canvassing. Similarly, our survey establishes that canvassing for Repeal provided opportunities for both new and experienced members to engage in conversations with strangers about the emotive and highly personal issue of abortion in Ireland.

Canvassing was organised at three levels, through: a buddy system, team leaders and social media. We began in mid-January 2018, after a training day in November 2017 attended by 15–20 people, when we decided to use a simple buddy system: a new canvasser is paired with a more experienced member (typically female/ male or female/female) until the new member gained experience and felt confident to go alone; with experience, the new member soon becomes a trainer. The group continued to canvass each week thereafter, and member numbers steadily grew as the weeks passed. A second training day was held in March 2018, organised in response to new members joining after the referendum had been officially called. About thirty people attended, many new joiners, and this training was led by an Abortion Rights Campaign (ARC) trainer. This juncture was a crucial time for the campaign as messages about the legislation were becoming solidified. Nonetheless, in our survey, members indicated that canvassing, rather than the workshops, helped them feel confident about the facts.

Eventually the campaign was able to divide the constituency into local canvassing groups, each with at least one team leader, all of whom were women and the majority of whom had their first canvass in January. For most of these neighbourhood-based team leaders, this was their first campaign. These women learned by doing; they became confident through the knowledge gained from more experienced members and were empowered to organise and lead their own local groups. Team leaders briefed canvassers before each night's canvass about our main message/s for that outing and debriefed them at the end of the evening, offering further opportunities for group discussion on issues that arose. A DBN member commented in the survey that the "debrief on how to address challenging questions, discuss strategies and share emotions" was especially important. Canvassers were given the opportunity to ask questions about specific material or raise concerns. Alongside briefs and debriefs by canvass leaders, our DBN FB and local canvassing WhatsApp groups fielded questions and posted the latest developments in the campaign and the press.

Initially, canvass leaders worked alongside others, and provided their group with white high-visibility vests, clipboards, pens, canvassing sheets, up-to-date leaflets and DBN window posters. The buddy system facilitated new members learning how to canvass with a more experienced member until they were confident to go alone and then train new people themselves. This was a constant process of sharing knowledge and support. The buddy system offered new members the space and time to grow in confidence without feeling pressured to canvass alone at any point. The buddy system also helped integrate new members into the group and build relationships with longer-term members, which also encouraged new people to return. This snowballing process enabled us to reach large sections of the constituency in the final weeks of the campaign, with team leaders directing 'buddies' to doors and streets. As the campaign intensified, large numbers of people would show up to canvasses, as illustrated in Figure 7.1, which was DBN Repeal's first monster canvass in Coolock in April 2018. For the last four weekends of the campaign, these 'monster canvasses' were organised, whereby 80–100 people would show up and work 2–3 hours. Thanks to the buddy system DBN Repeal could train such large numbers of new people at each monster canvass.

Canvassers recorded the date of the canvass, street name, house numbers and if the door was opened or the voter was not in. Initially, they rated residents' support for repeal from 1 to 5 (lowest to highest) and included a comments section (to direct return visits). By late April, DBN Repeal adopted the T4Y canvass sheet and recorded a Yes, Maybe, or No, with space for comments, feeding results back to the national campaign with canvass leaders uploading data after each canvass. At the door, enthusiastic Yes voters were given details of our public FB page and invited to join the group. These voters reinvigorated canvassers because

Figure 7.1 DBN Repeal first 'monster' canvass, 21 April 2018, Coolock, North Dublin
Source: Photo © Karl Leonard

they reaffirmed the commitment to seeing this change made in Irish society.

Meeting undecided voters at the door gave the greatest opportunity for dialogue about the impact of the 8th Amendment on the everyday lives of women and reasons to support its removal. Responses from these voters as to why they were undecided ran a broad spectrum: people hadn't thought about how they would vote; some felt the well-publicised cases (A, B, C, X and Y) were wrong, possibly indicating that the No campaign created uncertainty for them; whereas others wanted to know about the proposed legislation. If voters had specific requests for more information, canvass leaders had additional supplementary materials to hand, including Trade Union newspapers on the 8th Amendment, Doctors for Choice leaflets and Termination for Medical Reasons leaflets.

We will return to a discussion of our members' experiences of canvassing, but note here that our movement was impelled by solidarity with women who wanted a right to an abortion, and it mobilised very many women and some men. Many of these people were new to political activism and, specifically, to the canvassing which was the principal vehicle of the campaign. People sustained a very significant level of commitment and in this respect it is perhaps important that a majority felt that they influenced group decisions 'very much so' (14%) or at least 'pretty much' or 'sort of' (44%). The 42% who said that they influenced decisions 'not really' or 'not at all' were drawn mainly from the late-joiners. Even here there was a good degree of satisfaction with decision-making and the majority of those offering any explanation for their lack of involvement in decision-making said it was because they joined late, were happy to take instructions, chose not to be involved in decisions, or could not attend meetings. Of the fifty-one saying they were 'not really' or 'not at all' included in decision-making only three had any negative comments at all about the decision-making process while many more of this group commended the organisational structure or its inclusiveness.

The referendum and our campaign did not happen in a vacuum: it was the accumulation of decades of activism when abortion rights was a very hostile topic in Irish society. As bell hooks (1994; 2010) urges, it is critical to pay attention to previous ways that feminists organised around rights and support for women, and consciousness-raising work, and how they advanced feminist pedagogical practice. Before describing our members' experiences, we first acknowledge the hard and thankless work of many women and people who paved the way for groups like DBN to emerge in the next section. We then argue that DBN Repeal practised a feminist activist pedagogy through canvassing that was both empowering and effective. We describe how our members gained the confidence to speak and tell their own stories, to listen and interact with strangers on difficult issues, all the while feeling supported by other members.

The Irish women's movement and feminist pedagogy

The movement unleashed mass active involvement of people completely new to campaigning. Open activists' meetings, extensive and creative use of social media and a plethora of WhatsApp message groups for people to arrange canvassing and fundraising and suggest ideas, allowed people to step forward quickly into organising roles. In the Dublin Bay North group, for example, a seventeen-year-old school student, coming up to exams (and who was not even old enough to vote) threw herself into public speaking and had no qualms about doing so in front of large crowds. (Holborow 2018: np)

The Repeal movement drew upon decades of feminist organising in Ireland.[10] We identify three broad strands of feminist activism critical to the Repeal campaign: calls for women's and reproductive rights, detailed by Connolly (this volume) consciousness-raising about violence against women in Irish society and feminist pedagogies. Democratic female-led organising is central to all three.

Firstly, while organisations working both inside and outside established institutions adopted varying strategies to achieve aims, grassroots activism was always of paramount importance to the movement for reproductive rights in Ireland. Radical 'women's liberation' and female-led organisations like Irishwomen United focused on participatory democracy, consciousness-raising activities and political campaigns, calling for, amongst other things: free, legal contraception, including state-financed birth control clinics; the right to a free, legal and safe abortion; and the right to self-determined sexuality (Connolly and O'Toole 2005). This highlighted the intersections of socialist, lesbian, and class-based activism, which were critical to Irish feminists at this time. In advocating for women to control their own fertility, Contraception Action Plan (CAP) organised a national petition and large public meetings to oppose the 1979 Family Planning Bill (Galligan 1998) and later provided information on contraception and women's sexual health and the sale of non-medical contraception (*Irish Times* 1981). The Dublin-based Women's Right to Choose Group, the first abortion rights group in Ireland, supported the Irish Pregnancy Counselling Centre and supplied educational material and speakers to women's groups. Grassroots feminist activism continued to underpin the movement for reproductive rights in Ireland, focused energies on providing support and information to women who needed abortions and advocated for abortion access. Some DBN activists brought their experiences to the group having worked previously on earlier campaigns for women's health and reproductive rights, including CAP, Anti-Amendment Campaign (1983), Dublin Abortion Information Campaign (1985) and Defend the Clinics (1988).[11]

Secondly, activist consciousness-raising in practice drew connections between personal lives and political processes by calling attention to violence against women in the home and promoting women's bodily autonomy. Ailbhe Smyth (1995: 38) noted: "When the state failed to provide vital services in the area of violence against women, women established services themselves and have succeeded in forcing the state to recognize and (at least partly) fund them." The founding of voluntary organisations like Women's Aid (1976) and Dublin Rape Crisis Centre (1977) were important steps in making visible sexual and domestic violence. In the 1980s and 1990s, feminists mobilised on a number of core issues including divorce, contraception and abortion as well as the provision of services around violence, counselling and health centres. Important to DBN's informational campaign was raising awareness about these issues, through speakers at our regular and public meetings, including Midwives for Choice and Lawyers for Choice, and our leaflets. Furthermore, it was evident when canvassing that some voters understood issues of abortion access, bodily autonomy and violence against women as intimately connected.

Thirdly, alongside the Irish women's movement, community-based voluntary education groups developed feminist pedagogies as a necessary tool for examining and articulating women's experiences of oppression. The course content and scheduling of community groups were organised to accommodate women whose primary responsibilities were tied to the home (Inglis 1994). At the same time, the political and educational goals of women's studies projects and feminist education within academia were closely aligned to the women's movement (Connolly and O'Toole 2005). Trinity College Dublin Women's Studies Programme (1983) and the collective-run Women's Studies Forum (1987), which later became the Women's Education, Research and Resource Centre (WERRC 1990), were instrumental in establishing Women's Studies in third level education (Connolly and O'Toole 2005).[12] University College Dublin's Women's Studies Outreach programme (1990), an innovative

University-Community partnership with a certificate in Women's Studies, offered working class women pathways to university education previously out of reach (Moane and Quilty 2012). Some DBN members were educated through WERRC and other gender and women's studies programmes.

Feminist pedagogy in these programmes placed women's experience as the centre of inquiry to realise individual and collective empowerment through participatory learning. Owing to its activist roots, knowledge in the feminist classroom is generated through dialogue, with teachers and learners open to each other's viewpoints and is validated by or with experiences that are collectively recognised (Chow et al. 2003: 263). Transformative learning environments were created that were collaborative, non-hierarchal and 'safe' spaces, whereby instructors 'facilitate' and attempt to democratise the creation and sharing of knowledge, while students voice opinions and ask questions (Pileggi et al. 2015: 30). Experiential, 'hands-on' learning incorporates critical consciousness that enables one to generate new knowledge. Students thus gain confidence by developing critical thinking skills and political and social understandings of activism (Stake and Hoffman 2001). Emotion is an important tool in feminist transformative learning experiences, particularly when it causes discomfort, because these intense teaching moments generate different types of knowledge, requiring patience, collective inquiry and improvising (Pileggi et al. 2015: 31). Unpredictable teaching moments, born of intense responses to the social, political and affective relationships between learners, facilitators and content result in personal experiences of meaning-making (Ibid.). Moreover, acknowledging one's vulnerability is key to fostering a sense of mutual empathy in feminist experiential learning (Ibid.: 40). Dialogic, participatory and experiential learning in unpredictable moments was critical to the sharing of knowledge through canvassing in DBN, as we discuss below.

Canvassing for repeal as an empowering feminist pedagogy

I definitely became way more confident in the facts through canvassing and reading up. Listening to team mates really helped me also. (DBN member survey response, June 2018)

The Repeal campaign echoed these legacies and lessons of previous feminist practice. In particular, we found that the experience of canvassing was a transformative and empowering process for our members. The group's survey of open ended questions confirmed what we were witnessing during the campaign. Strangers, mainly women, came together for a common goal, supported each other, trained each other, built relationships and shared stories while fundamentally changing Ireland forever. Through our canvassing buddy system, we drew upon strands of dialogic, participatory and experiential feminist pedagogy that generated new forms of knowledge for the canvasser and citizen at the door. Our members raised their consciousness and knowledge and gained the confidence to share and listen to stories.

It is striking that 98% of our surveyed members described their experience of the campaign in positive terms, when considering that two-thirds of the same members had never canvassed before; further, two-thirds female and one-third male of first-time canvassers also had no previous experience with political activism. While almost half the early joiners (before March 2018) received some specific training, virtually none did who joined later. Instead, they were learning through experience. Certainly a few mentioned anxieties about canvassing. Asked if there were any factors inhibiting their engagement with the campaign, 27 of the 125 respondents raised a number of issues, but mainly about lack of time to do all that they would have liked. Only five mentioned a lack of confidence relating to canvassing, which is quite impressive given the general lack of experience among the group.

Our members, in other words, were empowering themselves and each other while carrying out actions that many thought they were unable to do or would never do. About three-quarters of those responding to the survey (77%) said that the buddy system we described above was very welcome, giving confidence to 22% of the women and 35% of the men, while 9% of the women and 12% of the men said it was important in learning the campaign's message. When asked which factors had developed their confidence in the campaign message, 45% referred to their own research, but one-third mentioned the information provided by DBN Repeal (33%) and one-fifth each mentioned their conversations with other members of the group (21%), the experience of canvassing as itself an education (20%) and the questions and replies on DBN WhatsApp (19%). Respondents felt supported and confident thanks to training, a buddy system and conversations within the group both in person and via social media.

The participatory nature of our approach was well received by our members. In an open-ended survey question, "What did you think about the buddy system we used?", people commented that it gave them confidence and companionship. A new canvasser stated, "[The system] was great for giving people confidence and showing you what to say to frequently asked questions"; an experienced canvasser said, "[It was] very good. I found it really encouraged the newbies and on bad days I needed the company myself". Not only was the buddy system useful for building confidence, but it provided a safety net for those who might have had concerns about going door to door. One canvasser responded that the buddy system was: "Excellent. My buddy had been knocking on doors for months, and gave me great advice, and boosted my confidence. It also made me feel safe". Another commented that not only did it buoy confidence levels but also served to integrate new people into the group. Members commonly referred to the friendships and camaraderie that resulted from the buddy system: "It is highly relieving to know that you have a friend with you that you know can back you up on the doorsteps and defend your points when the going gets tough".

We argue that the dialogic exchange of knowledge between new and experienced canvassers through the buddy system was a form of feminist experiential pedagogy. Initially, new canvassers observed how to engage in conversations with voters. When confident to try canvassing, the experienced canvasser offered feedback after leaving the doorstep, or suggested alternative responses if the new canvasser was uncertain how to respond to voter's queries or concerns. Individuals could immediately reflect on each experience based on discussion and feedback with their partner. Learning was also cumulative: new and old canvassers might test out different approaches, sometimes exchanging ideas about what worked with other pairs or asking for advice, which meant that pairs actively adapted and implemented changes to the way they canvassed as they went. For both canvassers, the conversations that happened on the walk between the doors provided a cyclical exchange between members. Indeed, a notable 11% of the women found the buddy system a source of solidarity and friendship. As hooks notes, creating a safe "woman space . . . where we can engage in open critical dialogue with one another, where we can debate and discuss without fear of emotional collapse, where we can hear and know one another in the difference and complexities of our experience, is essential" for political solidarity and moving the feminist movement forward (1994: 110).

Dialogic and participatory learning in a supportive environment created by relations between paired canvassers also encouraged canvassers to listen to and sometimes disclose personal experiences on the doorstep. As an experiential form of knowledge creation, storytelling resulted in powerful moments of self- and social-transformation. As hooks describes: "[S]tories

help us engage with the complexities of conflict and paradox . . .
Stories also help us heal" (2010: 52). All through the campaign,
activism solicited stories as one member remembered: "I heard
so many personal stories once I held a banner". One canvasser
reported that "our arguments were based on compassion and
real life experience". Another said that they were told by their
partner on their "first day of canvassing that speaking about why
I was pro-choice and speaking from the heart would sway people
which was something I was nervous about". Nervous or not,
confidence grew. One activist "learned from my co-canvassers",
including "those with personal experiences of how the 8th
Amendment affected them (oftentimes this was shared proactively
rather than me asking as I felt it was important never to ask
anyone why they were canvassing)".

Engaging in conversations with undecided voters was a significant way to break the silence and denial surrounding abortion in
their local communities. It drew citizens into conversations based
on the knowledge and experiences of both canvassers and local
residents, and became part of the doorstep education. As another
canvasser explained:

> Personal stories and individual experiences that weren't readily
> available on television or even on the web were key to the
> success of the campaign, and speaking with DBN members on
> a daily basis would produce different stories about how the 8th
> Amendment has affected them personally. I took these on board
> when developing arguments and they were highly effective in
> both educating the other side about the reality of what they were
> trying to defend, and in manifesting to ordinary and somewhat
> apolitical individuals just why they should vote yes.

This feeling of solidarity is the essence of the participatory learning in feminist pedagogy: the experienced activist and the newbie
each generated insights from shared experiences that can be
framed as liberatory knowledge. There can be few more engaged

forms of learning than trying to explain your evolving views to strangers who may not fully appreciate your standpoint. It takes creativity and courage, and the support of others.

Conclusion

> It was incredibly fulfilling. I think it is one of the best things I ever did. I never canvassed door to door or anything before so really pushed myself. Also the sense of belonging and support was important to me as this was a difficult personal issue close to my heart. (DBN member survey response, June 2018)

When women speak about abortion in Ireland: "There are so many things unsaid. So many stories remain hidden in Ireland, swept under the carpet, nudged into the shadows, silenced out of shame and pain" (Mullally 2018: 5). Canvassing for choice allowed some people to share these hidden stories with strangers. As a feminist pedagogy, it embodied decades of activism and annealed through an intense national debate about women's rights over their own bodies. Our survey indicated that canvassing offered new insights into the Repeal campaign, developed political strategies and useful arguments and empowered our members to 'find their voice'. The DBN paired buddy system in particular built confidence, served to integrate members into the group, resulted in friendships and created a level of group camaraderie that might not necessarily have been fostered by our other activities, such as attending meetings or using social media. By creating safe feminist spaces through dialogues while walking on the streets being canvassed, our buddy system allowed women to share and make political use of their personal insights and stories as part of a national campaign. This transformative experience, moreover, created a new cohort of empowered activists. Through experiential and participatory forms of learning, a new group of people were drawn into political participation, many of whom will continue to be active in years to come.

Acknowledgements

We extend our gratitude to all DBN Repeal members for their inspiring activism and incredible dedication to advancing women's rights and the rights of childbearing people to have the choice to decide on their own health, bodies and futures. We also thank DBN members for sharing their experiences through the survey. All errors of interpretation are ours.

Notes

1 All authors are members of the Dublin Bay North Repeal Research Group and were participants in the DBN Repeal/Together for Yes activist group. Callan, Kearns and Till are members of the Department of Geography, Maynooth University. Antosik-Parsons is affiliated with the School of Visual Culture, National College of Art and Design. McDonald was the chair of DBN Repeal.

2 Following the vote, with other DBN members, we formed a research group aiming to document and tell the story of our group's history and campaign from the perspective of our members.

3 The eleven taken here as Dublin comprise: Dublin Bay North, Dublin Bay South, Dublin Central, Dublin-Fingal, Dublin Mid-West, Dublin North-West, Dublin-Rathdown, Dublin South-Central, Dublin South-West, Dublin West and Dún Laoghaire.

4 The census data for the Dublin constituencies is part of the Small Area Statistics produced for the Census of 2016: http://census.cso.ie/sapmap/ (accessed 4 October 2018).

5 The breakdown of religion by age is given for the state in Statbank, Profile 8, Table E8078; www.cso.ie/px/pxeirestat/Database/eirestat/Profile 8 – Irish Travellers Ethnicity and Religion/Profile 8 – Irish Travellers Ethnicity and Religion_statbank.asp?

6 The eleven in 1983 are Dublin Central, Dublin North, Dublin North-Central, Dublin North-East, Dublin North-West, Dublin South, Dublin South-Central, Dublin South-East, Dublin South-West, Dublin West and Dún Laoghaire. This area is significantly smaller than the unit taken for 2018 as the boundaries of the Dublin region have extended and while Dublin North-Central and Dublin North-East were amalgamated, Dublin-Fingal was added to the north of them.

7 The share of electorate voting in favour of abortion rights is the valid vote against the 8th Amendment in 1983 and in favour of Repeal in 2018. The margin in favour of abortion rights is the share of the valid votes that were for abortion rights minus the share of the valid votes that were against abortion rights.

8 While the group did change its official name, it maintained independence from the national-level group. In this chapter, we use the short-hand DBN Repeal.

9 Membership estimated from social media. A voluntary online survey of group members was conducted in June 2018 on the nature, engagement and experiences of our members.

10 For a thorough history of women's rights in Ireland, see: Connolly (2001); Connolly and O'Toole (2005).

11 Some DBN members are involved with other activist groups including ROSA, ARC and IHN.

12 WERRC was founded by Ailbhe Smyth.

EIGHT | #Tá: pro-choice activism in the Irish language community

Lisa Nic an Bhreithimh

An Ghaeilge agus Éire ~ Ireland and the Irish language

For me, an Ghaeilge (the Irish language) is a distinctive way of thinking, feeling and communicating that is altogether different to English. Irish is my most cherished language, closely intertwined with my sense of identity as an Irish woman. Like many, I took an interest in the language through visits to the Gaeltacht (native Irish-speaking regions) throughout my life. There, I felt a connection to my national identity I hadn't felt before and Irish has been a core part of my personal and professional life since. As it is for many Irish speakers, it has always been important for me to be able to live my life through the medium of Irish.

The Irish language (or Irish Gaelic[1]) is an official language of the Irish State and the European Union. I will only skim the surface of its rich and lengthy history here. Irish is one of the oldest languages still spoken today and can be traced back as far as the 4th century AD. The relationship between the language and its people is complex. For many generations, the English language was seen as one of opportunity, a passport to Dublin or Boston to work and prosper, costing Irish much of its standing. Vast numbers of Irish speakers died during the Great Famine, when rural Gaeltacht regions were badly hit. Over time, there have been many factors resulting in a decline of the status of Irish and much work done on its revival. Nowadays, Irish is considered by many a 'minority language'. However, it has a growing base of speakers, in both urban and rural areas, among young and old, due to continued revival and promotion of the language by organisations like Conradh na Gaeilge (The Gaelic League), community-led initiatives such as the Pop Up Gaeltacht, Irish language media and Gaelscoileanna (Irish-medium schools) to name a few of many contributing supports.[2] Census data show that almost 40% of the population have the ability to speak Irish, approximately 4% speak it daily and approximately 2.3% said that they spoke Irish weekly outside of the education system (Central Statistics Office 2017).

The Irish language is vibrant in media and education in Ireland. Numerous Irish language radio stations exist as well as TG4, the state's Irish language TV station broadcast nation-wide and online. Online Irish language media outlets are becoming more prevalent and publications such as *Comhar* are still in print.[3] Universities across the world offer Irish programmes at degree level. The importance of the language is often recognised globally. On 23 May 2011, US President Barack Obama visited Ireland and in a speech in Dublin city he famously said: "*Is féidir linn*", a translation of his campaign slogan "Yes we can" (Taylor 2011). A president of a country with a population of over 300 million took the time to translate his motto to Irish for this speech – recognition of the status of Irish as an important, living language. This was an exciting and affirming moment for many Irish speakers. It was thus of great importance that the language be a part of the discourse around the 2018 referendum.

Stereotypes are sometimes projected onto '*Pobal na Gaeilge*' (the Irish speaking community), such as the assumptions that they are from a particular class or background, or in relation to how they feel about less fluent Irish speakers. The reality is that Irish speakers come from diverse backgrounds, places and age groups, making it difficult to tar them accurately with one brush (Ó Broin, 9 April 2017). Many stereotypes linger from the past or particular negative instances in people's lives. In my involvement with the Irish speaking community in media, education and indeed the Yes campaign, I have learned of the breadth and variety within the community and how it diversifies more and more with time. I see the Irish language community today as a microcosm of the population of Ireland. People take an interest in the language for various personal and professional reasons, and so the community itself is both diverse and no longer reflective of the narrow stereotypes that once defined it. In this chapter, I will examine the place and importance of the Irish language in the 2018 referendum campaign to repeal the 8th Amendment, taking this context of the language today and its community of speakers into account throughout. Although it might be more natural to write such a paper *trí Ghaeilge* (through Irish) itself, I will use English to share the story in this publication beyond the community of Irish speakers, while incorporating some Irish along the way.

Bunú Gaeil ar son Rogha ~ The formation of Gaeil ar son Rogha (Irish Speakers for Choice)

On the evening of 20 September 2017, a group of Irish speakers came together in Dublin to address a gap they saw in the work being done to call for a repeal of the 8th Amendment, and indeed in general public discourse about the Amendment. Ireland was already gearing into campaign mode, meetings were being held, local groups were forming and yet there was a vacant space in the Irish language media where we felt there should be regular, substantive coverage on the issue. Likewise, we identified a space within national events and meetings working for a repeal of the 8th Amendment where we felt there should be informed, intelligent, pro-choice dialogue through Irish. We wanted Irish-speaking pro-choice voices to be heard and to come together in their commonality. In return, we knew that a campaign conducted through Irish would add greatly to the national and indeed, international, campaign to repeal the 8th Amendment in that it would allow for a different set of voices to share the campaign message, a different way of communicating that message and another way to reach people on a personal level when asking them to vote Yes. I will elaborate further on these benefits throughout this chapter.

A similar group formed during the 2015 Marriage Equality Referendum called *Tá Comhionannas* (Yes Equality). Its reach was broad and significant with members taking part in regular media debates and interviews and a notable increase of discussion of the topic on Irish media. *Tá Comhionannas* representatives partook in the broader Yes Equality campaign meetings and the group is mentioned in *Ireland Says Yes*, published after the passing of the 2015 referendum, noting appreciation for its efforts towards the national campaign (Healy et al. 2016). The success of the campaign did not go unnoticed within the Irish language community either, where many recognised the effectiveness of campaigning through Irish. Abortion rights campaigner Ailbhe Smyth noted the significance of the crossover between the Yes Equality campaign and the campaign to repeal the 8th Amendment (Smyth 2018). Members of *Gaeil ar son Rogha* (Irish Speakers for Choice) recognised the successes of *Tá Comhionannas* and the value of such a campaign to a national effort and indeed to the Irish speaking community and Irish itself. Inspired by both the national campaign to repeal the 8th Amendment and *Tá Comhionannas*, and in no small part due to the drive of many hard-working Irish speakers, *Gaeil ar son Rogha* resolved to work together through Irish to campaign for a repeal of the 8th Amendment, or, later, for 'Yes'.

Gaeil ar son Rogha was made up of a range of age groups, genders, professionals and students, those from Dublin and other parts, native Irish speakers and those who learned Irish later, all joined in agreement on the following objectives:

1. To ensure that there would be a debate on the referendum in Irish and that the Irish language would have a place in the pro-choice campaign;

2. To make available to the people of Ireland information regarding the 8th Amendment/abortion rights;

3. To train spokespeople and to make them available to Irish language media in Ireland, including debates and interviews on radio, television and online;

4. To publish articles/blogs about the subject of the referendum through Irish;

5. To campaign for the referendum through Irish;

6. To give an opportunity to those who are in favour of repealing the 8th Amendment/abortion rights to participate in a group of Irish speakers who will be campaigning and promoting debate within the Irish-speaking community; and

7. To speak only on our own behalf, rather than anyone else (Gaeil ar son Rogha 2017).[4]

On 18 April 2018, around forty people gathered in Dublin for the launch of *Gaeil ar son Rogha*. Irish language writers and musicians performed, attendees had an open discussion on the amendment and journalists interviewed attendees. Our committee members ranged from a college student who had previously campaigned on the No side of the debate to a middle-aged man who had offered a place to stay free of charge in London to Irish women travelling there for abortions. Though we were small in number, we were a diverse group with a variety of reasons for coming together. Once formed, we knew it was important for our voices to be heard on Irish language media platforms. Aligning with the national campaign for Yes, through *Gaeil ar son Rogha* we found an abundance of empathy, a willingness to listen and kindness among the pro-choice Irish speakers we met. The more I learned more about who and what makes up '*Pobal na Gaeilge*' through our campaign work, the prouder I was to be part of it.

Na Meáin ~ Media

Gaeil ar son Rogha formed a committee of designated officers and began to build what would become an important Yes campaign group. The group's spokespeople could be seen and heard on Irish language media weekly from early on and gained hundreds of social media followers within weeks. The group reached 1,000 followers on Twitter[5] and over 800 on Facebook by polling day. As part of research conducted on the frequency of Irish language hashtags used on Twitter from September 2017 to June 2018, it was found that #Tá (Yes) was used almost 100 times, #GaeilarsonRogha 54 times and #Aisghair (Repeal) almost 150 times.[6] Taking into account that none of these figures include retweets and that the number of Irish speakers active on Twitter who confidently and regularly tweet about social issues through Irish is relatively quite small, these numbers are quite significant.

Irish language broadcasters can face challenges covering referenda due to the significantly smaller number of regular Irish speakers, compared to English speakers in Ireland (as referenced above). As a part-time broadcaster myself I have found that it can be significantly more difficult to find fluent Irish speakers who are willing to speak on television/radio and are comfortable speaking about the issue at hand as well as knowledgeable on the topic. One may find a speaker on a topic willing to speak on radio for example, but this person may not necessarily speak Irish, and among the smaller community of Irish speakers (compared to the English-speaking community), there are inevitably less available speakers, which can lead to a lack of speakers in certain areas at times. If, during a referendum, there are not enough speakers on one side, the issue may not be covered for the sake of balance, so there may be more limited coverage of news stories by Irish language media. *Gaeil ar son Rogha* brought together a panel of fluent speakers readily available to speak about the referendum. Similarly, individuals from '*Gaeil ar son na Beatha*' (Irish Speakers for Life) were available to speak on the No side. The mobilisation of Irish language campaigns, for and against repeal, was also the topic of debate and discussion on social media. Online commentary and appraisal of the existence of such groups reminded us in *Gaeil ar son Rogha* of our significance as part of the national campaign for Yes.

Scéalta pearsanta ~ personal stories

People's personal stories were a key driving force of the decisive results of both the 2015 and 2018 referenda. Irish writer Anne Enright was one of many to comment on the strong Yes vote in 2018 (Enright 2018; see also Reidy, this volume). Thousands of deeply personal stories were shared during the referendum campaign, giving the public a picture of the broad nature of the difficulties caused by the 8th Amendment. These personal stories, bravely shared, appear to have had a major impact on public sentiment towards the issues at hand.

As an Irish speaker, I felt a closer connection to stories told through Irish and many others spoke of feeling similarly. As a woman called Anja says in an Údarás na Gaeltachta video about Irish: "Each language is a way of thinking, (an) individual and unique way of thinking."[7] On 22 May 2018, *Gaeil ar son Rogha* shared a video of Tara Uí Adhmaill, a mother raising her children through Irish who spoke about the devastating effects the 8th Amendment had had on her life.[8] The video had a reach of almost 50,000 views, over 200 shares, almost 300 reactions and over 40 Irish speakers commented (in Irish) on the video. One person told us of an American friend who had seen the video in the Midwest of the USA and commented that seeing such a story told in the Irish language had a profound effect on her. By sharing her story with our Irish language campaign group through the medium of Irish, Tara shared something distinctive. The sharing of a variety of different stories from different places throughout the Yes campaign was crucial to reaching as many voters as possible. Because Ireland is a small place, stepping into the Irish language world is to step into an even smaller pocket of Ireland. Irish speakers were often somehow connected to the person telling the story. Generally, the closer we are to someone the stronger the impact they will have on us, so these stories told in Irish often had a greater impact.

Guthanna éagsúla ó áiteanna difriúla ~ Different voices from different places

Over an 8-month period (October 2017–May 2018), *Gaeil ar son Rogha* took part in over twenty-two radio interviews and debates, five TV interviews, wrote six articles in print and online and gave five online video interviews. On social media, we shared almost 700 tweets and hundreds of Facebook posts. As previously discussed, it is significantly more challenging to find suitable spokespeople for Irish language media. In *Gaeil ar son Rogha*, younger, less experienced speakers quickly rose to the challenge of taking on interviews, debates and news reports on behalf of the group. Indeed, due to the 'grassroots' nature of the Yes campaign, English language debates also involved younger or less experienced speakers, supported by professionals – trained activists, full-time campaigners, those with years of debating experience, politicians, medics and lawyers (see also McDonald et al., this volume). In the absence of many of these representatives, Irish language media coverage, for the most part, featured less experienced and untrained spokespeople.

I myself took part in a debate on Raidió na Gaeltachta representing *Gaeil ar son Rogha* alongside Sinn Féin TD, Donnachadh Ó Laoghaire.[9] Our opponents were Senator Rónán Mullen, one of the most vocal politicians in the anti-abortion campaign, and Niamh Uí Bhriain of the Life Institute, another longstanding pro-life campaigner. As two of the most prominent spokespeople of the No campaign, Mullen and Uí Bhriain would likely have had senior members of the Yes campaign as their opponents in an English language debate, so to find myself – a fairly unseasoned, untrained debater – partaking in an hour-long live debate on national radio against two experienced spokespeople was extremely challenging. Although I felt confident and passionate about my arguments, I recognised the differing levels of debating experience between us and the techniques my opponents had from their broader experience in debating on political platforms. Although challenging, the debate also provided an incredible opportunity for me to take on a debate at this level. I found that many *Gaeil ar son Rogha* spokespeople shared different messages than those shared through English. For example, one point we discussed in our campaign was how difficult it had been for native Irish speakers from Gaeltacht regions who were not so fluent in English to travel to other countries and discuss their crisis pregnancies through English in the earlier years of the 8th Amendment's existence. I believe that our varied messaging and ways of communicating added something not yet seen or heard elsewhere in the campaign for Yes.

After the referendum, I surveyed five key Irish language journalists, including one local and two national current affairs radio broadcasters and two national radio-television broadcasters. Those surveyed who also work in English language media told me that they saw the Irish language debates as more respectful. This may be a result of the size of the Irish speaking community or the existence of a spoken or unspoken mutual understanding between Irish speakers, wherein we recognise that we have each most likely actively undertaken to learn or continue to use Irish in recognition of its value. This may allow for a fundamental level of respect between Irish speakers because we share something in common – our respect for the status of the language as one still relevant and important enough to be used in this context – with most of our Irish-speaking opponents, something which could not often be said for opponents in English language debates. Another point noted by those surveyed was that the debate appeared clearer to understand in Irish than in English. The Irish language involves much more literal and direct communication than English. For example, the Irish word for midwife is '*bean chabhrach*' (helping/helpful woman). As such, some of the broadcasters surveyed found that the Irish language debates often came across as clearer and simpler.

For Irish to be considered a living, important language, it cannot be restricted to particular topics of conversation, rather it must lend itself to an in-depth debate of any important issue. By using the language to discuss a broad range of topics, those who speak it can free it from the confines of its historical context, or to the perception that it is only relevant in the education system. In this way, Irish speakers can show younger generations that it is useful and useable in their lives and allow it to continue to develop by creating new, relevant words like '*féinín*' (selfie) or '*ag treochtáil*' (trending). Equally in *Gaeil ar son Rogha* we had to quite literally choose our words carefully. The most commonly used word in Irish for abortion is '*ginmhilleadh*', which can be translated to 'the ruining/destroying of the child/offspring' – quite a loaded, and arguably, inaccurate term. Therefore, we often turned to other words such as '*foirceannadh*' (termination). Language is important and as many campaign groups did, we had an in-depth discussion about our words and messaging.

The Irish language itself had a significant place in the referendum campaign to repeal the 8th Amendment. The *Tá* (Yes) badges were highly visible (see Figure 8.1). The *Tá* badges brought an added sense of culture and identity to those who wore them. One Yes campaigner, Karen Fagan, coined a new phrase, '*Tágetherness*', which she termed the 'brief and potent connection felt with a passing stranger wearing the same badge as oneself' (Fagan 2018).[10]

Figure 8.1 TÁ badges

Often without even thinking about it, campaigners played with the language and displayed pride in it. The referendum called us to question who it is we are, as people of Ireland, and what it means to be Irish. Interestingly, in this questioning, in our display of who we are and what we stand for, Irish played a significant role and many wore Tá badges, regardless of their relationship with the language.

We found an interesting crossover with the Deaf Community Together for Yes in that we were the only groups campaigning for Yes completely through languages other than English, namely Irish Sign Language and Irish, the two other official languages of Ireland. Language was especially important to our two groups, for both our understanding and identity, and for an effective campaign. On 18 May 2018 *Gaeil ar son Rogha* released a collaborative video[11] produced with the Deaf Community group. In the video, the speakers say: "We both know how important it is, to the deaf community in Ireland and to Irish speakers, to be able to learn about this referendum and to discuss it in our own languages." Words and language were important throughout the campaign for Yes. We noticed just how important they were in our campaign through the medium of Irish and to the bilingual community to whom we spoke.

Dátheangachas ~ Bilingualism

The Irish speakers I met on the campaign trail felt that their bilingualism helped them to consider more easily a variety of opinions. Bilingual people are accustomed to seeing the world through the lenses of the different languages. I think that this made our campaign work easier in that many of the bilingual people we met had already done what we were asking them to do: to consider different ideas to their own. Psychologists who study bilingualism have argued that bilingual children possess a greater capacity for empathy than monolingual children because "children in multilingual environments have social experiences that provide routine practice in considering the experience of others . . . they have to think about who speaks which language to whom, who understands which content" (Kinzler 2016; see also Fan et al. 2015). Empathy was something Yes campaign groups sought from voters during the campaign – to deeply consider personal stories being shared.

Not only was the Irish language Yes campaigning an added benefit to the national campaign for Yes, the referendum in turn gave more visibility to the language itself and showed us the place Irish has in the hearts and minds of many of our people. To some in Ireland, the Irish language is stuck in between the pages of schoolbooks, rather than a language they see or hear around them every day. Many of *Gaeil ar son Rogha*'s social media posts were shared by regional Together for Yes groups and prolific Yes campaigners with large followings. I hope that this showed up on the radar of those outside of the Irish speaking community, making it clear that Irish is a living, contemporary language, a key part of modern Ireland. Women's stories of crisis pregnancies could be read, debates on the 8th heard, or information accessed through

Irish, emphasising its status as a living language – current, useful and important. Even if people did not speak Irish themselves, it was important to how Ireland as a nation is seen and conversely how Irish is part of Ireland during dramatic social change, that Irish language was a strong branch of the Yes campaign.

Cad atá foghlamtha againn? ~ What have we learned?

Similar to what the national Yes campaign saw of the country as a whole, *Gaeil ar son Rogha* discovered a strong will for activism, change, transformation and progress within the Irish speaking community. We learned that within the community there are those who are willing to get involved in campaigns that mean something to them. Conversely, it is clear, through the success of social media and media campaigns, public reaction and as a part of the overwhelmingly successful nationwide Yes campaign, that the existence of *Gaeil ar son Rogha* was important and significant to both the Yes campaign and to the language itself. To the national Yes campaign, *Gaeil ar son Rogha* provided a new way of reaching people, a different angle and a way to make a more personal connection. The campaign gave rise to discussion and debate on Irish language stations, helping to stretch the reach of the debate into homes where Irish language TV and radio stations are chosen.

For speakers of the Irish language, *Gaeil ar son Rogha* provided a reminder that Irish is an important and relevant language of our time and that, as one of our official languages and a language that thousands of people speak daily, it should be used in social and political campaigns. It reminded us that keeping a language alive means that we must use it to speak about all relevant topics. Tá badges seen all around the country and the informed discussions on Irish language media showed that Irish is still relevant, important and the first language of many.

Campaigns such as *Gaeil ar son Rogha* were crucial to the repeal of the 8th. Each community group was important to the

Yes campaign and its connection with people on a local and personal level. Through *Gaeil ar son Rogha*, we Irish-speaking Yes campaigners connected directly to our community of '*Pobal na Gaeilge*'. This Irish language campaign, I have argued in this chapter, made for a more effective Yes campaign. Drawing on the success of *Gaeil ar son Rogha* as part of the national Yes campaign, it is clear that similar Irish language campaign groups can and should be formed as part of social and political campaigns in Ireland in the future. They reach Irish speakers in a way English cannot, they broaden the scope of campaigns and as such, they are crucial to the future of the language. Not only are Irish language campaigns important for driving social change, the place of the Irish language is strengthened by such campaigning and how it leaks beyond the boundaries of those who regularly speak it, to make the language a crucial part of the Ireland after the 8th.

Notes

1 'Gaelic' usually refers to Scot's Gaelic, a similar language of Scottish origin.

2 For further information, see www.gaeilge.ie/?lang=en.

3 For example, Raidió na Gaeltachta (www.rte.ie/rnag/), Raidió na Life (www.raidionalife.ie/ga/) and Raidió Fáilte (www.raidiofailte.com/); TG4 (www.tg4.ie/ga/); Comhar (https://comhar.ie/).

4 *Gaeil ar son Rogha Terms of Reference*. 2017. Available at: https://drive. google.com/file/d/1ixOhTpkfmd1pqdPr8_E8J5sj1tBnXL_N/view, (accessed 10 October 2018).

5 See www.twitter.com/gaeilarsonrogha and www.facebook.com/ gaeilarsonrogha.

6 Scannell, K. *Indigenous Tweets*. http://indigenoustweets.com/ga/ (accessed 24 September 2018). See also http://indigenoustweets.blogspot. com/2011/03/welcomefailte.html.

7 Údarás na Gaeltachta. 2011. *The History of the Irish Language*. 13 October 2011. Available at https://youtu.be/9Uov9LHgyRY (accessed 12 October 2018).

8 Gaeil ar son Rogha. 2018. *Interview with Tara Uí Adhmaill – Gaeil ar son Rogha*. Facebook, 22 May 2018 [video] https://m.facebook. com/story.php?story_fbid=379917075824723&id=319315401884891 (accessed 12 December 2018).

9   The video for this debate is available online at https://m.facebook.com/story.php?story_fbid=378266712656426&id=319315401884891.

10 Fagan, K. 2018. Twitter, 11 May 2018. Available at https://twitter.com/karen_de_facto/status/994889685238460416?s=19 (accessed 11 December 2018).

11 Deaf Community Together for Yes and Gaeil ar son Rogha collaborative video, Facebook, 18 May 2018 [video] https://m.facebook.com/story.php?story_fbid=378487625967668&id=319315401884891 (accessed 12 December 2018).

NINE | Maser's 'Repeal the 8th' mural: the power of public art in the age of social media

Lorna O'Hara

Figure 9.1 The mural as it appeared in July 2016, Temple Bar, Dublin, Ireland

Source: Author (2018)

In the past six years there's been a significant change in how people talk about abortion in Ireland. It would have been completely unthinkable a decade ago to have a national campaign for reproductive rights that included the word 'abortion' in its name or large colourful murals calling for abortion access. The longstanding fight for reproductive rights – "free, safe and legal" in the words of the Abortion Rights Campaign – can be understood as a battle over access to public space. This struggle has been evidenced by pro-life billboards and ads attempting to shame women accessing abortion to pro-choice murals, graffiti, stickers and performance art. Feminist public art and social media are powerful and transgressive tools challenging hegemonic masculinist meanings of the built environment and public urban space (O'Hara 2016).

Dublin-based street artist Maser's 'Repeal the 8th' mural (Figure 9.1) serves as a metaphor for the larger issue of abortion politics in Ireland: representing a break with the hidden nature of crisis pregnancy historically and the accompanying shame, stigma and censorship. Indeed, as one of the mural's key collaborators Andrea Horan explained to me in an interview: "[I]f it's right up on the wall, there's no denying that it's there to talk about [. . .] and you feel more empowered to talk about it and confident to talk about it".[1] It is an important piece of feminist street art that boldly claimed public space for reproductive rights advocacy in a way that hadn't been done before; combining creative practice with technology and activism in innovative ways. While changes in how we talk about abortion have been gradual, involving years of hard work by grassroots activists (see Quilty et al. 2015), I argue that creative actions such as Maser's 'Repeal the 8th' mural have also been an important part of that change. The story of its appearance in Temple Bar in 2016, removal and subsequent appearance and re-removal in 2018, provides a significant case study in examining how street art contests gender-based norms in urban public space. Even after the referendum, the conversation started by the mural and its subsequent removal(s) continues to inform debates around planning and street art, and raises fresh concerns surrounding the censorship of political art in Ireland.

(Hybrid) public space and public art

The built environment is the materialisation of meanings which are created by dominant groups in society, mainly those who are white, wealthy, straight and male (Cresswell 1996). Indeed, public spaces continue to be shaped by gendered power relations and gender binaries (Gardner 1995; McDowell and Sharpe 1997; Doan 2010). Public art embodies how social power and social resistance are always spatial (Cresswell 1996). It also provides everyday users of urban public space with transformative and meaningful experiences, and in so doing reshapes the built environment (Zebracki and Palmer 2018). Bearing in mind varying limitations on access and mobility according to gender, race, class and ability, public space is both relatively open and accessible to all (Radice 2018). Public art is therefore not only public because of its location outside of the gallery, but also because of its impact on the 'public sphere': "the arenas where private individuals come together – 'as a public' – to discuss matters of mutual concern" (Ibid.: 57). Public space is also materially and digitally "hybrid". Both de Souza e Silva (2006) and Wilken (2008) argue that urban spaces aren't simply overlaid with digital technology, rather there has been a complete merging of physical and digital space through the use of mobile phones and other mobile technologies as social devices. Indeed, the "digitisation of our existence" (Bishop 2012: 435) means that public art needs to be examined as a "dialectic between the physical and the virtual" (Zebracki 2017: 441). It follows then that public art, or art situated in a public (relatively accessible and open) hybrid space, invites reactions, engagement and even participation via new technologies such as social media. When thinking of the public sphere's engagement with public art it is also important to bear in mind the ways in which the internet, in particular the use of smartphones and social media, have changed socio-spatial relations and produced new forms of communication (Dodge and Kitchin 2001). Digital interactions have become intertwined with temporary material artworks which are not necessarily an intentional part of the artwork as conceived of by the artist (Zebracki 2017).

While some scholars have examined how technology has created new and innovative ways for the public sphere to engage with cultural objects and artworks (Rose 2016; Zebracki 2017; Radice 2018), and how socially networked public art has even resulted in user-created content as well as in-situ protest (Zebracki 2017), the broader political and activist potential of this has remained overlooked. Maser's artwork is an example of public art that intentionally made use of social media engagement and embraced participation and reproduction of the work for political campaigning and activist use. The "publicness" (Radice 2018) of Maser's mural was not only contingent on its physical location in the street (as opposed to a gallery), but also on its ability to provide a space for individuals to come together to discuss the concerns it raised, in particular abortion access and censorship. Further, because the public's discussion and engagement with the mural resulted in multiple material and online forms, the artwork resisted its own removal through its extended lifespan in public (hybrid) space.

The appearance and disappearance of the mural
On 8 July 2016, the *Repeal the 8th* mural was unveiled on the exterior wall of the Project Arts Centre in Temple Bar. This piece was commissioned by a new feminist website, The HunReal Issues, and was produced with both the permission and overwhelming support of the Project Arts Centre.[2] Andrea Horan of HunReal explained to me that this collaboration started with the idea of having a few graphics that they could simply use on their website and Facebook. Once the designs were completed, Maser stated: "Find me a wall, and I'll paint it for you."[3] Just over two weeks after its unveiling, the mural was taken down (25 July) following an order from Dublin City Council (DCC) Planning Committee that the mural "violated planning law" after it had received a

number of complaints (O'Sullivan 2016). Despite Project Arts' compliance with removing the mural, the centre's artistic director, Cian O'Brien, was quick to point out how this was the first time that the centre had ever been asked to remove a piece from their walls (Murray 2016). The painting over of the mural caused outrage. A petition was circulated online pledging support for the mural when it was threatened with removal, reaching over 4,000 signatures.[4] Many decried the painting over of the mural as censorship, leading to a demonstration which took place the day after its removal, with people gathering where the mural once stood and painting themselves with blue paint, the same shade as used in the mural (see Devine 2016).

Two years later, Maser was invited to repaint the piece on the original wall outside of Project Arts. The centre was now allowed to display the image without planning permission because exemptions are made to planning laws for 'ads' in the run-up to elections and referenda (Hosford 2018). However, less than two weeks later, Project Arts was ordered to remove the mural by the Charities Regulator who stated that the mural put the centre in breach of the 2009 Charities Act, as it was considered to be "political activity" (Holland 2018). Rather than jeopardise the future of the centre, O'Brien stated before a crowd of people, who had gathered yet again to protest the mural's removal on 23 April 2018, that "through its absence this political artwork lives on in the thousands of people who have taken its heart into theirs. You can paint over a mural but you can't paint over an issue" (O'Brien, C. 2018). Rather than challenge the decision in court, they turned the mural and its removal into a public performance piece that would be broadcast via social media.[5] O'Brien called Project Art's online support, including videos of the mural being painted over again, an act of "defiant compliance". The centre purposefully painted over the mural in a way that left a watermelon-shaped part of it visible; a reminder of what they understood as censorship of political art (Figure 9.2). A mere week

Figure 9.2 A symbol of censorship: the painted over mural still appears days
after the referendum in May 2018

Source: Author (2018)

later, the mural also re-appeared (albeit in Amnesty's campaign
colours) on the side of Amnesty International's headquarters on
Fleet Street in Temple Bar. Drawing parallels between the painting
over of the mural and the way Ireland deals with abortion – hiding
it away and covering it up – Colm O'Gorman of Amnesty declared:
"No matter how hard the other side try to paint over the issue,
the 8th Amendment causes women immense harm and suffering"
(O'Gorman quoted in Duffy 2018).

The abortion debate: a battle over public space

O'Gorman's words are particularly salient when we consider how
the Irish state, in partnership with the Catholic Church, heavily involved itself in regulating the sexuality of its citizens. While
abortion and contraception had already been outlawed (1861
and 1935 respectively), the adoption of the 1937 Constitution
restricted married women from working outside the home and
introduced a ban on divorce (Smyth 1998). Gendered attempts

at controlling the sexuality of citizens also played out spatially; enforcing what Crowley and Kitchin (2008) have referred to as a "spatialised grid of discipline" on women. In an attempt to produce "pure" Irish women, the state relegated them to the home and restricted their access to public and work spaces, all the while threatening them with new sites of ostracisation and reformation, for example Magdalene Laundries and mother and baby homes (see also Olund, this volume). In addition to this, art, literature and film that discussed issues that were considered "indecent" were heavily censored in the Free State under the Censorship of Publications Act (1929), specifically any reference to contraception and abortion (O'Callaghan 1998). Indeed, the censorship of Maser's mural sits within a long history of censorship of art that discussed the state's treatment of women and girls. Project Arts itself had emerged out of a two-week festival at the Gate Theatre in 1966 where writer Edna O'Brien, known for writing about sexual and social issues during the particularly repressive 1950s, came over to talk about the censorship of her work and the work of others in Ireland.[6]

It's no surprise then that abortion was traditionally spoken about in hushed tones. Cian from Project Arts Centre made reference throughout the interview to the particular atmosphere of fear that persisted when it came to speaking openly about abortion. He felt it was this fear as well as shame around the topic of abortion that informed the way the various state bodies responded to the mural, "censoring" what they considered was an uncomfortable truth.[7] Abortion was clearly seen by both those who had made complaints to DCC, the DCC themselves and then later the Charities Regulator as something that did not belong in the streets – an issue, like many issues relating to the lives of women in Ireland, that had no place in the public realm. Abortion in Ireland continues to happen despite its illegality, rather it simply happens clandestinely, shrouded in a legacy of shame and stigma which so often characterises discussion around abortion. While other well-known Irish artists such as Sarah Browne,[8] Jesse Jones,[9] Siobhán Clancy[10] and others have dealt with the issue of abortion in their work in recent years, it was the public nature of Maser's piece and the way it allowed its collaborators to digitally engage the public sphere in discussion which made it so controversial. It reflected a shift in the debate over abortion access in Ireland and this shift is something that is very clearly reflected in the urban landscape.

The controversy created by the mural not only succeeded in being what Sarah Pierce, chair of the board of the Project Arts Centre, described as "a reminder that art matters" (quoted in O'Sullivan 2016) but also serves as a reminder that, as geographer Doreen Massey argued, space matters too (Massey 2005). Until relatively recently, pro-life groups completely dominated public spaces with their posters and advertisements, attempting to control public discourse about abortion. Youth Defence's 'Abortion Tears Her Life Apart' outdoor billboard campaign was launched in 2012 and featured images of an ultrasound or an image of a young woman quite literally torn apart. This campaign purposefully targeted spaces such as airports, bus stations and train stations – public spaces where women travelling to access abortion services in the UK would undoubtedly pass through (Doherty and Redmond 2015). In one particularly cynical move, a billboard truck even parked outside the Rape Crisis Centre in 2013 (Hosford 2013). Until Maser's mural was unveiled, it appeared that only those who could afford a large ad campaign, such as the pro-life lobby, had any power to shape public space towards their discourse. While people did challenge this campaign through defacing the billboards as well as petitioning the advertising company that hosted them, Maser's mural marked an important turning point in the representation of the pro-choice movement within the Irish landscape. The mural was a powerful public challenge to the dominant power structures shaping our public urban landscapes at multiple scales; becoming a symbol of hope for a grassroots movement who frequently found themselves standing up to those with more power and money. Not only this, but it was this particular mural's removal that began an important debate about street art and planning permission requirements in Dublin city, which has since inspired street artists such as those in the group Subset to pursue a project highlighting the issue now known as the Grey Area Project (Subset 2018).

Street art in particular "challenges the dominant dichotomy between public and private space. It interrupts the familiar boundaries of the public and the private by declaring the public private and the private public" (Cresswell 1996: 47). This is exactly what the Maser mural did. The piece took the issue of abortion, something considered the private matter of women rather than a public health concern, and literally put it into the streets – demanding us to take responsibility for those women. The mural's unapologetically bright and cheerful style located outside in such a prominent part of Dublin aimed to make visible what for so long had been systematically hidden. Indeed, one of the key things Andrea Horan wanted the mural to do was to act as a public source of support to the twelve people a day in Ireland accessing abortion. This is another reason why its location outside of the gallery as opposed to inside was so vital. Women experiencing crisis pregnancies had been historically stigmatised and hidden away: from those put in Magdalene Laundries to those forced to travel because of Ireland's restrictive abortion laws. Through the mural she wanted to send a clear message to them: "[W]e put the mural up to start a conversation, but also for people who had to travel for abortions, to know that we've got your back."[11] The particular site of the mural also had a previous political history. Another mural had been painted in the exact same spot by Sums1 in the run up to the marriage equality referendum (2015) and, as Cian informed me, was also the site where gay rights activist Will St Leger painted another piece called 'Troubles Fade Out in the Open'. It's worth noting that neither of these murals had required planning permission.

Political public art and activism in the digital age

While the mural was an important political intervention in public space, technology and digital mediation of the piece also played a significant role. Today, mobile phone technologies and the internet are transforming our understanding of place as well as how we experience and interact with physical urban space (Dodge and Kitchin 2001; de Souza e Silva 2006; Wilken 2008; Nash and Gorman-Murray 2016). This has an impact on how we engage with public art, turning audiences into users who exercise their agency by engaging with public art in new and innovative ways (Zebracki 2017). Social media and the internet were important not only in responding to Maser's mural and its subsequent removal, but also in campaigning for abortion access in general (Doherty and Redmond 2015). Indeed, one of the first pro-choice demonstrations I attended in 2012 was organised by a Facebook group set up in response to the Youth Defence billboards.[12] Social media not only allows people to access and share information and organise politically, but it also allows us to get direct access to 'experts' – politicians, celebrities, academics and journalists – in ways that would have been unimaginable before. The political potentialities of this are significant.

For Andrea, social media is particularly important in helping people shape their own opinions, get politically active and engage with the pro-choice campaign. While the mural itself is obviously a powerful piece, Cian felt it was Andrea's mastery of social media and her role as a "social media influencer"[13] that played such a critical role in the mural's overwhelming popularity. Indeed,

Cian directly linked the unprecedented amount of backlash – as well as support – that Project Arts received to the very specific way that social media had been strategically used from the very start to rapidly spread the mural's image. The motivation behind public art is also about allowing people to interact with a piece as they wish, and that was one of the key aims for both Andrea and Maser: "[W]ith public art people will take ownership of it and the message will spread. And it did" (Maser quoted in Duffy 2016). Indeed, just hours after its removal people were changing their Twitter and Facebook profile photos to images of the mural, articles were being written about it, a protest was being organised and stickers featuring the mural were appearing in the streets. Rather than silencing the pro-choice movement, the mural's removal created online and offline debate not only about abortion rights, but the way that we talk about them, i.e. publicly, loudly and colourfully.

One of the innovative qualities of digitally networked public art is that it allows a piece to "live on" digitally once its material form has been removed (Zebracki 2017). As an act of resistance to its removal, Maser made the mural's digital image copyright-free, encouraging people to use it and reproduce it as they wished. Maser himself often shared pictures featuring the work of people who re-used the image, from the giant projected images of the mural used by Generic People in Cork to a small embroidered 'Repeal' heart sewn on to a young woman's t-shirt or to trade union UNITE's recreation of the mural on the wall of their headquarters. These images on Maser's public Instagram often featured the caption "taking ownership".[14] HunReal also made t-shirts and badges featuring the mural's image, the profits for which went directly into funding for the repeal campaign. People even reproduced the mural on banners at demonstrations not only in Ireland but also abroad, for example, as part of Repeal Global's solidarity demonstrations with the March for

Choice in 2016 in places such as Glasgow, Berlin and Montreal (Kenny 2016). Other murals also appeared which were clearly influenced by Maser's work, for example, a pro-choice mural featuring a heart with the words "Solidarity with Irish Women" appeared in Porto, Portugal in 2017. As it turns out this mural was painted by Berriblue, a Polish-Irish artist, who created the piece originally as a banner for Porto's Repeal Global solidarity demo in 2016.

Technology also played another significant role in the story of the 'Repeal the 8th' mural. Following the initial removal of the mural in 2016, Andrea wanted to get it back up as soon as possible in any way, shape or form so that it could continue to serve as a source of solidarity with those accessing abortion services.[15] While they could not get the mural back up physically (at least not until 2018), they had come up with an innovative substitute; creating an Augmented Reality (AR) version of the mural that people could access with their smartphones. By clicking on a link and then holding their phones up to a piece of paper featuring a QR code (a type of barcode people scan with their phones) placed on the wall where the mural

Figure 9.3   Berlin Ireland Pro-Choice Solidarity/Repeal Global 2016 demo, Berlin

Source: Nate Eileen Tjoeng (2016; with permission)

originally stood, it would re-appear on the wall once viewed through their phone. This offers an innovative method of returning the mural to the wall; it was literally and figuratively a merging of on and offline space. This can be understood as a particularly literal version of what Heidi Rae Cooley termed "screenic seeing" a "material experience of vision" where "hands, eyes, screen, and surroundings interact and blend in syncopated fashion" (Cooley 2004: 145). People are physically present in the place where the mural once stood, with their attention split between the physical wall and the screen of their smartphone where they're experiencing the mural. This type of seeing really highlights the embodied experience of using technology as suggested by earlier scholars such as Haraway (1991), forcing us to consider the more fluid relations between the human and non-human and between the material and the virtual. Technology is not only transforming street art itself by helping it overcome its transient nature through such tactics, but it's also developing new ways for audiences to engage with it, all the time posing new questions about participation, ownership and even city planning.

Conclusion

Some scholars have examined how public art can be co-created in a "spatio-technological" sphere (Radice 2018) using mobile phone technologies connecting with material city spaces. Others have examined how receptions and interactions can digitally intertwine with temporary material artworks and empower users (Zebracki 2017). Yet, scholarship around the broader political potentialities of these "empowering" interactions remains scarce. I argue that Maser's mural provides an important case study for examining these. The mural was an overtly political piece of street art which sought to make the topic of abortion in Ireland unashamedly visible through its bright colourful style, its public location and its collaborators' strategic use of social media. In a country where women's bodies have been systematically controlled and regulated by the state – from Magdalene Laundries and symphysiotomies to restrictive abortions laws – artistic projects such as Maser's mural are powerful public challenges to the dominant power structures shaping the Irish landscape at multiple scales. Public art, such as street art and murals, can engage the public sphere in meaningful discussion around issues of social justice. While city authorities were successful in removing the material mural, images of it continued to live online, keeping it alive in the public imaginary. The mural, which brought the pro-choice message quite literally to the streets, even seems to have given others the confidence to start creating their own graffiti around Dublin, which appeared in the period immediately following the mural's removal in 2016. This trend appears to have continued, with pieces growing ever more detailed and complex with pro-choice murals, such as the Savita mural by Aches and Subset's 'Her Body NO Choice' mural, both appearing in Dublin mere days before the referendum.

Furthermore, political engagement with the mural also happened offline, resulting in two in-situ protest actions at the site of the mural. Indeed, following the second removal of the mural in 2018, the debate spilled out onto the Dáil floor. It was reported that Taoiseach Leo Varadkar even repeated the words Cian uttered during Project Arts' act of "defiant compliance": "[W]hile you can paint over a mural you certainly can't paint over an issue" (quoted in Halloran 2018). Social media and other new technologies not only transform the possibilities of street art itself by creating other expressions of its materiality and developing new ways for audiences to engage with art, but its material and subsequent online forms were a direct political intervention in public space. Combining political public art and technology suggests new possibilities for public participation in advancing reproductive rights and making visible the inequality and oppression that women continue to experience.

Notes

1 Horan, interview, Dublin, 2016.
2 O'Brien, interview, Dublin, 2018.
3 Horan, interview, Dublin, 2016.
4 The closed online petition 'Pledge Your Support for Maser's Repeal the 8th Mural at Project Arts Centre' can be viewed at http://chng.it/SrxrRyt7Ns.
5 'Defiant Compliance': https://twitter.com/projectarts/status/988423284852129793.
6 O'Brien, interview, Dublin, 2018.
7 O'Brien, interview, Dublin, 2018.
8 See Sarah Browne and Jesse Jones collaborative project 'In The Shadow of the State': www.create-ireland.ie/in-the-shadow-of-the-state/sarah-browne-and-jesse-jones-in-the-shadow-of-the-state-2016.
9 See Jesse Jones' solo project 'Tremble Tremble': https://projectartscentre.ie/event/tremble/.
10 See Siobhán Clancy's piece 'Metronome': https://vimeo.com/50730626.
11 Horan, interview, Dublin, 2016.
12 The 'Unlike Youth Defence, I trust women to decide their lives for themselves' Facebook page was set up in 2012 and remains online, although largely inactive: www.facebook.com/notalwaysabetteroption.
13 O'Brien, interview, Dublin, 2018.
14 MaserArt. 2016. 'Taking ownership #repealthe8th'. Instagram, 4 August 2016. Available at: www.instagram.com/p/BIsCyVXgDrb/?utm_source=ig_web_copy_link.
15 Horan, interview, Dublin, 2016.

TEN | Repealing a 'legacy of shame': press coverage of emotional geographies of secrecy and shame in Ireland's abortion debate

Eric Olund

Introduction

"Ireland may be known internationally as a country of saints and scholars. But it has, for a long time, also been a country of secrets and shame. Most of these have revolved around women, what we do with our bodies, and what comes out of our bodies" (Douglas 2018: 32). Donna Douglas' full letter to the *Irish Independent* went on to describe Ireland's landslide decision to repeal the 8th Amendment on 25 May 2018 as a "collective scream for freedom" from the country's patriarchal institutions that denied women their sexual and reproductive autonomy. Her coupling of secrecy and shame reproduced a recurring theme in mainstream press debate about abortion. 'Secret shame' framed women's experiences of Ireland's many ideological and material constraints on their bodies, the institutions in which those restraints were felt and enforced, the scandals they occasioned, and when all else failed, the export of those who fell short of Ireland's double standard. Thus, secret shame was not simply presented as an individualised psychological state. It was a collective production with a complex geography.

This chapter explores the discursive production of secret shame in the press, then goes on to focus on one particular geography of secret shame that was ubiquitous in Ireland's newspapers, 'Going to England', a euphemism for going abroad for an abortion.

Debate over abortion in the public sphere went well beyond print media, as several chapters in this volume explore. But newspapers still have influence not only through their print circulation, diminishing as it is, but also through their online presence. Collectively they continue to be a locus for both (re)producing and contesting norms (Altheide and Schneider 2013) in a markedly divided imagined community (McGill, this volume; cf. Anderson 1983).

But this discourse of secret shame has hardly been confined to the island itself, thanks in part to Ireland's long history of emigration, a shared global language and an exceptional status as a 'last holdout' on reproductive choice among Western countries (Browne and Nash, this volume). British and American press coverage of the referendum campaign offered headlines such as "Shrouded in Shame" in *The Guardian* (Kalia 2018) and "Scarlet Letter in the Emerald Isle" in *The New York Times* (Dowd 2018). These predictable spatial metaphors caught my attention as a US citizen of Irish descent, raised Roman Catholic, working in England as an academic geographer and *relieved*, oddly so given my many-generations' distance, about Ireland's rapid cultural shifts on sexuality and gender. Having grown up where abortion is an ongoing focus of its culture wars, and subsequently living where it is a much more settled social question, I seek here to unpack this notion of 'secret shame' that appeared to me so distinctive about the Irish debate. What I show is that, appropriately enough for a country with a long history of emigration, including those who were sexually and gender non-conforming (Luibhéid 2006: 62–8), the very *necessity* to go overseas for an abortion emerged as a significant locus of secret shame in 'going to England'.

My focus here will be on the narrative of secret shame that emerged in what reporters and editors saw fit to print in the Republic's mainstream press. Starting with 1992 coverage of the X Case and ending in September 2018, 4 months after the 8th was repealed, I searched Nexis and the Irish Newspaper Archive using key words referencing abortion, secrecy and shame, including variations and synonyms. I included the Belfast-based *Irish News* given its island-wide coverage and circulation. Excluding coverage of abortion in Northern Ireland, approximately 164 returns comprising letters to the editor, regular columns, book and other arts reviews, personal testimonial features and standard articles offered contextual and/or substantive contributions to the discourse of secret shame. Non-tabloid papers dominated numerically, especially the *Irish Times* at 37% of the total, followed closely by sibling publications the *Irish* and *Sunday Independent*, together at 32%, and the *Irish Examiner* at 15%. A significant limitation of this study is that not all Irish tabloids are included in either database, especially the *Sunday World*, the Republic's second Sunday paper in terms of circulation according to the Audit Bureau of Circulations' latest figures. Thus, I have excluded tabloids from the actual analysis – but notably, references to secrecy and shame in abortion coverage were scarce in the tabloids I could access, whether Irish or British titles.

Even before formal coding for themes surrounding secrecy, shame and space, it was apparent the discursive construction of secret shame was remarkably consistent across the broadsheet-cum-compact press, with differences between individual contributions greater than differences between papers, hence in the analysis to follow I largely treat the press collectively regardless of political leaning. As Sinéad Kennedy, academic and co-founder of the Coalition to Repeal the 8th Amendment, recalled about press requests about abortion, reporters sought a particular type of 'abortion story' emphasising the emotional and physical hardships of 'difficult cases'.[1] Thus, this discursive object of 'secret shame' is a particular, limited construction of these papers' reporters and editors, however much it intersects with accounts of secret shame elsewhere, public or private. It is *a*, not *the*, discourse of secret shame, and as the rest of this collection shows, it is also only one facet of the larger debate about abortion in Ireland.

The production of shame

Shame is one of the 'self-regarding' emotions because it concerns judgment of the self by another – whether that 'other' is internalised or not (Taylor 1985). Shame is often felt in tandem with guilt, which concerns conduct, but they are distinct (Nussbaum 2004). As with any emotion, shame is not simply an individual experience, state of being or property of the psyche. It is a social, historical and geographical production (Reddy 2001; Scheer 2012). Furthermore, shame is often a particularly embodied emotion, as it can prompt a facial flush and a physical turning away (Ahmed 2004; Probyn 2005). This combination of a character defect (potentially) visible to another – a stigma – and the act of turning away from them underscore the body's orientation in space in producing shame. Thus, any specific experience of shame is constituted through an emotional geography that is necessarily material (Johnston 2007; Katigbak 2017; Waitt et al. 2007).

In Irish newspapers' coverage of abortion, shame's geography extended well beyond the clinic in which the procedure takes place to a larger topography on which women's varying experiences were mapped. First, commonly cited prompts for shame for actions taken varied, such as enjoying bodily pleasure, sex, pregnancy and motherhood out of wedlock, adoption, having an abortion and/or committing an illegal act. Second, the cited sources of judgment of the self before others constituted through these acts ranged from family, to friends, community, co-workers, doctors and nurses and the law – of God, church and/or state. As I will argue below, the dual requirement to travel abroad for the procedure, and to do so in secret, was also shaming such that the distinction between shame *for* and shame *before* became meaningless. Through this conflation, the press spatialised shame's distinctive prompt to 'turn away' through a travel itinerary, an Irish "abortion trail" (Rossiter 2009; Calkin and Freeman 2018) that materially, though only temporarily, distanced women from the sources of judgment at home that made 'going to England' necessary in the first place. Paradoxically, the act of escaping from shaming in itself became articulated as a locus of shame as the abortion debate unfolded.

Secrecy, shame and space in the press

Secret shame only occasionally featured in Ireland's newspapers until the mid-2000s, with most attention (such as it was) given during the 1992 and 2002 referendum campaigns. More specific narratives of its itinerary became at least an annual feature in one or more paper after the 2007 Miss D case, and then more frequent after the Citizens Assembly began considering the 8th Amendment in late 2017. This itinerary, which I will detail below, was remarkably consistent over this time, even after the availability of the (illegal) abortion pill through internet pharmacies reduced the numbers of women going abroad for terminations (Calkin, this volume). This was because coverage was situated over time in two important ways that inflected how the itinerary was narrated – the revelations about historical institutional abuse and the increasing authorisation of the victims' voices in the late 2000s.

In this context, secret shame was framed as a self-perpetuating 'legacy'. Thus, its past was very much alive in the present, not only through exposés of scandals such as the Magdalene Laundries and the Church's sexual abuse and its cover-up, but also of the secret memories and stories that individual Irish women were still carrying with them, whether of their own, their mothers or their grandmothers. These were stories of sexual abuse, rape, naivety and broken condoms; stories of crisis pregnancies and forced adoptions; and stories of abortions, whether back-alley or legal. The press began to acknowledge Ireland's particularly harsh treatment of non-conforming women, especially those who were poor, who previously could be confined in the laundries or other abusive homes for the 'unfortunates' (Fischer 2016). Memories of this 'carceral geography' (Morin 2013) at home both haunted and impelled going abroad in secret shame. Indeed, as Karen Weingarten argues in the US context, shame's mobility makes the emotion "a 'neater' mechanism for regulating bodies than the disciplining technologies of site-specific locations, such as school and church" (Weingarten 2016: 36). Ireland's historical legacy of incarcerating women coupled with the still-present threat of ostracism and imprisonment materialised shame and secrecy in the past and perpetuated it in the present.

Irish Examiner columnist Louise O'Neill summarised the legacy's message succinctly: "You can have sex, young woman, but if you get in trouble, you must travel alone, you must tell no one, you must keep your dirty secret to yourself" (O'Neill 2016). But secrets exist to be shared – they can become a selective inheritance and even an open secret (Derrida 2008). This was so while first-hand accounts of abortion were nearly non-existent in this discourse before the lead-up to the referendum. Between 1992 and 2007, I counted six instances significantly centring women's voices in the form of first-hand accounts of their own experiences of shame and secrecy. However, the 2009 release of the Ryan and Murphy reports on state care homes and clerical abuse in the Dublin Archdiocese saw an upsurge in women's testimonials in the press.

A few years later, especially when the founding of the Abortion Rights Campaign shortly followed by Savita Halappanavar's death rekindled the *national* debate (Connolly, this volume), a narrative emerged *about* the fact that Irish women had begun to speak more openly about their stories and experiences of unplanned pregnancies and their decisions. Some felt liberation upon learning how many others shared similar experiences, sometimes hearing these stories from close friends and family for the first time. Others still felt 'ashamed of feeling ashamed' and remained anonymous, but with repeal of the 8th, they hoped future generations would not have to feel shame as they did.

'Going to England'

This bequest of secret shame forced generations of single, pregnant women to 'go to England'. Earlier in the 20th century, this euphemism usually described a woman 'in trouble' going abroad before the pregnancy became visible to give birth and give the baby up for adoption. Since its 1967 legalisation in Britain, the euphemism has referred more often to going abroad to have an abortion. While pregnant women might go to a number of countries, the vast majority of Irish abortions have been and still are, as of this writing, performed in Great Britain, where with the crucial exclusion of Northern Ireland, abortion is legal up to 24 weeks. This means pregnant Irish women seeking a safe, legal termination physically *must* cross the Irish Sea, with all of the obstacles and burdens this entails – finding options, raising funds for travel, accommodation and the abortion itself, bringing a partner, friend or family member along for support if wanted and available, arranging for time off work or school, actually getting to the clinic, having a termination as an Irish woman in a foreign, usually British clinic, and returning after the procedure to a place in which aftercare and support are question marks at best, and secrecy is an ingrained expectation.

This secret itinerary has been well-travelled for over a century, and in the 2000s, it was a common fixture in newspaper histories of secret shame that collectively articulated emotional continuities between adoption and abortion in the experience of what was effectively forced emigration for sexually 'deviant' women (Luibhéid 2006). As investigative journalist and filmmaker Mary Raftery[2] (2006) put it for the *Irish Times*: "Long before it became a safety valve for Irish women in terms of abortion, the boat to England was the last refuge for those too fearful to give birth in this country." The shame of adoption continued for much of the 20th century. As *Irish Times* journalist Kate Holmquist (2008) described a friend who gave up a child in the late 1980s: "She is angry that the Catholic Church shamed her and that society and her own parents turned a blind eye to her going on a boat alone to England to give birth and surrender the baby. This secrecy still affects her because she is afraid to talk about the adoption." But while the stigma of pregnancy out of wedlock was a shared factor in the shame of going to England for adoption or abortion, the temporality of each decision was and is quite different. Going to England to give birth and surrender a child for adoption required *staying* in England for a period of time, often months if the pregnancy was to be hidden. But going to England for an abortion can now be a daytrip thanks to Ryanair, and this shortened timeframe shifted the locus of shame's production.

What comes through consistently in first-hand framing of going to England or elsewhere for an abortion is that it is *the need to have to travel at all* for a short, out-patient procedure that is shaming. While this also provokes resentment, that emotion is left implicit in discussions of shame. As the itinerary narrative continued to develop, regardless of whether addressing so-called difficult cases (especially prevalent after the 2010 European Court of Human Rights ruling) or more prosaic ones, the refrain was much the same. Women felt an "added burden of guilt and shame through being forced to make an expensive and often secret trip to Britain or mainland Europe" (DeWan 2010). This was especially ubiquitous in the personal testimonies emerging after the 2009 abuse reports. Siobhan G, who was pregnant with twins with fatal defects, said: "I was forced to leave home and do everything in secrecy . . . I was made to feel that I was doing something wrong" (Ring 2010). Another (still anonymous) woman said: "I flew to Liverpool, to a country I had never been in before and felt I was being made to feel like a criminal for doing something sensible" (*Irish Independent* 2013). The illegality of abortion in Ireland was a state-imposed stigma, a 'shaming before', that trailed these women as they exercised agency through crossing the Irish Sea, an act worthy of 'shaming for'. Secret shame was a transnational production of crossing between spaces of illegality and legality, one that was reinforced by the Irish state's inconsistent approach to the legalisation of 'going to England' after the 1992 referendum (see also Freeman 2017).

The itinerary of secret shame

The press presented women's first-hand accounts of going to England for an abortion through fragmentary memories of the emotional extremes of the trip, often in concert with other women's particular, punctuated recollections, but always supplemented with the reporter's or editor's voice. Thus, the linear itinerary I assemble here emerged collectively over time, and unevenly so in terms of which voices spoke of which stops in the itinerary. In this coverage the itinerary usually started at the airport and first-person voices about the *start* of the trip are remarkably absent in the newspapers' narrative. The effect is a lacuna, a spatial gap, in the first-hand narratives emerging before the referendum campaign. Whether this was the choice of women reluctant to speak about their experience in departure spaces or of editors looking for a more exciting story is unanswerable from the coverage itself, but its narrative effect is important. In place of first-hand experience, the departure point was framed as the last-chance *political* space for pro-choice and pro-life activists alike, as pregnant women prepared to leave to have a legal abortion, especially as the 8th was being considered by the 2016–17 Citizens Assembly and afterward.

One pro-choice campaign that was highlighted in a regional paper, *The Sligo Champion*,[3] was the Out of the Shadows project by artist/activist Will St Leger for the Abortion Rights Campaign and Amnesty International Ireland. Life-sized silhouettes of women were put in airports, along with bus stops and train stations, to publicly represent the women forced to go abroad for abortions. The artist explained the rationale in familiar terms: "Women forced to travel feel a sense of exclusion from their health care system, the stigma of travelling, and the burden of secrecy, shame and fear that comes with knowing they are doing something that is a criminal offence at home. This project is designed to bring these women out of the shadows so that we can stand in solidarity with them" (Healy 2017).

The prominent pro-life group the Irish Centre for Bio-Ethical Reform (ICBR) had a rather different notion of solidarity with pregnant women leaving the country for abortions, so-called education projects for which Dublin and Cork airports refused permission, coincidentally or not after the United Nations Human Rights Council ruling (Knox 2017). "'Departing abortion passengers', its proposed sign reads, 'Stop! We are here to help you and your baby'" (O'Mahony 2017). *Irish Independent* editor Catherine O'Mahony responded to the plan: "Well, an offer of help can't be scoffed at", and went on to enumerate the material help the ICBR might give instead. "Expressing anti-abortion views is one thing. Waving posters of dead foetuses at women who are about to board a plane having decided to undergo a possibly traumatic procedure is quite another." In the lead-up to the referendum, some readers were not aware of airports' decisions not to allow pro-life protestors. "Why are the pro-lifers not picketing at our airports and ports?" asked one letter to the editor (Turloughmore 2018). It continued: "If you are OK with women travelling to access abortion outside of Ireland, then your issue isn't with abortion – your issue is with women and exerting your control over them."

A characteristic motif of pro-life discourse before and during the formal referendum campaign was one of keeping Ireland pure from the act of abortion and disavowing the secret shame that the pro-choice movement sought to expose. Thus, both pro-life and pro-choice activists were given the platform to narrate the departure airport as a political space in which both the secrecy and shaming of women seeking abortions was alternately contested and reinforced as public debate increased. In so doing, for this first stop of the itinerary, the newspapers gave voice to everybody about the first stop of the itinerary except the women themselves.

Centring women's experiences of secret shame

Women's experiences, if not voices, began to feature in the itinerary upon their arrival in England, with particular interest shown after the release of a 1999 Green Paper on abortion. "In the arrivals hall in Stansted Airport, three cab drivers await the flight from Dublin, holding up name-cards: Flynn, McGann, Ryan . . . They are all from the same cab-company, all awaiting passengers bound for the same destination: the nearby Marie Stopes Clinic" (McCarthy 2000). The clinic's head nurse noted the emotional state of her many Irish patients. According to the *Irish Times*: "Irish women are harder on themselves than British women, Marie believes. Confidentiality is primary for them, and they tend to berate themselves with guilt. 'English women are upset too – of course they are – but the Irish women are full of shame. Religious factors play a bigger part with them too'" (Ibid.). This initial interest in British observations of Irish women continued. British abortion provider Dr Patricia Lohr, medical director of the British Planning Advisory Service (BPAS), made a similar observation about their plight. "It is a tragedy that women have to travel from Ireland. The travel is hugely stressful" and having the abortion "under the radar" only makes the experience worse (Mitchell 2012).

The wait to return home could amplify the shame, as the airport, a 'non-place' of transience, anonymity and isolation (Augé 1992), prompted reflection – a self-surveillance that mirrors the airport's securitising disciplinary gaze (Adey 2004). And it was here, *after* the procedure, the experience of secret shame's itinerary became intensely physical in the press. *Irish Independent* columnist Martina Devlin wrote of the case of a 28-year-old single Irishwoman. "She described fainting in the airport as she waited five hours for her return flight to Ireland, and the guilt, shame, and above all secrecy, which added their weight to this daunting experience" (Devlin 2009). This corporealisation continued on the plane, as in the case of a woman who received a medical rather than surgical abortion profiled in a 2015 BBC documentary, 'Abortion: Ireland's Guilty Secret?' The broadcast prompted considerable commentary, and *Independent* columnist Carol Hunt wrote: "Listening to the story of Lauren on the programme, an Irish woman who travelled in secret to the UK and had her miscarriage in the cramped, tiny toilet of the aeroplane on the way home, was heart-rending – how dare we do this to our own citizens?" (Hunt 2015). In a letter to the editor, an Irish obstetrician-gynaecologist related the story of one patient who returned home from England sooner than advised. "She was so anxious to get home, she feared having to explain her absence" (Rigney 2018). She started haemorrhaging on the plane and nearly died. "She wondered how she would explain her admission to hospital. She lay alone unsupported by friends or family. I held her hand. I felt ashamed that this is how women living in Ireland are treated." She admonished No and undecided voters in the upcoming referendum, "If the No vote passes you will go on your way, and I will go back to work with my head held in shame, hoping that the plane gets here on time."

Conclusion

On the eve of the referendum, Taoiseach Leo Varadkar addressed the nation's legacy of shame. "170,000 women have had to travel, sometimes in secret, to another jurisdiction to end their pregnancies." He declared, "I hope that a Yes vote will help to lift that stigma and help to take away that legacy of shame that exists in our society" (Loughlin 2018). It is worth noting that Varadkar, being openly gay and of Indian heritage, has himself served as an emblem of a 'new Ireland'. But he is also a Fine Gael neoliberal whose position on abortion 'evolved' after hearing about 'hard cases' during his tenure as Health Minister. But it was not only testimonies of those so-called hard cases, but also women's accounts of more ordinary circumstances for choosing abortion that also came to shape the emotional topography of the secret shame of 'going to England' in the press. For, in contrast to the sympathy (or scare) stories of health complications in the 'hard cases' explored above, in many accounts the itinerary of secret shame was travelled with little fuss, and ended back home in more prosaic ways, often showing off the 'souvenirs' bought to verify the woman's 'holiday' in England and thereby sealing her secret.

Physical souvenirs of secret shame can be given or thrown away. What effect the Health (Regulation of Termination of Pregnancy) Bill passed by the Oireachtas on 13 December 2018 will have on the emotional *legacies* of secret shame of countless individuals, and its collective cultural legacy in Ireland, remains to be seen. Discursively reframing a requirement for secrecy as a right to privacy by extending abortion's legality from across the seas to the Republic itself *may* eventually end the secrecy and shame. But there is no guarantee – Weingarten (2016) has shown how the *legal* framing of the right to abortion as a right to privacy in the US has reinforced the individualisation of abortion as a choice to be delimited, judged and shamed. In Ireland itself, Sheldon (2018) has shown how the experience of taking abortion pills in private, despite advice and assistance from online collectives providing abortion support, can be alienating rather than empowering, as "privacy collapses into secrecy" and "widespread practices of nondisclosure serve to distort public debate and to obscure the harm done by punitive criminal laws" (Sheldon 2018: 825).

Weingarten's and Sheldon's points are crucial, for public debate about abortion will continue in Ireland, as the new law has, in the words of legal scholar Máiréad Enright, "seemed to pull further and further out of the grasp of the movement that gave life to the demand for abortion law reform" (Enright 2018: 3). Except for the so-called hard cases, abortion will be legal only up to 12 weeks, compared to Britain's 24 weeks, thus, the stigma of illegality will still follow women seeking 'late' abortions across the Irish Sea. Further restrictions are in store. For legal abortions, a mandatory 3-day waiting period is set to shame women as unreliable decision-makers about their own fertility. This, plus two mandatory consultations, will also add the material burden of multiple trips to a provider which may be distant (possibly still in England) due to a local lack of provision or a woman's desire for privacy. This burden will also be increased for many women for whom 12 weeks will really be 9 weeks, as past that date abortions must be provided in hospital.

Finally, the circumstances for legal 'late' abortions are ill-defined, and while the law does decriminalise abortion for women, it does not fully do so for the doctors performing them. As Enright argues: "[T]he shadow of criminalisation will deter more cautious doctors from providing care . . . As we know in Ireland from our long experience with treating abortion as a crime, the mere possibility of prosecution will often have disproportionate chilling effects on legal abortion access" (Enright 2018: 5). The *geographies* of secret shame are, therefore, predictable: the need to 'go to England' will not disappear for the foreseeable future and a new, domestic itinerary of secrecy and shame will emerge.

I had hoped to conclude on a more optimistic note, that perhaps Ireland's distinctive reification of secret shame in the form of a 'legacy' during the repeal campaign would enable a different outcome, one in which abortion is collectively normalised, and this legacy of shaming judgment of church, state, family, friends and community is made history. But beyond the exhaustion of the repeal campaign and the anger and frustration at the government's refusal to address women's concerns about the legalisation bill, and beyond the inevitable post-mortems of the repeal campaign's strategy, much more work will need to be done to change the law to eliminate its inherently disciplining and shaming restrictions, recentre women's voices in defining the ethics and emotions of abortion access and render 'going to England' a cautionary tale about an emotional geography that is truly past.

Notes

1 Kennedy made this comment at a workshop organised by this book's editors at Maynooth University on 15 November 2018. I thank her, the editors and the rest of the participants for a collective reality check on this research. Any errors or omissions are of course my own.

2 Raftery's investigative work was instrumental in the 2009 Ryan and Murphy Reports.

3 The paper is owned by the same parent company as the *Independent*, but the latter apparently did not regard this as a 'national' story.

PART III | Futures: Ireland and beyond

| Placing the Catholic Church:
the moral landscape of repealing the 8th

Richard Scriven

Introduction

> But, for Catholics, the result is about more than just
> abortion . . . [it is] a decisive and public rejection of Christianity
> in Ireland. It is agonising for believers in Christ to witness the
> public thrashing of what the [sic] hold to be good, true, and
> beautiful. (McDonough 2018)

Writing for *The Irish Catholic* in the immediate aftermath of
the vote, Fr Conor McDonough equates the referendum result
to a denunciation of Christianity. His absolutist position treats
faith and being pro-life as synonymous, ignoring the nuances
of denominational and individual positions. While this polemic
was found in religious and popular responses to the referendum,
I, instead, argue that the vote reveals how the historical moral
monopoly of the Catholic Church has been replaced by a more
pluralist moral landscape where individual conscience and civil
society play a larger role. This diversity is equally manifest within
the church itself with some clergy and bodies acknowledging
the range of opinion on this fraught topic, and groups such as
Catholics Together for Yes actively campaigning for repeal.

As well as being socio-cultural barometers, Irish referendums have been interpreted as an assessment of the Catholic
Church's position (Barr and Ó Corráin 2017). The slim passing
of the divorce referendum in 1995 (passed 50.5%) is cited as a
clear mark of its waning (Inglis 2003). The scale of the passing

of both the abortion and same-sex marriage (2015, 62.1% voted Yes) referendums demonstrates a moral landscape informed by liberal democratic values. This contrasts greatly with the passing of the 8th Amendment in 1983 (66.9% voted Yes) which manifested church teachings in the constitution granting significant rights to the unborn.[1]

I use the 2018 referendum campaign and its aftermath to examine the place of the institutional church, alongside considerations of the various affiliates and the role of the laity and believers. My treatment intends to reflect the complexity of the 'church' which is not a monolithic organisation but is rather a layered and assorted gathering of local diocese, religious orders, lay organisations and individuals that exist separately (and sometimes in tension) while committed to common principles. The doctrinal position is that "[h]uman life must be respected and protected absolutely from the moment of conception" meaning that "procured abortions" are morally evil (Catholic Church 1994: 2270–1). Their pro-life position is rigorously promoted by the church and its organs globally. This stance is increasingly being challenged by members, most visibly Catholics for Choice, an international organisation that promotes women's rights to follow their conscience in sexual and reproductive health (Catholics for Choice 2018). Contributions to the campaign and reflections on its outcome capture the nuances of institutional teachings and how clergy and laity respond to them.

This chapter unfolds by firstly discussing the historical moral monopoly of the Roman Catholic Church in the Republic of Ireland and its role in the 1983 referendum. From this basis, reflection is offered on how the clergy and lay associations deployed their messages in the 2018 campaign, as well as the other Catholic and Christian voices that presented alternative positions. I then use different responses to the vote to examine how it is cast as a defining moment for the church, both internally and externally.

The chapter concludes with speculation on the future of Roman Catholicism and its place in society.

Moral monopolies

For most of the 20th century, the Roman Catholic Church had a ubiquitous presence in both the Republic and parts of Northern Ireland. It had vast presence through education, health and welfare provision, and it was marked by high levels of religious practice and clericalism (Barr and Ó Corráin 2017). Inglis (1998) describes a Roman Catholic "habitus" that shaped social and political life according to church teachings. This moral consensus was regulated through a partnership between clergy and politicians, especially concerning the family and sexuality (Barr and Ó Corráin 2017). Virtuous living was enforced through affective structures, including religiously dominated education, the illegality of contraceptives and the control of socialising through lay Catholic associations or monitored spaces (Luddy 2017).

While abortion was outlawed by legislation in Ireland, a shifting social and legal setting prompted conservatively (mostly Catholic) groups to pre-emptively preserve the rights of the unborn (Field 2018; Spreng 2015). Against a background of modernisations and Pope John Paul II's call for Ireland to uphold Catholic values during his 1979 visit, this issue served as a rallying point to assert conservative morality and stem creeping liberalisations (Brown 2011). Moreover, it was cast as a nationalistic endeavour further asserting Irish distinction from (Protestant) England and its abortion policies (Smyth 2005).

It is noteworthy that the campaign was driven by the lay Pro-Life Amendment Campaign (PLAC), which was formed in 1981 by numerous organisations most of whom were Catholic, including the Irish Catholic Doctors' Guild, Guild of Catholic Nurses and the Catholic Young Men's Society (O'Toole 2014). The hierarchy firmly supported the campaign with prelates such as

Dr Kevin McNamara, Bishop of Kerry, defending the absolutist position and criticising Protestant churches for their stance that recognised the potential moral cases for abortion in cases of rape, incest and fatal foetal conditions (McAvoy 2015). This partnership between conservative groups and clergy is important in highlighting the role of lay people in embodying and mobilising church teachings.

While the 8th Amendment passed with a clear majority, the campaign was not the affirming process some had intended. Instead, it was a bitter and divisive process, referred to as a moral "civil war" in some commentaries, ending in a poorly attended vote (53.7%) and a significant minority that was unwilling to adhere to the religiously defined ethics (Brown 2011). Moreover, the vote occurred during the early fragmentation of the church's moral monopoly resulting from social liberalisation, greater equalities and increased capacities to challenge authority (Inglis 2003). Then, the waves of scandals, primarily the sexual abuse of children and its cover up by ecclesiastical authorities, served to definitively displace the church (Barr and Ó Corráin 2017). Nonetheless, the hierarchy and allied lay organisations actively pursued pro-life agendas, especially on key debates around the Miss X case, and the 1992 and 2002 referendums (Spreng 2015). This trajectory culminated in the vast mobilisation of the 2018 campaign.

The Catholic Church and the Vote No campaign

Gradually, the efforts of activists, combined with larger social changes, resulted in a concerted effort for repeal in the early 2010s, which was crystallised by the death of Savita Halappanavar (O'Connell 2018). In contrast, the hierarchy and its affiliates were organising their own campaigns and initiatives to ensure the preserving of the severe restrictions on abortions (Quinn 2013; Martin 2013b; Rally for Life 2018). Reflecting international anti-abortion discourses, the focus was on humanising the unborn and casting terminations as the intentional killing of the vulnerable (Martin 2013a).

A noteworthy aspect of the church's involvement in the Vote No campaign was the manner in which they divided the activities and communications. The hierarchy and clergy primarily focused on the 'internal' message through weekly sermons at masses, episcopal pastoral letters and vigils, novenas, pilgrimages and prayer events (Choose Life 2018; O'Sullivan-Latchford 2018). This discourse combined Scriptural references with church teachings and quotes from Popes Frances and John Paul II, which spoke to regular practicing believers. One of the more controversial aspects was the use of external pro-life speakers during masses which was welcomed by some (Save the 8th 2018b), challenged by the Association of Catholic Priests (2018) and attracted media attention with reports of people leaving mass in response (Kelleher 2018; McGarrigle 2018). This strategy resulted in the mobilisation of Catholic spaces generating distinct geographies with religious locations becoming political arenas on a scale uniquely reserved for this topic.

Citing moral grounds the church justified its role in the campaign, with Dr John Buckley, the Bishop of Cork and Ross, emphasising in a pastoral letter that "[w]e will never again have a more important vote" (Buckley 2018). The referendum allowed the hierarchy and clergy to assert a moral authority by claiming that "silent infants in the womb call on us, out of our common humanity, to protect them and to give force to that protection by rejecting this proposal being put to us" (O'Reilly 2018). These arguments, as with others in the No campaign, blended morality, legalities and medical science in a focus on the personhood of the unborn and their subsequent inalienable rights.

Clergy and the hierarchy were largely absent from the public-facing campaign with lay people (including medical and legal professionals) and proxy bodies acting primarily through the umbrella groupings 'Save the 8th' and 'Love Both' who articulated a non-religious message emphasising the human rights of the unborn, people with disabilities and children and women's welfare (Save the 8th 2018a).[2] The Iona Institute, a socially conservative Roman Catholic organisation, was one of the most significant players working in the background with both groupings (McGee 2018); more publicly, its members represented the No side on media debates and in weekly newspaper columns, and they had a national billboard campaign targeting the proposed legislation. In her *Irish Times* column, Breda O'Brien (2018), patron of the Institute, conveyed the Roman Catholic position:

> The question is, why do people who are pro-choice believe that compassion for the newer human cannot co-exist with compassion for the older human? Why do they think that taking life is a compassionate action?

The argument combines a stance that simultaneously stresses the humanity of the foetus and that there is always an alternative to abortion. The observable approach of the Roman Catholic position being articulated differently to internal and external audiences suggests a strategy to reaching as many people as possible. Similar to 1983, in 2018 the church's No campaign mobilised all of its assets and remaining social capital to resist any change to the constitutional restriction on abortion. However, the views and stories of pro-choice Catholics and others presented alternatives for believers and non-believers alike.

Other voices
The campaign illustrated both how many people's morality was informed by personal and civic principles rather than religious arguments, and the diversity of opinion amongst Irish Catholics. Not only was the moral landscape of Ireland more complex and varied,

but the simplistic model of a monolithic Roman Catholic stance was fractured. Individual believers and groups articulated relativistic and nuanced positions often borne from experiences of tragedy and suffering under the restrictions of the constitutional ban.

Catholics for Choice presented a framework for believers who disagreed with the church's official position. Cynthia Romero (2018), director of communications at Catholics for Choice, explained:

> Catholics in Ireland are coming to terms with the notion that Ireland's proud Catholic tradition is not at tension with repealing this law. Quite the contrary, as Catholics revere individual conscience as the final arbiter in moral decision-making and respect a secular state that allows all citizens to make their own ethical decisions.

Centring on the role of individual morality they illustrated how practicing Catholics could in good faith vote Yes. While this principle was mentioned in some of the bishops' pastoral letters, it was nonetheless emphasised that morally believers had to reject the proposal (Choose Life 2018).

Alternative positions were fostered by Catholics Together for Yes and Grandparents for Repeal who drew on their personal experiences of suffering as a result of the restrictive laws (Catholics Together for Yes 2018; Fegan 2018). In their social media, Catholics Together for Yes demonstrated how one could be both pro-choice and religious with posts such as: "After we vote yes we will still be good Catholics. We will still have our own moral code. Nothing will change for us. What we will have done is let others decide for themselves" on 1 May[3] (Catholics Together for Yes 2018). On a more intimate scale, the Termination for Medical Reasons (TFMR) group, who supported a Yes vote based on their experiences of diagnoses of severe and fatal foetal anomaly, highlighted that religious funerals were still held as an important part of the grieving process.[4] They illustrated how personal beliefs were still extremely important to people despite the church's stance. This range of perspectives articulate a greater role for the laity in shaping Catholic morality by stressing how practicing believers can, based on their experiences and informed decision, hold a position contrary to the hierarchy.

Different groups from within the church recognised the validity of this position centring on respect for the numerous voices that make up the body of the faithful. In expressing their unease with pro-life political speakers at masses, the Association of Catholic Priests (2018) explained that "there are, among faithful, church-going Catholics, a great variety of opinions on this vote". Similarly, the Society of St Vincent de Paul, a large Roman Catholic social justice charity, did not take a stance on the referendum, recognising that it is a personal decision, for which it received criticism from within the church (Ryan 2018). Although these strands were denounced by more traditionalist factions, they illustrated a realistic understanding that there was not a singular position among Catholics.

Other Christian perspectives also contributed to the moral landscape of the campaign, illustrating a greater diversity of theological understandings than argued for by Roman Catholic authorities. The Church of Ireland Archbishops of Armagh and Dublin considered legislation to be a more appropriate means to regulate abortion, but they opposed the unrestricted access to abortion up to 12 weeks (Clarke and Jackson 2018). Dr Laurence Graham (2018), President of the Methodist Church in Ireland, explained that they would not advocate how members should vote, but he also took serious issue with "abortion on demand". The Presbyterian Church in Ireland opposed the constitutional change on the basis of the "unrestricted access to abortion up to 12 weeks" (McNeely et al. 2018). These more relativistic positions are informed by the more participative nature of the denominations with lay people having an active role in decision-making.

More broadly, the Yes campaign revealed markedly more pluralistic conditions than in 1983. While the political establishment largely supported a Yes vote, the campaign was led and populated by a range of civil society organisations, local volunteers and the women and families who shared their personal tragedies, including Termination for Medical Reasons and In Her Shoes. Field (2018: 17) highlighted how the Together for Yes campaign was driven by a "non-traditional, non-hierarchical, women-led" movement. This assemblage, which was by these criteria a polar opposite to the Roman Catholic leadership, embodied a new civil-oriented morality which carried the vote.

Catholic Church responses to the referendum outcomes

The scale of the referendum outcome resulted in renewed evaluations of the role of the Catholic Church. The core message from church authorities and conservative viewpoints was the need for them to continue to pursue their pro-life campaign. However, the margin by which the vote passed revealed that many practicing Catholics had voted Yes, underlining the diversity of moral positions within the church. In response, the hierarchy, some clergy and prominent commentators rejected the legitimacy of these positions insisting on an absolutist stance.

In a homily during a pilgrimage in Knock the day after the results, Dr Eamon Martin (2018), Archbishop of Armagh, outlined: "In the midst of so much disappointment for those who voted No to repealing the 8th, it remains as important as ever to affirm the sanctity of all human life." In this immediate response to an audience of active Catholics, he articulates disenchantment and the need for dissent against the majority. In their summer statement, the bishops concluded:

> With the repeal of the Eighth Amendment a new situation now exists in Ireland. It is essential for us as a Church which

cares passionately about the gift of life, and wants to support
both mothers and their unborn children, to seek better ways
of responding to this new and very challenging reality. (Irish
Catholic Bishops Conference 2018)

They continue to assert the righteousness of their position as
presenting "better ways". As part of this process they are going
to establish a "Council for Life" to "advise and advocate for the
Catholic Church in Ireland on a consistent ethic of life and care
for those most at risk" (Ibid.). This seems to reproduce the campaign model of utilising lay professionals and organisations to
communicate the church's perspective.

More conservative Catholic commentators go further, presenting
a siege mentality. An Iona Institute (2018) blog post argues for the
need to dissent from the new "moral consensuses" by advocating for
"the right to life of the unborn as the pro-life movement has done,
and is doing, in other countries". This certainty not only propels
them to continue their campaigns and lobbying, but also to emulate
transnational pro-life strategies. An article in the right-wing Catholic
newspaper *Alive* claimed the results were "a massive earthquake in
Irish society . . . In essence, it was a profound rejection of Christian
faith and Christian civilisation" (Alive 2018: 3). While the loss of
power and status among religions generally can be seen as an assault
on faith by believers, it is an adjustment that needs to be contextual-
ised as a transition from a position of dominance to a new place in a
more diverse moral and spiritual landscape (Ammerman 2010).

The reality that many Catholics had voted for repeal was
responded to differently, reflecting perspectives on church moral
teachings. Jon O'Brien (2018), President of Catholics of Choice,
commented:

[I]t is clear Irish Catholics trust women with their religion, in
spite of the views of the Catholic hierarchy. It is clear Catholics
can be and are in favour of abortion rights.

He reflects the position of some Catholics and illustrates the prelates' unwillingness to engage with these perspectives. Similarly, Catholics Together for Yes expressed their gratitude to those who had voted Yes (Catholics Together for Yes 2018). These reactions reinforce their arguments on a greater role for dialogue in the church and recognition of the importance of individual conscience. A contrasting stance was presented by Bishop Kevin Doran who suggested that Catholics who "voted Yes, knowing and intending that abortion would be the outcome . . . should consider coming to confession" (Ní Aodha 2018). As well as displaying the distance between the Catholics who had voted Yes and church authorities, this and other church responses overlooked the moral agency of the conscientious decision reached by individuals and society. His comments were challenged by the prominent priest Fr Brian D'Arcy who advocated the importance of people following their conscience and that he "wouldn't like to attribute sin in this matter, at all" (*Irish Examiner* 2018).

While the questions of how the church balances doctrine and social change, and its conservative and liberal wings are perennial, it appears as though the leadership of Irish Catholicism are determined to follow more traditionalist interpretations into the future. Fr D'Arcy suggests other approaches, which acknowledges that doctrine does not have to change but how it is pursued and how pro-choice believers are treated can be more considered (*Irish Examiner* 2018). The diverse responses to the referendum exhibit different understandings of the church from within and its contemporary role in people's lives and society more broadly. This refuses a singular narrative of the Catholic Church, in relation to its stance on abortion, as well as that of its clergy or laity.

A pluralistic moral landscape

The repeal of the 8th Amendment is a significant event in Irish social and political life, a change that has revealed a complex moral landscape. For the Catholic Church in Ireland, the campaign and its aftermath has highlighted the diversity of perspectives on how doctrine is lived and enforced. While most of Irish society has moved beyond the church's moral monopoly, the hierarchy and traditionalists have become more entrenched in their stance (Inglis 2003). Conservative values are becoming more prominent in a declining church across Europe and North America, and now the Irish branch is taking on the mantel of a virtuous minority. It is apparent that lay people and organisations will take on an increasingly important place in promoting and defending doctrine. The church's abortion referendum tactics discussed in this chapter illustrated how the laity were central to the church's campaign, often being more visible and vocal than clergy. This aspect is also found in the management of Catholic services and institutions being transferred to trusts operated by lay people in response to the declining numbers of clergy and religious orders. Following trends elsewhere, the Roman Catholic Church in Ireland will continue to exert its influence on social and state policy, but it is likely to do so from a diminished position centring on conservative principles mobilised through lay organisations and affiliates.

Despite the significance of social changes, Ireland's context is still relatively distinct with the church remaining in control of hospitals and welfare organisations, as well the vast majority of primary schools and more than half of secondary schools. Ongoing conversations with government and civil society are attempting to divest some of these institutions, however, it is an onerous and slow process. Now, fresh tensions are emerging over the provision of reproductive health care in Catholic healthcare settings. A "code of ethics" from the Bishops Conference suggested that they would refuse to provide abortions (Coyne 2018), while Simon Harris, the Minster for Health, has insisted that publicly funded hospitals will provide legal health services (Ring and Ó Cionnaith 2018). Until these infrastructural contexts are addressed, the church will continue to have a disproportionate effect on Irish life. Institutional secularisation is lagging behind social secularisation, which has occurred primarily through societal liberalisation and the contraction of the church (Barr and Ó Corráin 2017; Inglis 2003). Nonetheless, the church, given the historical and cultural context in Ireland, will still have a privileged religious and moral position for some time (see Ammerman 2010).

Yet, the diversity of Catholic voices in the referendum campaign demonstrates how prominent conservative approaches are only one (albeit more likely) possibility. Lay and liberal clergy contested official positions and dictates. The campaign opened a new space for progressive Catholics and other believers to assert the validity of their position. While prelates and conservative viewpoints gain more attention, the role of these active grassroots believers should not be overlooked. Building on this momentum they may play an important role in the church as it enters a new model in response to clerical shortages and declining practice.

The 8th Amendment "demonstrated the power of the Catholic Church in the Irish political field" to define practice and discourse (Inglis 1998: 85). Its repeal indicates the waning of this power with the church becoming the source of morality amongst a more varied set of social and civil society actors. The campaign indicated how religious and ethical topics are becoming increasingly matters for individuals with new forms of civic moralities emerging. The hierarchy's determination for the church to be a dissenting voice and the commitment of its adherents is already manifest in attempts to prevent access to abortions in healthcare settings and add barriers through policy and legislation. The influence of more liberal Catholic voices remains to be seen, but their presence is statement in itself. It is clear, even at this early stage, that abortion will continue to be a contentious issue, but one that will be discussed and performed in a more diverse and pluralistic setting, within as well as without the church.

Notes

1 Reflecting the constitutional language for the 8th Amendment, the unborn is used as a generic term to refer to foetuses during prenatal development.

2 It is difficult to definitely trace the links between the Roman Catholic Church and these groups as their websites did not declare all affiliated groups at the time of research for this chapter.

3 See for example the Facebook and Twitter pages for Catholics Together for Yes: www.facebook.com/catholicstogetherforyes, https://twitter.com/catholics4yes?lang=en.

4 Termination for Medical Reasons (TFMR Ireland). Twitter. 6 May 2018. Available at: https://twitter.com/TFMRIRE/status/993247090649325571 (accessed 12 December 2018).

TWELVE | Losing Ireland: heteroactivist responses to the result of the 8th Amendment in Canada and the UK

Kath Browne and Catherine Jean Nash

Introduction

The resounding Yes vote to the repeal of the 8th Amendment in the Republic of Ireland on 26 May 2018 reverberated around the world with multiple effects. This chapter focuses on the responses by those who campaigned against abortion, in places where there are legislative regimes entrenching supposedly unassailable liberal laws supporting gender and sexual equalities. In our research to date, we have argued that resistances to sexual and gender rights and equalities can be best understood as heteroactivism – a form of resistance that seeks to reassert the primacy of heterosexual, monogamous, appropriately gendered marriage as best for children and society (Browne and Nash 2014, 2018; Nash and Browne 2015). Heteroactivist opposition has surfaced not only around same sex marriage but also around sex education curricula in public schools and appeals to freedom of speech to support anti-queer and/or anti-trans sentiments (Nash and Browne, forthcoming). This chapter considers how heteroactivist resistances surfaced in the context of the Irish reproductive rights battle by examining how organisations that oppose lesbian, gay, bisexual and trans (LGBT) equalities in Canada and the United Kingdom (UK) reacted to the Irish vote in the immediate aftermath of the referendum. This highlights the increasingly interconnected and emergent heteroactivist ideologies linking anti-LGBT and anti-abortion groups across these seemingly disparate issues. More particularly, we offer insights into the transnational geographies of heteroactivist resistances being crafted in the aftermath of the vote on the 8th.

We begin from the premise that certain groups campaigning against LGBT equalities also campaigned against abortion rights (although there remain some single-issue groups). Whilst these might seem to be different campaigns with diverse agendas, common ground is found around the perceived threats that sexual and gender rights (including abortion rights) pose to society and to the common good these rights arguably disrupt, including the 'natural' family based on male/female heterosexual procreative relationships (Browne et al. 2018). Current scholarship on the United States (US) Christian Right has shown that those opposed to LGBT rights are networked with groups opposed to abortion (see for example, Stein 2001; Burack 2014). However, these sorts of networks are not always or necessarily mirrored in the UK and Canada, given some resistances are not expressly Christian or right wing and that left wing heteroactivists are actively visible as well. These distinctions are not surprising given the unique relationship of the Christian Right to the American legal and cultural systems which are different from the UK and Canadian experience (see also Kuhar and Paternotte 2017; Saurette and Gordon 2016). Thus, while the US Christian Right does seek to further its influence through transnational alignments (see Rao 2014), this chapter focuses on the unique transnational geographies underpinning resistance to the Irish abortion vote by considering how heteroactivist arguments were formulated in the vote's aftermath.

Understanding distinctive resistances requires a specific geographical analysis trained on the UK and Canada given that legal, social and cultural contexts matter to how resistances can operate, what form they take and how they interact. In deliberately moving away from the USA, and whilst recognising its desire to influence other countries (including the Irish referendum), this chapter, and our work more broadly, shows how transnational connections and resistances are recreating different modes of opposition beyond a US-centric focus, which have yet to be fully understood. Decentring American activism opens up the possibility for seeing multiple distinct – but linked – manifestations of heteroactivism in the anti-abortion movement. This is evident in the shock and upset regarding the Irish referendum result that reverberated internationally, with heteroactivist groups struggling to accept the result in the 'Emerald Isle', which was once considered a "uniquely safe place for pre-unborn babies" (Chretien 2018). With the Yes vote, a place that had to be "defended" (McAuliffe and Kennedy 2017) was lost.

This chapter explores the initial reactions in the UK and Canada to demonstrate how 'losing Ireland' was understood in places where legislative and cultural norms uphold sexual and gender diversities and inclusions. Following a brief discussion of the methodology, the chapter examines some of the key tropes that emerged in our data. These tropes reflect traditional narratives that relate to religion, women, sex and the foetus. We then examine the discourses focusing on losing Ireland's exceptional status in an increasingly developed world. We focus on what opponents term 'the coalition of the powerful' that supposedly duped Irish voters into a Yes vote, and how opponents understand the 'next battle' in terms of Northern Ireland. Our focus on what are perceived as 'accepting' and 'tolerant' nations such as Canada and the UK allows us to explore heteroactivist anti-abortion discourses, as they circulate within hybridised transnational responses to local events that have global effects and ramifications.

Methodologies

For this chapter, we gathered data for one month after the vote to focus on immediate reactions to the loss of the vote by heteroactivist groups before these groups consolidated and reframed their reactions into a more coherent narrative. The groups selected are those we have followed throughout our 'Resisting Recognition' project.[1] We wanted to answer the question, what are heteroactivists in Canada and the UK saying about the results of the 8th Amendment referendum? We explored all the Canadian and UK heteroactivist websites on our databases and captured any articles published between 25 May and 25 June about the 8th referendum. Emails and newsletters we received from these groups were also saved and included in the data set. This yielded a total of forty-eight articles and allowed us to explore key points of mobilisation and the discourses that were informing key responses and debates (see also Saurette and Gordon 2016).

The analysis focused on identifying patterns in the data through thematic data coding, followed by an analysis of how these themes were discussed. We then developed an understanding of the key ideas and patterns in play to create a broader understanding of the commonalities as well as the differences within these responses. In what follows, we reflect on our in-depth analysis and then offer key quotes to explore the multiple, fragmented and sometimes contradictory reactions that emerged in the month after the vote. The chapter now moves to discuss the key tropes, beginning with the traditional tropes associated with anti-abortion arguments/activism.

Keep your rosaries off my ovaries: repositioning traditional tropes

Saurette and Gordon identify the traditional portrait of academic studies of anti-abortion activism as "a male dominated, extremist, religious and anti-woman movement that opposes abortion because of the fundamental belief that abortion kills a human being" (2016: 16). They contend that the anti-abortion movement in Canada (and to an extent, the US) is attempting to develop more woman-centred discourses that move beyond its 'in group' to create a more effective politic. In this section, we discuss how the traditional understanding of the anti-abortion movement was manifest in the initial reactions to the vote in a way that mainly spoke to their in-group as they attempted to understand the result. These initial reactions had a religious focus, but in heterogeneous ways, and also displayed anti-woman/anti-sex themes, including claims about the loss of 'Irish babies' through 'murder'.

Many heteroactivist groups initially focused on the secularisation of Irish culture, and the loss of 'Catholic Ireland' (which is associated with the Republic) was understood as having a key role in the referendum result, with recriminations aimed at clergy and laity alike. Part of their critique was focused on the perceived failure of the church to take a strong and public stand on the abortion vote. Some claimed that, historically, the Catholic Church had not stood up to the liberalisation of abortion laws, including, for example, opposing the 1992 legislation that allowed girls and women to travel overseas to access abortions (Smeaton 2018a). This is, of course, a predominant concern given the pivotal role the Catholic Church has assumed in Irish life in the modern era. Heteroactivists also turned their vitriol on fellow Catholics who voted Yes, both ridiculing and chastising them for their vote and for having the audacity to take communion, thereby "compound[ing] the evil they have done" (Adamus 2018). Groups were particularly upset with Catholics who are baptised but voted Yes, arguing such individuals were both in need of repentance and were traitors to the church itself. A slightly different narrative emerged from the Protestant Church of Ireland, where there was perhaps a more circumspect approach, with calls to "repent and reflect soberly when the Church has sought a kind of control which looks more like an earthly Empire than the Kingdom".[2]

Despite critiques about the silence of the Catholic Church in the lead up to the vote, others noted how the church was nevertheless a key focus of those looking to repeal the 8th in terms of painting the church as anti-woman:

> Despite the No campaign tactfully limiting the voice of the Catholic clergy, lacking any moral authority after years of scandals, some pro-abortion activists seemed hell-bent on portraying the call to retain the Eighth Amendment as an insidious anti-women Catholic conspiracy, aptly summed up with placards reading "Keep your rosaries off my ovaries". (Newman 2018)

In direct opposition to the church's failing to stand up to abortion reform, this commentator links "years of scandals to the Catholic Church" which now lacks moral authority to the notion that the clergy's voices need to be tactically limited. The activists who would not allow the connections between child sex scandals and histories of institutional abuse to be "limited" were seen as "hell-bent" on refusing the secularisation of the campaign, pinning the No campaign to religious and misogynist histories.

There is considerable diversity in how the history of these scandals and the links to institutional abuse were read by commentators. A heteroactivist re-narrating of Irish Catholic heritage claimed that opponents created a 'myth' about the Catholic Church around past abuse, avoidable deaths and the neglect of those who came under her care. This myth is associated with the church's past (not its present) in order to challenge efforts to limit the moral authority of the Catholic clergy in the abortion debates and to contest the deployment of an "insidious anti-woman" narrative against the church:

> Human beings like to find good reasons for doing bad things, and the grim myths of Ireland's Catholic past have provided comforting justification for the demolition of all legal protection for the unborn . . . The sad truth is that in an age of high infant mortality, illegitimate babies were probably not the healthiest; all orphanages had high death rates and the victims had to be buried

somewhere. The workhouses were also terrible, but they were
never empty, because for many, to be outside the workhouse was
even worse than being inside it. The past was indeed grim, but
is death the lesson that abortion campaigners should have learnt
from it? Does it mean that in an age of plenty, unwanted babies are
to be killed in the womb and not even given a grave, provided they
appear as a statistic in a spreadsheet somewhere? (Farmer 2018)

This quote both seeks to represent these histories as a myth
and also to claim that matters might have been worse but for
the church's interventions. In this reading, proponents seek
to rework the dominant discourses that see church history as
abusive and link that abusive history to broader Irish patriarchal culture (for a fuller exploration of Ireland's reproductive
histories and institutional abuses see Gilmartin and Kennedy
2018). Key here is the desire to consign what happened to history, and in this way minimise the impact of these abuses and
their effect on Ireland, as well as the Catholic Church. This
allows for a portrayal of "unwanted babies" in the contemporary era as subject to a far worse fate. The death of children
who were buried in unmarked graves during Ireland's history
of institutionalising unmarried women but were "unhealthy"
is equated with the foetus. This seeks to make equivalent the
death of women and children found in places such as the septic
tank of Tuam's mother and baby home. Imposing this narrative
on what is commonly read as historical institutional abuse of
women and children at the hands of the church, seeks to suggest a hypocritical view of those who wish to legalise abortion.
In this view, all become unwanted babies, and aborted foetuses
are read as not grieved for because they are not given 'appropriate' graves. Instead they are uncared for, sterile and emotionless
"statistics". This reworking of the institutionalisation and
death of an unknown number of women and children is done
without acknowledging the denial of information by the Catholic

Church for those who seek to know their histories/families of origin following church involvement in their (early) lives.

The narrative of women irresponsibly having sex was key in the stigmatisation of women who became pregnant out of wedlock in Ireland in the 20th century (McAuliffe and Kennedy 2017). The 'wayward woman' was a spectre that reappeared (or indeed never disappeared) throughout the 2018 referendum. The phrase "abortion on demand" was used to evoke the image of the woman who had (irresponsible) non-reproductive sex. Framed this way, these women were not 'victims' but threats to not only moral order, but life itself:

> [T]hey believe that it is legitimate to treat babies before birth differently to those after birth – on the basis of their age, size, dependency and mental capacity.
>
> This is profoundly discriminatory but is being advanced ironically on grounds of equality, diversity and tolerance . . . [T]he roots go back to the sexual revolution and the widespread acceptance of sex outside marriage[,] it is also stark witness to the ineffectiveness of free contraception in preventing conception and the legacy of believing that people who are not willing or ready to be parents should be having sex . . . A society will always be judged on how it treats its weakest members. Women are not the victims here. (Saunders 2018)

> [T]hey went with sex, and said it will be the babies who must be put to death. As one meme making the rounds of late puts it: "Abortion is the world's resounding answer to the question: If you had to murder in order to have an unfettered sex life, would you?" (Muehlenberg 2018)

The equating of sex and murder in these quotes supports a central contention of heteroactivists, that is, that people who do not want to be parents should not have sex. This fetocentric narrative places "babies" as the victims of women who seek to have sex without parenting. This serves to claim that the "hard cases" associated with foetal abnormalities are "vanishingly rare" and make "bad law", while vilifying young women who were "unwillingly pregnant" (McDonagh 2018). In these claims, the babies are the ones being discriminated against, with accusations of double speak around "equality, diversity and tolerance". This pushback against and challenge to the notion of equality is central to heteroactivist tactics of resisting sexual and gender rights that are seen as dominant. It is also worth noting that it is not just women, but "parents" who are implicated, in a reworking of anti-woman narratives. This may be, on the one hand, an argument that gives men a role in abortion decisions, but might also be read, on the other hand, as moving beyond blaming only women for unwanted pregnancies by acknowledging the role of men in sex/pregnancy as well.

Following from the fetocentric narratives, heteroactivist articles also condemned the celebration of the Yes vote success as a celebration of the "loss of countless lives of Irish babies killed before birth" (Smeaton 2018b). Heteroactivists represented the Yes campaign as frivolousness while claiming that they, with the "plucky infantry" of the No side, had done their best to frame this campaign in a positive, life affirming way (McDonagh 2018). These claims seek to demonstrate how heteroactivists sought to move beyond the negative portrayal of abortion as death towards a more 'affirming life' message. The obvious contrast of these metaphors reflects the seriousness of the issue (as well as evoking a war, where babies are being defended), where one side (No) is associated with foot soldiers (Lucie-Smith 2018). This is contrasted with the other side who are literally consumed by and consuming death through choice.

Perhaps in contrast to these anti-woman, anti-sex discourses there was some attempt by the heteroactivist groups in the immediate aftermath to formulate more pro-woman narratives, as identified by Saurette and Gordon (2016). Women were evoked as "countless mothers [who will] mourn their babies, often in silence". There was also a "sobering" thought in the face of the celebrating Yes side that sought to upend the myth of the bloody choice of abortion "magically making women 'unpregnant' so that they could go on to live happily ever after" (Farmer 2018). However, these pro-women discourses were largely secondary to the "unseen, unacknowledged" foetus (McDonagh 2018).

This section has highlighted how the initial responses to the Irish referendum in Canada and the UK were framed within more traditional anti-abortion arguments/activism. We have not distinguished the Canadian and UK discourses here but instead explore their transnational formulation in order to present the variety of ways heteroactivists in 'tolerant nations' responded to the Irish referendum. These formulations reflect more "traditional narratives" around abortion, including fetocentric and anti-woman narratives grounded in religious precepts. However, these responses also illustrated the complexities of these claims as well as attempts to be more supportive of women considering abortion. These arguments were positioned against the 'silence' of the Catholic Church (see also Scriven, this volume). Heteroactivist movements also made arguments about the equality of the foetus while deriding "liberals" for failing to recognise fundamental human rights (van Maren 2018b).

Losing Ireland, holding on to the North: exceptionalism, elites and the ongoing contest

While traditional narratives were clearly visible in explanations about the loss of the abortion vote, oppositional groups also drew on specific imaginings of the Republic of Ireland that made the Yes vote a "particular sort of dark day" for the Emerald Isle (McAvoy 2018). As one Canadian reflected:

> And we, like the pro-life Irish are now asking, wondered, How is it possible? We tried so hard. We did so much. We called

on God. We believed. Why didn't it work? Why do some
interventions save some lives and others don't? (Gray 2018)

This quote highlights the transnational impact of the loss of the
vote. "We" are "like the pro-life" Irish and together "We tried
hard" and "did so much"; the feeling of loss and failure in spite
of the effort is palpable. The collective transnational community
is implicated in the loss, it is not just about Ireland. Yet, the
exception of Ireland in this globalised world was also held to
be a loss:

> That it has been welcomed by most Irish is a stunning judgement
> on just how far the country has slid in the last 40 years . . . Ireland,
> having held out for some decades against the rest of the so-called
> developed world, has now joined the pack with a vengeance.
> (Saunders 2018)

A form of Irish exceptionalism was understood as defeated by the
forces of social and cultural globalisation, against which Ireland
had once 'held out'. This was framed as the 'death' of Ireland
itself and as a betrayal of the historical, religious and political men
who are seen as 'fathering' the nation through independence from
the British. Evoking these men, commentators worked to create a
specific version of a now seemingly lost past and framing the vote
as a betrayal of the Irish nation:

> Rest in peace dear children. Rest in peace dear land. A nation
> has voted to kill its children. The Ireland of St. Patrick,
> O'Connell, Pearse and Plunkett was sacked on 25 May as the
> sovereign people turned persecutor with the stroke of a pencil.
> The carefully crafted Constitution was also destroyed by
> inserting a fundamental right to kill . . . Who else could celebrate
> a nation choosing to kill its own children but a propagandised
> and vacuous generation, bereft of love for country or feeling for
> the innocent to be slaughtered. Is there a more treasonous deed
> than this? (van Maren 2018a)

Historically, the original "carefully crafted constitution" made no mention of abortion or the right to life. The 8th Amendment was not included until 1983 (see introduction, this volume). The call to the nation's fathers, Pearse and Plunkett, references the referendum campaign where No vote posters quoted Pearse who exhorted the Irish to "Cherish all the children equally". This quote by Pearse was not about abortion but to the Catholic/Protestant divide and calls to cherish Protestant children. The call to cherish children then was appropriated by the Vote No campaign to link Irishness, the constitution and pro-life positions. The break in these connections through "the stroke of a pencil" is read as creating a nation that celebrated the right to "kill its own children". The importance here is placed on *Irish* children, those who should be "owned" and "loved" as generative of, and linked to, the historical creation of the independent nation.

Yet, younger people were also derided as a "propagandised and vacuous generation" (van Maren 2018a). They were seen as engaging in groupthink and their overwhelming support was juxtaposed against those who are older and wiser and who saved the lives of those who voted No through the inclusion of the 8th Amendment into the constitution:

> It is a sad irony that thousands who voted to repeal the 8th Amendment probably do not realize that they are only alive today because they were protected by law in the womb. (van Maren 2018b)

The idea that those born since 1983 were 'only alive' because of the 8th Amendment harkens back to an 'abortion-free Ireland' that protected hundreds of thousands of its own children. Whereas, as Gilmartin and Kennedy (2018) have shown, those who were forced to be pregnant through this law were not only those who could not afford to travel, but also those who would be seen as 'foreigners', those who could not travel because of citizenship, regardless of health concerns. More broadly, opponents claimed the Irish voters had been sold "the Big Lie" (Gomes 2018):

> Irish voters were told "that the right thing is the right thing" and were sold the big lie that "abortion is healthcare necessary to save the mother's life". Which, of course, make it the right thing to do. The Big Lie repackages murder as life-saving healthcare with a pink ribbon of morality, blue wrapping-paper of compassion and a "Mommy, get well soon" Hallmark card. (Ibid.)

For those opposed to the repeal of the 8th Amendment, the selling of this lie is crucial. Part of the success of this lie, so it was claimed, was the absence of "a balanced media" that helped to dupe Irish voters. The ridiculing of sick mothers also reflects the anti-woman rhetoric where life-saving healthcare is read as "murder". The failure of the Irish populace to see the big lie is read as voters being "told" the "right thing" and believing it unquestioningly.

The media was also represented as reproducing the narratives of the British liberal elite. Opponents claimed that Irish media reports were intimately linked to some of the British media but that they did not do this in a 'balanced way' because they did not report the arguments of the far right. Thus, readers are asked:

> [I]imagine the Brexit campaign without Boris Johnson, Michael Gove, Gisela Stuart and the Mail, Telegraph and Spectator. That's how fair and representative it was. Oh and let's not forget the wording. The Brexit vote was an impartial choice between Leave or Remain; in Ireland it was Yes (positive, upbeat) for Repeal; No (sad face, negative) for retaining the amendment. It could have been put the other way round but of course it wasn't. The internet and social media was stymied as a debating arena, not least because Google banned online referendum advertisements, though it was notable that the Yes side used a device – RepealShield – themselves to block debate. (McDonagh 2018)

In this telling, traditional media was not only "biased" but online debate was deliberately "stymied", reflecting another key hetero-activist trope about the undermining of freedom of speech. Claims about the need for free speech are often used to argue there is no fair debate, or to emphasise their worldview. Opponents claimed that the Google ban on all advertising (not simply from one side) and the opt-in RepealShield on Twitter was used by those who wanted to block accounts and keep discussions for those "genuinely undecided" (McDonagh 2018). These actions were seen as limiting debate in ways that were supported by politicians. The political preference for a Yes vote ensured the referendum question was framed as a yes or no question by a "new dominant political elite" who wanted to create a "new political reality". Together this is seen as producing:

> A coalition of the powerful – Irish politicians who ran on pro-life platforms a few short years ago before abruptly betraying their supporters, the international abortion industry, the media, much of academia, a gaggle of celebrities, and the European elites – have finally prevailed in their relentless efforts to persuade the Irish people to become the first to bring in abortion on demand by popular vote. (van Maren 2018b)

The relentless efforts of the "coalition of the powerful", it was argued, served to manipulate and undermine the "popular vote" thereby not reflecting the "will of the people". The earlier contrast with Brexit also serves to create this narrative. Whereas Brexit is read as a vote against the elite, Irish people capitulated to those same elite (the distinction between Britain and Ireland being negated in these narratives). Voters were "persuaded" by politicians who "betrayed" pro-life supporters, as well as by the international forces of the "abortion industry". These claims return again to equating the referendum loss to the globalisation of Ireland and the loss of exceptionalism to forces beyond the Emerald Isle's control. To its supposed shame, Ireland was purported to be one of the first countries to bring in "abortion on demand" which opponents used to evoke the irresponsible sexually active woman, or parents who refuse to take responsibility of having sex outside heterosexual, married parenthood. The assertion then is the inability of Irish voters to think for themselves and to make decisions informed by the evidence presented to them particularly given what was construed as the unbalanced nature of the debate. These voters are juxtaposed with those who could move beyond group think, as evidence that there is hope that the fight was not over.

There were at least two key tropes regarding the future for Ireland and more broadly the fight against abortion on the Island. The first focused on 'lessons' from the UK and Canada:

> There is another even more disturbing aspect to this new political dispensation. It is liberal in name only. In reality, it is wholly intolerant of the pro-life position. As in Canada and the United Kingdom, such views will now be deemed 'offensive'. Never again will Irish pro-lifers be given access to the media in the way it did during this past campaign – not that it was ever a fair fight even then. Slowly but deliberately the pro-life case will be consigned to the dustbin, thought of as trash, unworthy of discussion. Just like the tiny victims of the new abortion regime that is about to become a facet of Irish life. (Turley 2018)

Turley offers insights into the dystopian futures opponents can expect in Ireland. The supposed lack of balance and impartiality ensured that heteroactivists in Canada and the UK were positioned as outsiders and their views not tolerated by the 'liberal elite'. Both countries have liberal abortion regimes, reflective of successful abortion advocacy, which has supposedly resulted in a dearth of publicly aired debates around abortion and in politicians' reluctance to engage with the issue. The move towards a liberal, yet 'intolerant' position is how the UK and Canada are read by heteroactivist groups who have mostly unsuccessfully sought to open up debates and create new legislation in both countries. This was seen as inevitable for Ireland where heteroactivists would not be able to access the media to influence the Irish populace again. Dystopian predictions were, however, contested by narratives, claiming the battle is just "beginning" and exhortations about the need for persistence given claims that a significant proportion of the Irish population is pro-life.

The second trope deals with Northern Ireland which is within the jurisdiction of the United Kingdom and yet does not offer citizens access to abortion due to devolved governance. In the aftermath of the referendum, the attention of both camps quickly shifted to Northern Ireland, where Prime Minister Theresa May congratulated the Irish on the referendum outcome and MP Stella Creasy introduced a motion into the House of Commons to remove parts of the 1861 law that prohibits abortion – the Offences Against the Person Act – because repealing portions of this law would have immediately decriminalised abortion across all parts of the UK, including Northern Ireland. In the view of heteroactivist commentators, British (read English) politicians were not properly distanced from the issue with grave consequences, illustrating the transnational reverberations of the Irish vote:

> The abortion issue may come to haunt Mrs May and even destroy her government. Given that there is pressure, in the aftermath of the Irish vote, to extend abortion legislation to Northern Ireland, something that the British government could do by Order in Council, Mrs May is in a bind, as her government relies on the votes of the DUP [Democratic Unionist Part, see Smyth, this volume] to survive, and the DUP are staunchly pro-life. It is not impossible to imagine a scenario where the government falls over divisions on abortion legislation for

Northern Ireland. Governments have fallen over less. What an
irony that would be: not the Northern Ireland border issue but
the abortion issue finishing off Mrs May. (Lucie-Smith 2018)

At the time of writing in 2018, the geopolitics of Brexit is such that
there is an unstable British government with no overall majority
in the House of Commons and one that is currently engaged in
bruising negotiations with the EU regarding Britain's exit from
the block. The government is propped up by the Democratic
Unionist Party (DUP) of Northern Ireland, who is both strongly
unionist and anti-abortion (Northern Ireland voted against
Brexit, but the DUP campaigned for it). This combination of factors places the abortion issue much higher on the political agenda
than it has been in decades past.

It also means distancing Northern Ireland from the UK.
Supporters of the union between the UK and Northern Ireland,
who are usually keen to be within and part of Westminster governance, had to distance themselves from the will and the rule
of Westminster to 'protect' Northern Ireland from both the
Republic of Ireland and the United Kingdom:

> The whole point of devolution, which is generally supported
> by self-identifying liberals, is that laws can be varied to suit
> the purposes of the people and legislatures of the kingdom's
> component parts. But not, obviously, if they contradict the
> prevailing wisdom of the liberal 'elite'. (Littlejohn 2018)

The return to a narrative of 'liberals' betraying 'liberalism' reiterates a key heteroactivist trope. Liberals in heteroactivist narratives
refuse free speech, and in the Northern Irish context reject legislation that is decided by devolved (democratic) governments.
Indeed, in arguing against a popular vote and arguably more
inclusive democratic processes, the Society for the Protection for
Unborn Children (SPUC) accused:

abortion advocates in the House of Commons of trying to intimidate the people of the Province and impose their ideology upon them. Liam Gibson, SPUC's development officer in Northern Ireland said: . . . "Attempts to exploit the decision of the referendum in the Irish Republic and sweep aside the consistent opposition to liberal abortion in Northern Ireland shows how little respect some in Westminster have for the devolution settlement. Their calls for a similar referendum . . . would have no legal precedent in our system of government and would only serve those who seek to bypass political opposition to the abortion agenda", said Mr Gibson. (Society for the Protection for Unborn Children 2018)

Here the popular vote cannot be called upon as it has "no precedent" and might well lead to a referendum on the reunification of Ireland. Bypassing "political opposition" is unconscionable when key tenants of Unionist politics are at stake: both the Union of Great Britain and Northern Ireland and the pro-life position of the DUP.

The positioning of Northern Ireland as the "next battle" opens up new frontiers that create particular geopolitical tensions (see Smyth, this volume). This reminds us that the Emerald Isle that has been "lost" is not uniform, Northern Ireland retains its anti-abortion legislative position. Here the "English elite" in Westminster House of Commons cannot impose their will on a devolved nation. The connections to England are both crucial to unionist identities and politics, and yet distanced, creating moral geographies that emphasise the difference of Northern Ireland from both England and the Republic.

Conclusion

Heteroactivism is a form of resistance that seeks to uphold the opposite-sex, monogamous, appropriately gendered marriage as best for children and society in places that have robust sexual and gender equalities legislation particularly for same-sex marriage (Browne and Nash 2018; Nash and Browne, forthcoming).

What we argue here is that heteroactivism as an analytical category largely focused on opposing same sex marriage, can also be used to engage with discussions of anti-abortion activism. Heteroactivism is geographical sensitive and enables insights into the transnational formulations of new resistances and alliances that nonetheless are reproduced in and through grounded cultural and legal contexts (Browne and Nash 2017). Using Canadian and British narratives of Ireland and Irishness, we have illustrated how these heteroactivisms have played out in transnational and hybrid ways. Heteroactivist groups in these debates deployed traditional, fetocentric, religious and anti-woman narratives, with newer emerging tropes condemning liberalism, 'coalitions of the powerful' and the globalisation of anti-family rhetoric.

These emergent tropes reflect the widening reach of heteroactivist discourses which seek to buttress traditional patriarchal family structures through direct attacks on LGBT and pro-abortion stances as well as through more subtle and less obvious claims about freedom of speech, religion and expression, and attacks on academia, social justice activism and the notions of tolerance, diversity and equality. While the Irish referendum might seem a narrow and geographically-specific battle, the underlying heteroactivist arguments require detailed examination, and the formulation of coherent and trenchant responses. Heteroactivists are operating across regional, national and international boundaries in their quest to reassert heteronormative sexual and gendered regimes beyond merely anti-gay rhetoric.

Notes

1 This research is part of a larger project entitled 'Resisting recognition: opposition to LGBT equalities in Canada, the UK and Australia' funded by the Social Sciences and Humanities Research Council (Canada).
2 Evangelical Alliance. 2018. *Reflecting on the Referendum*. 1 June [email].

THIRTEEN | The primacy of place: in vitro 'unborn' and the 8th Amendment

Noëlle Cotter

Introduction

In 1983 Ireland voted in favour of the 8th Amendment to the Constitution enshrining the 'right to life of the unborn' by referendum. In this same year, Louise Brown, the world's first 'test tube' baby, celebrated her fifth birthday, and cryopreservation of embryos was a burgeoning technology (see Trounson and Mohr 1983). Within three years Ireland's first fertility clinic offering assisted human reproduction opened. At the same time that Ireland was gripped by a debate to provide Constitutional protection to Ireland's laws criminalising abortion, assisted human reproduction was rapidly developing and had become relatively accessible. The use of the term 'unborn' in the 8th Amendment, while intending to ensure abortion would never be allowed in Ireland, had potential repercussions for these recent advances in reproductive medicine. While a conservative approach to the practice of assisted human reproduction was taken, it continued quietly and largely without controversy.

Embryos are perceived differently across a spectrum of opinions and beliefs, and perception and interpretations can be context dependent. Embryos are value-laden bodily commodities with a liminal status; embryos are not uniformly perceived as an insignificant cell cluster or a bodily product such as saliva or blood, and they are interpreted as human life along a continuum of development (and location) in a myriad of ways (Cotter 2009). Ireland's paradoxical understanding of the embryo is evidence of this, whereby the Constitutional term 'unborn' is interpreted to mean its physical location. In other words, destruction of the 'unborn' embryo while implanted in the womb was considered abortion, while cryopreservation of the 'unborn' embryo which until recently was an endeavour with limited success, or destruction within the laboratory of a fertility clinic, did not fall within the interpretation of 'unborn' in the 8th Amendment.[1] This chapter will outline this significance, or primacy, of place to the understanding of 'unborn'.

This paradox is not unique to Ireland; the regulation of fertility medicine (as well as abortion) in many jurisdictions has led to grapples with philosophical questions of when life begins, in a difficult task of turning this into a series of clear, secular, laws and governing regulation. Ireland is not alone; however, Ireland's debate has been limited and few other jurisdictions have had ambiguous terminology in their constitutions adding to this complexity. It is not possible to exhaustively explore the implications of the interactions and intersections between sociology, law, philosophy, theology and science with regard to the human embryo as debated across the globe; rather it is the intent of this chapter to note the parallel but different treatment of abortion and assisted human reproduction in the context of the 8th Amendment, how this was facilitated and the implications, if any, of the repeal of the 8th Amendment for the practice of assisted human reproduction in Ireland. This chapter will also briefly discuss methods and technologies that were not pursued in Ireland due to the lacunae of legislation for assisted human reproduction and the ambiguity of the 8th Amendment, against the backdrop of forthcoming legislation from the Department of Health.

Assisted human reproduction

Abortion and involuntary childlessness are, in the main, two very different experiences provoking divergent debates. This is evident in the silence during the recent 8th Amendment referendum campaign of healthcare practitioners in the area of infertility, client-patients and legal professionals in invoking the in vitro embryo as subject to this same Amendment.

Abortion and involuntary childlessness are two extremes of the female reproductive experience; decisions to begin and end pregnancies are shaped by diverse intimate, social, cultural, medical and economic factors. However, these extremities of experience have an important commonality in discourse: the potentiality of life. This potential is a legal, philosophical, ethical and religious quagmire. Gillon (2001) argues that this is not primarily a moral debate, but rather a metaphysical and/or theological debate with significant moral implications. Gillon (2001) outlines the various arguments from consideration of full moral status from the point of conception through to birth or some time thereafter, with the point of viability often used as the legal parameters for abortion laws. However, there are frequently significant disparities between the law and practice across the globe with the 'unborn' often existing in a liminal space (Marecek et al. 2017). The discussions around abortion diverge from embryo debates at this point.

Steptoe and Edwards, the physicians who presided over the in vitro fertilisation (IVF) that led to Louise Brown's birth, developed a method that at its core has not altered in the last 40 years.[2] The most common route to IVF treatment is a well-trodden road of failed less-invasive fertility treatments and it is often considered the "last chance saloon" (Mahon and Cotter 2014).[3] IVF is a practice of ever-diminishing returns and the odds are played to increase the chance of pregnancy; not all eggs produced through superovulation will be viable, and following that, not all eggs will fertilise, and if they do, not all fertilised ovum will survive to be considered viable for transfer to the womb. However, where multiple embryos are created (which also may not all be viable) this provides individuals with a greater chance of achieving at least one pregnancy. Cryopreservation of embryos has become increasingly important; not only has vitrification improved survival rates (Kushnir et al. 2017) but practice is moving increasingly towards single embryo transfer and possibly even freezing all embryos for later transfer (Konc et al. 2014; Dyer et al. 2016) – all with the objective of optimising pregnancy potential. As cryopreservation and associated methods improve, this is at the same time as fresh cycle success rates have improved and this potentially leads to a situation whereby frozen embryos are not wanted by their gamete owners. People who have undertaken this treatment may achieve their desired family size with 'surplus' embryos remaining. Setting aside national regulations, there are six options broadly considered available: use in own treatment, placing in the uterus when implantation is impossible, donation to others, infertility research, general research, or destruction (Nachtigall et al. 2005). However, when national practices are taken into account, there are generally significantly fewer options (Busardò et al. 2014). Although Ireland has no national regulations, it did have the 8th Amendment. Without clarity on the definition of 'unborn', clinics trod carefully to ensure they would not fall foul of the Constitution. However, some guidance from a government commission and the courts has been forthcoming since 2005, providing the clinics with clarity around the primacy of place: the embryo was not, strictly speaking, 'unborn'.

Assisted human reproduction regulation and Ireland

Ireland's abortion referenda have been incredibly divisive; incorporating debates and decisions of 'the right to travel'. However throughout this era, Irish people have accessed assistive reproductive technologies across member states and beyond relatively unproblematically.

Ireland has no official body or legislation for the regulation and licensing of clinics offering IVF or other associated reproductive technologies, despite their presence in the country since the late 1980s (Ibid.). Thus far, physicians in Ireland have been guided by the Irish Medical Council (Ibid.). The sixth edition of the Irish Medical Council's conduct and ethics guide (2004) is clear in stating that "the deliberate and intentional destruction of in-vitro human life already formed is professional misconduct" and "any fertilised ovum must be used for normal implantation and must not be deliberately destroyed". However, by the seventh edition (2009) this reference is deleted in favour of informing medical practitioners that they should "not participate in creating new forms of life solely for experimental purposes". The (2016) eighth edition reiterates this 2009 statement. The EU Cell and Tissues Directive (2004/23/EC) gave the Irish Medicines Board a role in regulating IVF laboratories due to their designation as tissue establishments;[4] this included a licensing system for human embryology laboratory operations. While that focus is on the laboratory, the Commission on Patient Safety and Quality Assurance produced recommendations in 2008 for regular clinical audit and a licensing system for clinics (Sills and Murphy 2009).

To date, the most comprehensive official consideration of regulation in this field was initiated in 2000 by the Minister for Health and Children in establishing the Commission on Assisted Human Reproduction (CAHR). The Commission, in dissent, stated that the Constitutional protection should be granted once embryo transfer into the uterus has taken place. The member disagreeing with this recommendation had at the centre of his objection that he could not agree that the embryo's status was dependent on its location, or its primacy of place (Commission on Assisted Human Reproduction 2005: 80). However, the CAHR did agree unanimously that superovulation should be allowed and that appropriate guidelines should be put in place to govern cryopreservation of excess healthy embryos, disagreement around this recommendation was based on what should be done with 'excess' embryos.

To consider the moment of conception as the beginning of human life is conceptually appealing in its clarity and simplicity. However, the logic would therefore continue that embryos either outside or inside the female body have the same rights; albeit regulatory deliberations have concluded that without implantation there is no potential for onward development into a foetus (for example, see Warnock 1984; Commission on Assisted Human Reproduction 2005). This has been the means to set the in vitro embryo outside the definition of unborn. However, and as recognised by both the aforementioned regulatory deliberating bodies, there is a high rate of embryo loss when in the body due to miscarriage or not implanting. Therefore, the in vivo embryo may have considerably greater potential for its location, but this potentiality is still on a spectrum with the in vitro embryo. In sum, the embryo has the potential for human life both inside and outside the body, however, outside the body the embryo's potentiality is deemed non-existent in current regulatory debates. Sills and Murphy (2009) argue that this fails to reconcile the distinction between what is and what could be. However, in both situations, for the embryo outside and inside the body, the potential is non-existent without successful implantation. Place is paramount. The Warnock Committee (1984), the UK's original deliberating body, concluded that the embryo outside the body did not have potential without considerable scientific intervention and therefore differed in its potentially from the in vivo embryo. This was the same understanding adopted by the Commission on Assisted Human Reproduction which therefore was able to set aside the 8th Amendment in its deliberations, albeit not in a consensus decision. However, implantation of the embryo, even if successful, gives rise to the capacity to be born but does not give it the separate capacity to be born alive (McGuinness and Uí Chonnachtaigh 2011). Therefore, this distinction, which has been accepted as the difference between in vivo and in vitro embryos, is not necessarily on solid ground. Primacy is given to place for its convenience rather than its logic.

In the 2009 case, *Roche v Roche*[5] (see Mulligan 2011; Staunton 2018), against a former husband's wishes, a woman wanted to use their cryopreserved embryos; both the High Court and Supreme Court decided in favour of the husband, on the understanding that no one could be forced to become a parent against their wishes. This is particularly interesting in the context of the 8th Amendment, because the courts decided that the individual had the right to avoid procreation even when fertilisation had occurred. This is precisely the right that was circumvented by the 8th Amendment which was, technically, placing people in the position of becoming parents against their wishes in the case of a crisis pregnancy. Ireland's primacy of place of understanding the embryo was, at best, enmeshed in a legal paradox and, at worst, was an entirely unregulated environment available for controversial practices (see Ibid.).

Ireland's pronatalism[6]

The influence of the Catholic Church in Ireland has been particularly evident in attitudes towards abortion. Not content with abortion being illegal, placing the 'right to life of the unborn' into the Irish Constitution by referendum was intended to guarantee its prohibition in perpetuity. The 8th Amendment did not jar with the Constitution; instead it reflected the Catholic moral code already evident in Ireland's constitution.

The Catholic Church has traditionally held a privileged place in the Irish State; Inglis refers to it as a "power bloc" with a "moral monopoly" in Irish society (1998). Inglis eloquently describes this influence as "a sacred Catholic canopy which hung over most aspects of Irish life" and describes residues of Catholic culture as lingering "in the Irish collective consciousness" (Ibid.: 253). *Bunreacht na hÉireann* (the Irish Constitution) was, and remains, a mirror to Irish societal values and mores. Beaumont (1997) emphasises how the Constitution was influenced by Catholic thought and phraseology; for example, until deleted in 1972, the Constitution explicitly enshrined the Church-State relationship. Twentieth-century Ireland was dominated by the Church's rule which, although in decline, evident through developments in the latter years of the century and the early years of this century, Catholic values, norms and mores are embedded in Irish society, culture and psyche. The primacy of Catholic values in Irish life is learned and incorporated from an early age and across the generations (Inglis 2005). Ireland's activities and laws with regard to reproductive health were particularly influenced by Catholicism. Condoms were not allowed to be sold without prescription until 1985 and then from named outlets; deregulation only occurred in 1992, and until 2018 abortion was (almost entirely) illegal and unconstitutional.

It is unlikely, given the duration of Catholicism's influence in Ireland, that all Catholic values could rapidly dissipate (see Scriven, this volume). In its place, "cultural Catholicism" may emerge; certain morals and attitudes associated with the Church may prevail despite abandonment of the official religion (Inglis 2007). Thus, as Catholic values and norms have been embedded in Irish society and culture and reproduced through Irish institutions, the population has been socialised by these values and norms without conscious adherence to the institution of the Church (Cotter 2009). The slow dismantling of this embedded religious force in Irish society and institutions has lifted the silences surrounding significant injustices and crimes perpetrated by religious orders and individuals within the church, serving as a feedback loop advancing the secular drive in Irish life. The shame bestowed upon unmarried pregnant women by Irish society, imbued with Catholic values, and the response, is a clear indicator of the 'wrong' kind of parenthood made right by babies being given to the right kind of parents – married couples (see Olund, this volume; McGill, this volume). Similarly, assisted human reproduction was only available until relatively recently to married couples according to rules made by individual clinics.[7] In addition, assisted human reproduction is only available privately and, until recently, was not available through private health insurance. Couples undergoing assisted human reproduction in Ireland had to have considerable resources to access these services, albeit the majority of drug costs were borne under the Drug Refund Scheme.

Ireland's historical pronatalism is, at least in part, attributable to the Catholic Church's traditional dominance. Ironically, the family form that is most supported is also frequently the nuclear family that assisted human reproduction seeks to create, albeit using technologies that have been denounced by the Vatican (Congregation for the Doctrine of the Faith 1987; 2008). Therefore, Ireland's pronatalism, rooted in Catholicism, quietly accepted assisted human reproduction while abortion remained abhorrent and divisive. However, it is interesting to note that this oxymoron may not be unique to Ireland. Präg and Mills (2017) in a cross-European analysis, note that being a predominantly Catholic country has no relationship with use of assisted human reproduction technologies. This discrepancy between religious identification and practice is potentially indicative of this Catholic pronatalist ethos that may lead individuals to undertake treatment that is abhorred by this very institution that encourages childbearing. Ireland rarely debated this intersection. In a pronatalist context, where abortion was abhorrent, there was no contradiction with assisted human reproduction practice in this State enabling individuals to align with these traditional values. Ireland's dichotomy was reconciled through the framing of unborn to refer to place: with embryo implantation in the womb being interpreted as the working definition of unborn.

Ireland and 'the unborn'

The Health (Regulation of Termination of Pregnancy) Act 2018 is clear in its definition of a foetus to which this Act refers; an embryo or foetus after implantation in the uterus is within the remit of this Act. This is sharply juxtaposed with the 8th Amendment 'right to life of the unborn' text which offered neither definition nor clarity and was criticised for its vagueness during the 1982/3 referendum campaign.

Language reflects and shapes cognitive processes; and use of the term 'unborn' (particularly instead of 'foetus') reflects attitudes about the ontological nature of certain beings (Bilewicz et al. 2017). Bilewicz et al. (Ibid.) note that, as the moment when the 'potential to live' is arbitrary, cultural expectations and beliefs about biological mechanisms may shape the way cells or gametes and their personhood are conceptualised. The embryo is frequently considered to have a liminal status; existing in a grey area and interpreted and reinterpreted based on different framings (Cotter 2009). Thompson (2005) utilises the concept of ontological choreography to understand the coordination required for common understandings within assisted human reproduction. This concept also provides a useful framework for considering the co-existence of the Constitutional right to life of the unborn and how primacy of place facilitated assisted human reproduction in Ireland.

If the term 'unborn' was interpreted to provide constitutional protection from the moment of conception, the ramifications for assisted human reproduction in Ireland would be substantial, leading to debates relating to donation, third party gestation and unwanted pregnancies, in the latter paralleling with the repeal movement. If embryos have an equal right to life, cryopreservation has the potential to be an affront to this right. Cryopreservation increases the likelihood of embryo destruction as survival rates through thawing were relatively poor until recently. This would remove superovulation as a possibility in assisted human reproduction in Ireland,[8] thereby not permitting the potential production of multiple embryos. However, as vitrification has improved both the chances of frozen embryo survival as well as pregnancy rates, embryo freezing could be permitted. However, if frozen embryos have a right to life, they could not be permitted to be frozen indefinitely. They would have to be given an opportunity to be implanted in a womb, although this could be impossible due to death or contrary to the wishes of embryo-owners for a variety of reasons. Therefore, the embryo would have to be donated, leading Ireland into the quagmire of surrogacy and donation (assuming such alternative gestational mothers are available), not to mention considerable issues around birth registration and adoption. Recommendations by the Commission on Assisted Human Reproduction (2005) and the *Roche v Roche* ruling (2009) opined, for the first time, that the in vitro embryo did not have the protection of the 8th Amendment. However, human embryo stem cell research or other emerging techniques were not introduced to Ireland in the period 2005–2009 through present day, despite the human embryo technically not having any Constitutional protection (see Staunton 2018). The primacy of place of the embryo did not give rise to a plethora of practices and interventions which technically could have occurred ironically and in parallel to the abortion ban.

Ireland's 'Brave New World'?
The Health (Regulation of Termination of Pregnancy) Act 2018 provides a succinct definition of what it is actually referring to; it definitively sets aside the in vitro embryo as falling within the remit of this abortion legislation. However, without further legislation, the in vitro embryo may be falling outside the Health (Regulation of Termination of Pregnancy) Act

2018 and also falling between the cracks. The extracorporeal embryo remains in a liminal place.

The Constitutional protection of the unborn had potential implications for IVF treatment as practiced in Ireland: as discussed above, this practice includes superovulation for the purposes of counteracting the diminishing rate of IVF returns and potentially facilitates less invasive and cheaper frozen cycles in the future. The treatment of embryos in this manner, even if all embryos produced were transferred at different times, could have been considered an affront to human dignity if 'unborn' were interpreted as on a par with an adult human. The freezing, thawing and potential for destruction during these processes, as well as thawing for the purposes of destruction, should have been more controversial in Ireland. This controversy may have been mitigated by the Commission on Assisted Human Reproduction report (2005) and the *Roche v Roche* ruling (2009) where the in vitro embryo was not considered unborn, by virtue of location. However, practice of these methods in Ireland predated these findings.

In spite of this somewhat laissez-faire approach, Ireland has taken an overall cautionary approach to practice. However, it must also be noted that governing/advisory European bodies have also avoided an ethical debate, albeit they could not interfere with national laws, leaving these considerations at the Member State level (Staunton 2018). In other jurisdictions, regulation facilitates practices such as preimplantation genetic diagnosis, while experimental research follows a 'use animal first' rule that some object to as a waste of time, effort and money, or consider ethical gatekeepers as placing obstacles in the path of scientific advancement (Gizzo et al. 2016; Jans et al. 2018). This is further complicated by less controversial methods of deriving stem cells for research purposes, which can be a driver for the (perceived) necessity for human embryo stem cell research (Staunton 2018).

Laboratory-based researchers may (or may not) view ethical guides for research on human embryos as an inconvenience, but this view is certainly juxtaposed with the conservative approach to assisted human reproduction at the patient level (Konc et al. 2014). In the period between the repeal of the 8th Amendment referendum and the enacting of the Health (Regulation of Termination of Pregnancy) Act 2018, the issue of conscientious objection[9] came to the fore from a mobilised group of General Practitioners stating that they should not be obliged to provide a referral to another physician willing to provide services.[10] In this conservative context, where (some) physicians are unwilling to refer patients, it is unlikely that Ireland will become a beacon of embryonic research. In addition, the Catholic Church's waning influence over Irish maternity hospitals also has the potential to complicate the introduction of abortion; even before repeal of the 8th Amendment, many fertility clinics are physically aligned to maternity hospitals.

In the time lag between the removal of the 8th Amendment and commencement of State-oversight a proliferation of controversial practices in the area of assisted human reproduction did not come to pass, but it certainly provides the space within which to consider Ireland's 'Brave New World'. Individuals have already accessed these practices in other countries through so-called reproductive tourism (see Ferraretti et al. 2010). As with abortion, many couples will have been provided with the information but not the services by their Ireland-based physician (Cotter 2010). These practices may not have been any more at odds with the 8th Amendment than standard IVF and embryo storage, however, their potential for controversy in the absence of legislative clarity may have cautioned Irish clinics against directly providing services.

Ireland's Department of Health published the General Scheme of the Assisted Human Reproduction Bill in 2017. It deals with gamete and embryo donation and research, posthumous assisted human reproduction, pre-implantation genetic diagnosis and sex selection, surrogacy, embryo and stem cell research and provides for a regulatory authority to oversee assisted human reproduction in the State. It defines the embryo as an entity formed at the point of fertilisation, but also facilitates destruction and embryo research. This Bill has been criticised, perhaps unfairly given its context and cultural milieu, for being restrictive, outdated and not aligned with current practice in other jurisdictions (Bracken 2017; Staunton 2018).

Current research points in a direction in which assisted human reproduction and associated experimental research may develop, for example, mitochondrial manipulation, removal of gene sequences for inheritable diseases, gene therapy, cloning, production of chimeras or hybrids and the possibility of ecto-genesis (Gianaroli et al. 2016; Busardò et al. 2014). However, the regulatory body will have to immediately grapple with issues likely to be controversial given their social implications, such as duration of storage, guidelines on death or divorce of a couple (particularly where the woman might not be able to have children by other means), surrogacy in its various forms of parentage (gestational, biological) and remuneration and access for different family forms. This regulatory body will need to have the capacity to keep on top of advances within the field of fertility treatments and associated research, this may include grappling with significant advances in areas such as genomic medicine which seep into areas relatively untethered to assisted human reproductive practices. However, this body must also be mindful to not be distracted by developments in this evolving area, but also must be clear about the mundane and common practices. It is likely that clarity will be welcomed by practitioners and researchers, while the ability to have a mature discussion, whatever the outcome, will be a testament to significant change within Irish society.

Notes

1 Evident in the conclusions of the Report of the Commission on Assisted Human Reproduction (2005) and the *Roche v Roche* ruling (2009).

2 *In vitro*, or in glass fertilisation, as opposed to *in vivo*, or in body fertilisation, is particularly named after the technique with the most scientific intervention, however, there is significant body work (Throsby 2004) undertaken by women up to that point and beyond. The significant physical toll that IVF places on a woman's body is frequently ignored; this is also evident in considerations of stem cell research. The production of embryos solely for the purposes of research is rarely discussed with consideration of this toll.

3 New technologies may alter that perception albeit all of these treatments will involve at least some form of IVF protocol.

4 This role included oversight for compliance with international standards regarding quality and safety for the donation, procurement, testing, processing, preservation, storage and distribution of human tissues and cells.

5 *Roche v Roche* 2010 2IR 321.

6 Pronatalism refers to a policy, practice, or in this case, a cultural milieu, that is pro-birth and pro-families.

7 Ireland is not alone in this; across Europe assisted human reproduction is predominantly only available to married or 'stable' couples, able to verify their relationship has lasted circa 2 years (Busardò et al. 2014). Thompson (2005) refers to this as "selective pronatalism".

8 Unless success rates for egg freezing were to significantly improve. In theory, eggs and sperm could be frozen and thawed for fertilisation; one embryo created at a time, albeit this is impractical.

9 The Council of Europe Parliamentary Assembly (2010) provided for the right to conscientious objection in medical care. See http://assembly.coe. int/nw/xml/XRef/Xref-XML2HTML-EN.asp?fileid=17909&lang=en; The Irish Times (2018) GPs demand freedom to opt out of plans for abortion services, 26 September 2018. www.irishtimes.com/news/ ireland/irish-news/gps-demand-freedom-to-opt-out-of-plans-for-abortion-services-1.3642086 (accessed 11 October 2018).

10 For further information on conscientious objection, see Part 3, Miscellaneous, Health (Regulation of Termination of Pregnancy) Act 2018.

FOURTEEN | Northern Ireland after repealing the 8th: democratic challenges

Lisa Smyth

Introduction

What does Ireland's repeal referendum mean for abortion access in Northern Ireland? This question is considered here in terms of the tensions between institutional and cultural opportunities for campaign groups to mobilise the public around the issue of abortion. While the politics of abortion in this region, as elsewhere, link moral and political life (Boltanski 2013; Sanger 2016; Smyth 2016), the political and historical context shapes the debate in particular ways. The chapter examines the organised efforts of the two major political groups in the region to frame what is at stake in abortion legislation: whether as a matter of democracy in a devolved post-conflict context or of equal citizenship. The chapter examines pro-choice and anti-abortion[1] organisational efforts to engage in core political tasks of frame building and bridging, establish relevance to everyday life and motivate support. In Northern Ireland these tasks are pursued within a restricted political context which is at the same time culturally open. The challenges abortion politics poses to democracy and post-conflict constitutionalism form the core of the chapter's analysis.

Northern Ireland has some of the most restrictive abortion laws in the world. Abortion is a crime punishable by a maximum sentence of life imprisonment, under the 1861 Offences Against the Person Act. The only exceptions are in circumstances where an abortion is necessary to preserve a woman's life, or to protect her from becoming a "physical or mental wreck" (see Sheldon 1997). Abortion in cases of rape, incest, fatal or serious foetal abnormality are all criminal offences.[2] Britain's 1967 Abortion Act was not extended to Northern Ireland, a result of repeated pressure from Northern Ireland's political parties (Bloomer and Fegan 2014; Fegan and Rebouche 2003; Smyth 2006). At the same time, more than 900 women from Northern Ireland travelled to Britain for abortions in 2017 and 724 in 2016 (BBC 2018a). For those who cannot travel, abortion pills can be purchased online, although these are taken without medical supervision and at the risk of criminal prosecution (BBC 2018b; Gentleman 2016).

What follows examines political contestation over the significance of abortion access in Northern Ireland. This is a context where norms of equality and citizenship have gained prominence through the post-conflict settlement. At the same time, the region tends to be treated as politically and socially exceptional – "a place apart" – requiring differentiated rights from Britain (Side 2006). This chapter argues that the deployment of common frames of meaning by conflicting organisations in this context indicates the importance of cultural politics in generating change, particularly in contexts such as this, where institutional structures reinforce the political stalemate.

The politics of signification

Social movement organisations, such as those engaged in abortion politics, can be understood as 'norm entrepreneurs' (Sunstein 1996), who seek to change the accepted meaning attached to a social phenomenon. Such organisations are primarily caught up in 'the politics of signification', namely those efforts to secure public acceptance for a specific way of framing what is at stake with the phenomena in question (Benford and Snow 2000: 613). This politics is not straightforward, as competing frames are developed and deployed in the face of contestations, both within social movement organisations and in the wider political context (e.g. Baird and Millar 2018; McDonnell and Murphy 2018). Political tactics can include adopting an opponent's meaning frames so as to confuse the terms of debate (Rohlinger 2006: 540). Efforts to generate successful meaning frames which define the moral, political or social significance of a specific phenomenon are continuous, as norm entrepreneurs cope with dissent from both within and beyond their organisational contexts. A number of core tasks and processes have been identified as driving efforts to frame and re-frame political significance. These include diagnosing the issue at stake, developing prognoses for how to address this issue and motivating political support. These tasks are pursued in several ways, including by building bridges to other congruent frames and connecting otherwise disparate events or attitudes to amplify the frame's significance. Other strategies involve demonstrating the frame's relevance to the everyday lives of wider publics, resonating with contemporary cultural norms, and deploying strategic vocabularies to motivate support, for instance, by attaching claims of severity, urgency or moral duty to the frame in question. The success of a frame depends on how inclusive and flexible it is, since these attributes allow meaning frames to develop broad appeal, respond to unexpected events or situations that may arise and become amplified in the process, for example, through the successful dissemination of slogans or catchphrases (Benford and Snow 2000).

Political opportunity structures: institutions and norms

The success of framing efforts depend not only on the strategic efforts of social movement organisations, but also, crucially, on the political opportunity structure within which the politics of signification takes place (Ferree et al. 2002: 106). This refers to the opportunities which a political system's institutional and normative structure makes available to social movement actors. If a frame does not resonate with the context's political concerns, meanings and institutional arrangements, it is unlikely to take hold and become the lens through which questions are posed and public debate plays out (Benford and Snow 2000: 628; Crossley 2002).

Cross-border campaigning has long been a feature of both pro-choice and anti-abortion campaigning on the island of Ireland, and changes in the regulation of abortion access in one jurisdiction have resonances in the other. However, the political opportunity structure in Northern Ireland is different both from that of the Republic of Ireland and Great Britain. Northern Ireland is not a state but instead is governed as a UK region with devolved political institutions. Legislation is caught up in the broader UK framework as well as local political interests. It is inhabited by two conflicting "imagined communities" (Anderson 1983) rather than one, making appeal to 'the people' as the source of political legitimacy difficult (McEvoy and O'Leary 2013).

Northern Ireland's devolved Legislative Assembly was suspended in January 2017 (Carroll 2018) and seems unlikely to be reinstated in the foreseeable future. Westminster's minority government relies on the region's Democratic Unionist Party for political support, giving that party's fundamentalist position on gender and sexual equality some influence at the centre of UK politics (Cabinet Office 2017). Northern Ireland currently operates in a state of crisis and uncertainty. Thus, despite devolution, abortion politics take place within the confines of limited institutional opportunities for contesting current legislation.

Nevertheless, there have been some important changes. Although access to legal abortion is highly restricted inside Northern Ireland, in October 2017, the UK government introduced funding for women in Northern Ireland to travel to Britain to access abortions through the NHS; it also made some travel funding available for low-income women (BBC 2017). This was followed by national and international judgements in 2018 which found that the region's current abortion law violates women's human rights (Committee on the Elimination of Discrimination against Women 2018). Although there have been some significant attempts by Westminster MPs to call for UK-wide decriminalisation of abortion (Bowden 2018), Brexit has dominated Westminster's political agenda throughout 2018 and beyond.

By contrast, the normative opportunity structure is more favourable for pro-choice reforms. Recent attitudinal survey data from Northern Ireland shows that 68% of the population believe that abortion should not be criminalised; 67% of DUP voters polled supported decriminalisation (Kolirin 2018). The changed constitutional and legislative context of the Republic and the pressures brought to bear by international bodies such as the United Nations have opened up new opportunities for building bridges to other congruent frames which justify abortion access around the world. Most notable here is the claim that abortion should be understood as a key aspect of women's equal citizenship and specifically as a social right to reproductive healthcare. The efforts of the two major campaign organisations in the region to resonate with this wider political context by framing abortion law in Northern Ireland as raising issues of equal citizenship, in both liberal and illiberal ways, will be examined below.

The politics of signification: framing abortion politics in Northern Ireland after the 8th

Political actors seek to establish frames of meaning at local, national and international levels. What follows considers this politics of signification as it played out during the summer and autumn of 2018, following the result of the 8th Amendment referendum in May. The public statements of Northern Ireland's two most prominent abortion rights organisations are the focus of this analysis, namely the anti-abortion group Precious Life and the pro-choice group Alliance for Choice. Campaigning material posted on both organisation's websites between late May and September 2018, in the aftermath of the repeal referendum, was collected. This has been analysed inductively, supported by NVivo qualitative analysis software. The analysis is informed by debates in moral and political sociology on social movements and abortion politics, drawing in particular on Ferree et al.'s approach to frame analysis of public abortion speech (2002).

The major frames apparent in material posted to each organisation's websites during this period are outlined below. The master frames deployed by both groups during this period are those of Democracy and Equal Citizenship. These are put to use in conflicting ways by each group, as they struggle to build bridges which resonate beyond the immediate political context, to amplify the significance of their political agenda and motivate support. Political strategies are differently oriented towards either the political or the cultural opportunity structures, as each side seeks to lever widespread support for their agenda, in light of the cultural impact generated by the result of the Repeal the 8th referendum in the Republic.

Democracy: the anti-abortion frame

Both pro-choice and anti-abortion organisations frame their competing perspectives in terms of democracy. Anti-abortion responses to the outcome of the Repeal the 8th referendum emphasised that post-conflict devolved power in Northern Ireland requires that abortion legislation should not be changed by Westminster or Dublin. Precious Life insisted that Stormont debated abortion law in 2016 and decided to leave it unchanged, a position which should be respected despite the absence of a Legislative Assembly in 2018.

The suspension of the Assembly was treated as threatening democratic control over Northern Ireland's abortion laws in the wake of repeal. Deploying slogans which reflected this, such as 'our laws matter because every life matters', Precious Life framed their defence of Northern Ireland's abortion laws as a defence of democratic institutions:

> [B]ecause of the stalemate at Stormont in restoring power sharing in Northern Ireland, pro-abortion MPs in Westminster are trying to ride roughshod over the democratic process here and force abortion on Northern Ireland. But the legislation governing these issues is a devolved matter for the Northern Ireland Assembly only. (Precious Life 2018i)

In the wake of the repeal of the 8th Amendment in the Republic of Ireland, Precious Life emphasised the centrality of the Good Friday Agreement to Northern Ireland's devolved democratic institutions and framed the possibility of Westminster making direct changes to Northern Ireland's abortion laws as a threat to devolution and peace:

> Meddling with the Agreement could undermine and endanger the peace process here. The spirit of the Good Friday agreement was all about respecting devolution, and was founded on the principles of full respect for and equality of all rights, and of freedom from discrimination for all people in Northern Ireland. Our unborn children must never be discriminated against. Their most fundamental right – the right to life – must always be respected and upheld. (Precious Life 2018f)

The Republic's government similarly came under attack for threatening Northern Ireland's democratic institutions:

> Simon Harris [Minister for Health in the Republic of Ireland] has no respect for the fact that laws in Northern Ireland are a matter for public representatives in Northern Ireland. Abortion is illegal in the North. Our laws protect unborn babies and their mothers. This is the reality that Simon Harris and other

pro-abortion politicians need to acknowledge as a matter of
urgency, and stop interfering in our affairs. (Precious Life 2018g)

Such efforts to frame abortion as a democratic issue insisted that
the restricted political institutions structuring opportunities
for political change should be respected given the fragility of
democracy in the region. This ignores key provisions in the
Good Friday Agreement allowing for island-wide governance (Good
Friday Agreement 1998). Anti-abortion framing efforts instead
suggested that political 'interference' would threaten the post-
conflict settlement and undermine peace.

A communitarian rather than an egalitarian account of
democracy underpinned this position. Democracy from this
perspective entails the representation of a united moral community, rather than morally diverse individuals. Characterisations
of Northern Ireland as morally unified are commonly made in
Precious Life's online materials, alongside depictions of liberal views as destructive of that unity. This allows for claims
to represent 'the people' in moral rather than contested political/
nationalist terms. Precious Life claims to represent and
defend a moral community in the face of threat, not only from
Westminster but also now from the Republic, as abortion
seemed likely to become more accessible for Northern Ireland
inhabitants following repeal.

Contrasting Northern Ireland's alleged 'pro-life' collective
morality with "a culture of death in Britain stemming from half
a century of legalised abortion" (Precious Life 2018d), Precious
Life insisted that 'we' in Northern Ireland would defend against a
similar situation developing:

Before the official results were even announced, the pro-
abortionists were baying for the blood of Northern Ireland's
unborn children. But we will not stand idly by in Northern
Ireland and let pro-abortion groups, in collusion with

pro-abortion politicians, try to legalise the killing of our unborn children by attacking our prolife laws. (Precious Life 2018e)

The language of war is deployed here by Precious Life to rally support for the moral community in the face of a threatened return to bloodshed and terror were abortion to be decriminalised. This can be understood as an effort to generate solidarity by provoking a sense of outrage against a shared enemy, the all-island pro-choice movement (Joas 2013: 61).

A call to arms made at a 'Rally for Life' held at Stormont, Belfast, in July 2018, similarly combined militarist and populist tropes to mobilise support:

> This is our land and we will not rest until it is a pro-life light to the world once again. We will rebuild the culture of life in Ireland, we will stand strong, we will walk tall, we will fight on – in the North and the South – a people united together for life – because a child's life is always worth fighting for. (Precious Life 2018i)

A coalition of anti-abortion groups participated in a public march in August 2018 organised by Sinn Féin to commemorate the 50th anniversary of the Civil Rights movement in Northern Ireland. While this was not an anti-abortion event, Precious Life participated, a 'piggybacking' strategy adopted to increase public attention (Rohlinger 2006: 540). Their speeches drew parallels between the history of violent political conflict and the struggle against abortion: "There has been enough bloodshed in Northern Ireland since 1968, without now legalising the killing of our unborn children" (Precious Life 2018h). Following the May referendum result, the threat to democracy was treated as heightened, as attitudes liberalised and the Republic's abortion laws changed. The response evident above called for a hardening of moral boundaries between Northern Ireland, the Republic and Britain (see also Browne and Nash, this volume).

Democracy: the pro-choice frame

Pro-choice groups similarly relied on the Democracy frame in public statements during 2018, although emphasizing individual freedom rather than claims about the moral character of the culture. Alliance for Choice identified barriers to abortion access as a threat to a morally diverse democratic society. Democratic polities are expected to treat women as moral agents whose individual decisions concerning pregnancy should be respected: "It is the time to confront the abortion issue in Ireland and Northern Ireland, and to build toward a more progressive future where women are heard, respected, valued and trusted" (Alliance for Choice 2018a).

Framing abortion access as an aspect of democratic respect for individual moral agency is captured in Alliance For Choice's campaign slogan 'Trust Women', and gained fullest expression through the public recounting of personal stories of abortion-seeking women.[3] The moral complexity and personal intensity of abortion decision-making was demonstrated through individual testimonies made available through the Alliance for Choice website. This also allowed the organisation to underline both moral diversity in abortion decision-making and the personal cost of the abortion regime in ways which potential supporters might identify with. As Ferree et al. argue, such stories are present in strongly democratic contexts, characterised by an expectation of moral disagreement rather than unity (Ferree et al. 2002).

Seeking to capitalise on the cultural momentum for liberalisation that the Republic's referendum result had generated, Alliance for Choice developed slogans such as 'The North is Next'. This effort to build political pressure was explicitly framed in terms of Democracy: "[U]ltimately we need . . . Westminster to do it's [sic] job and support the people, not the politicians of Northern Ireland in enacting access to abortion healthcare NOW" (Alliance for Choice 2018f). This call on Westminster to "do it's [sic] job" demands majority representation, given the failures of locally elected politicians and parties.

The threat to democracy included barriers to representation created by party politics: "We believe that abortion and reproductive rights and the corresponding discussions should be led by those affected, not by politicians" (Alliance for Choice 2018b). Emphasising the disjuncture between attitudinal surveys showing support for liberalisation and the perspectives of political parties Alliance for Choice argued: "We have been let down by our representatives who either refuse to take seat in Parliament or refuse to acknowledge the public will in Northern Ireland for change" (Alliance for Choice 2018c). This insistence on the responsibility of democratically elected politicians to actively represent majority views is a standard political strategy of liberal and left social movement organisations as they seek to demoralise and secularise contentious issues in order to win support (Rohlinger 2006: 542). From this perspective it is the failure to represent majority views rather than supposed moral cultures that threatens democracy.

Pro-choice articulations of the Democracy frame sought to resonate with newly established norms governing abortion access in the Republic following repeal. This frame was deployed in pro-choice public speech in ways that sought recognition for individual moral authority, in sharp contrast with anti-abortion efforts to signify democracy as a mechanism for representing a putative 'pro-life' moral culture.

Equal citizenship: the anti-abortion frame

The second major frame evident in post-May 2018 abortion politics in Northern Ireland is that of Equal Citizenship. This frame has particular value in political conflicts over the role of states in recognising and interpreting competing rights and has wide resonance beyond Northern Ireland (Ginsburg and Rapp 1995).

Anti-abortion organisations commonly frame abortion access as a threat to women's equal status, seeking resonance with pro-woman norms (Condit 1990). Arguing that "[Repeal the 8th] has highlighted the situation north of the border where action is urgently needed to protect the human rights of women", Precious Life characterised women and girls as victims of industrial abortion, suffering psychological as well as physical harm as a result (2018a). The rights of disabled future citizens and minority racialised populations were also framed as threatened by legal abortion. Precious Life shared stories from the US of "abortion racism", where non-white women are apparently targeted for abortion advertising and so are potential victims of a "silent genocide" (Precious Life 2018b):

> 75% of the abortion centres – lucrative killing machines – are in minority areas. Dr Alveda King, niece of Martin Luther King Jr., who had two abortions she severely regrets, exposed that around ¼ of the black population in America are missing because of the abortion industry. (Ibid.)

The availability of abortion as a matter of choice when foetal abnormalities are diagnosed was similarly framed as a eugenic effort to undermine equal citizenship for future disabled populations: "This choice I think it is very much directed towards eliminating Down Syndrome, it's almost like they want to make part of the human race extinct" (Precious Life 2018c). The eugenic agendas of early birth control movements in Britain and the US are also underlined in statements such as this, as is the disproportionate use of abortion services by ethnic minority women in Britain. This is explained not as a reflection of the structural position of such women with respect to choices about family formation and size, but instead as an indication of the racist and eugenic agenda of abortion providers.

Central to anti-abortion deployment of the Equal Citizenship frame, captured in the slogan 'Civil Rights begin in the Womb', is that 'the unborn' should be accorded rights equal to those of women: "[W]e seek to be a voice for the voiceless, and as we argue for more modern and humane abortion law that upholds not only the dignity and rights of women but the dignity and rights of the unborn child" (Precious Life 2018d). This assumption that citizenship can be held prior to birth reflects an effort to resonate with the individualism of late modern societies (Beck and Beck-Gernsheim 2002). At the same time, no account is offered of how the duties of citizenship might be discharged when the 'citizen' is not yet born (Holc 2004).

Equal citizenship: the pro-choice frame

Pro-choice efforts to frame abortion access as an issue of women's citizenship similarly relied on individualist norms, emphasising the differential rights accorded to women in Northern Ireland, in contrast to both Britain and Ireland. Personal storytelling, an important feature of complex political deliberation (Polletta and Lee 2006), was used to demonstrate the impact of unequal rights on girls and women in a variety of situations, in ways designed to underline the relevance of this frame to the everyday lives of potential supporters.

Within this frame, the introduction of funding and a central booking system for women in Northern Ireland to access NHS abortions in Britain in the weeks following May 2018 was welcomed, but did not address the full extent of underlying inequalities:

> Although Alliance for Choice welcome this scheme, it sadly leaves behind those in precarious employment, those without childcare, those in abusive and controlling relationships, those who are unable to travel easily due to disability and many more. (Alliance for Choice 2018e)

The organisation responded in a similar way to the commitment from Ireland's Minister for Health to ensure access to abortion services to those in Northern Ireland following repeal:

[T]his is still not a solution to the lack of abortion access for us in the counties we call home. Women and pregnant people who travel for abortion care face practical and financial barriers which may be lessened by travelling to Dublin rather than Liverpool. However, they still exist and the details for accessing healthcare outside of our usual jurisdiction will require a great deal of co-operation and diplomacy from our representatives in Stormont. (Alliance for Choice 2018b)

The resonance and flexibility of this frame not only allowed it to be deployed in different ways on both sides of the conflict, but also, crucially, generated international pressure on the UK government to introduce change. Local pro-choice organisations were able to mobilise international interest and support by emphasising the implications of Northern Ireland-specific abortion legislation for equal citizenship (*The Guardian* 2018). This extended normative opportunity attracted the attention of international citizenship and human rights bodies, who contributed to the amplification of pro-choice frames beyond the confines of Stormont and Westminster. Following the judgement of the Committee on the Elimination of Discrimination against Women (CEDAW) and the UK Supreme Court's statement on Northern Ireland abortion law, Alliance for Choice insisted: "We urge the government to act now. Human rights do not need an electoral mandate, the rights of abortion seekers deserve immediate action" (Alliance for Choice 2018d).

Conclusion: Northern Ireland after the 8th

Tensions between the institutional and normative aspects of democracy and citizenship have become central in conflicts over abortion access in Northern Ireland following the 8th Amendment referendum result. Anti-abortion politicians sought to reinforce existing constitutional arrangements following May 2018, despite the suspension of the regional Assembly. By contrast, pro-choice politics sought to capitalise on the significant normative opportunity created by the referendum result, and particularly its resonance with wider politics of gender equality and women's rights (Messerschmidt, Martin and Messner 2018).

The shared frames employed by these groups, on opposite sides of the abortion issue, speak to Northern Ireland's post-conflict political culture and institutional position. Pro-choice and anti-abortion groups both advocate for abortion law through the frame of democracy. For the pro-choice lobby, this supports the demand that laws should represent the majority of the electorate, understood as morally diverse, as reflected in opinion polling data. At the same time, democracy frames anti-abortion assertions of moral unity and distinctiveness, underpinning calls to respect post-conflict institutional arrangements. Arguments framed in terms of citizenship similarly connect conflict over abortion access to patterns of inequality, although again in quite different ways. The political and social conflict over abortion access in Northern Ireland raises questions of devolved power, democratic legitimacy, citizens' rights and the representation of morally and socially diverse populations. Indeed, abortion became an important site of unity and alliance for otherwise divided conservatives from across the sectarian divide in the post-conflict era, allowing for a consolidation of interests amongst those seeking to define the parameters of gender and sexual citizenship in the region's newly established political institutions (Smyth 2006).

The events of May 2018 in the Republic removed an important supporting structure for anti-abortion politics in Northern Ireland, as individual women south of the border have been newly recognised as the source of moral authority in pregnancy, at least in the first 12 weeks, Northern Irish women will be able to access abortion in the Republic, although they will have to pay for the service (Government of Ireland 2018). The end of the 8th Amendment regime and the introduction of abortion in the

Republic of Ireland has in turn added momentum to pro-choice activities in Northern Ireland despite the suspended Assembly and barriers to change at Westminster. Indeed, a Bill to decriminalise abortion across the UK, introduced in October 2018, attracted majority cross-party support at its first reading (BBC 2018c). Although it ultimately failed (Simpson 2018), the willingness to support change, evident amongst Westminster MPs, signals a significant shift in political attitudes towards abortion access in Northern Ireland following repeal, perhaps reversing the tendency to treat the region as an exceptional 'place apart'. However, while cultural politics have become a major route for generating normative pressure for change, the very limited institutional opportunities for political decision-making, combined with the turmoil over Brexit, have not yet delivered on the hopes of those who are pro-choice for 'The North is Next' raised by repeal of the 8th Amendment.

Notes

1 Since terminology is itself a focus on conflict in abortion politics, I adopt the widely accepted liberal rather than conservative nouns throughout this chapter. For a critical discussion of this terminology, see Smyth (2002).

2 Committee on the Elimination of Discrimination against Women. 2018. *Report of the inquiry concerning the United Kingdom of Great Britain and Northern Ireland under article 8 of the Optional Protocol to the Convention on the Elimination of All Forms of Discrimination against Women*, United Nations; The Supreme Court of the United Kingdom. 2018. *In the matter of an application by the Northern Ireland Human Rights Commission for Judicial Review (Northern Ireland)*. Reference by the Court of Appeal in Northern Ireland pursuant to Paragraph 33 of Schedule 10 to the Northern Ireland Act 1998 (Abortion) (Northern Ireland), [2018] UKSC 27.

3 See Alliance for Choice: www.alliance4choice.com/partner-projects. Alliance for Choice originated the 'Trust Women' slogan, but stopped using it by 2018 because the group decided the slogan was trans exclusive and the political party Sinn Féin began using the slogan in their messaging (Alliance for Choice, personal communication).

FIFTEEN | Reflections after the Irish referendum: abortion, the Catholic Church and pro-choice mobilisation in Poland

Dorota Szelewa

Introduction

The referendum to repeal the 8th Amendment that took place on 25 May 2018 was widely interpreted as a turning point in Irish societal history dominated by the Catholic Church. Led by the church hierarchy and with the support from the Vatican, Irish citizens had decided to insert the Amendment into the Constitution in 1983, which resulted in one of the strictest abortion regimes in Europe. Thirty-five years later, a considerable majority of citizens decided to reject the existing law. At the same time in Poland, where a right-wing populist party has been in office since 2015, a conservative agenda dominates the discourse on gender roles and women's reproductive rights, while the Catholic Church has been actively engaged in consecutive attempts to introduce a complete ban on abortion, although the existing legislation is already very strict.

The Irish Referendum raised a great interest among the Polish public and its results provoked widespread comment, with various reactions from disappointment from the Catholic media (Bortkiewicz 2018; Falkowski 2018; Gądecki 2018) to excitement and euphoria in the case of pro-choice organisations (Borowicz 2018; Diduszko-Zyglewska 2018; Gostkiewicz 2018; Paciorek 2018). The feeling of empowerment and encouragement was evident among those who drew links between the mobilisation of Polish women and the effective strategies of the feminist movements in Ireland. One feminist activist suggested: "Ireland has showed us how to do it. The rest belongs to us" (Diduszko-Zyglewska 2018).

The goal of this chapter is to examine the circumstances for the possible shift in abortion law in Poland, in the context of the Irish Referendum. As the two countries seem to share many important characteristics, such as national identities coupled with Catholicism and relatively recent modernisation, the Irish 'revolution' might serve as a blueprint for the pro-choice movement to effectively mobilise for change to take place in Poland as well. Such transfer of ideas, to be successful, would need to be supported by a specific constellation of factors, such as a weakened position of the Catholic Church, a shift in the political composition of the government (currently composed of right-wing populist party) and a strong, institutionalised pro-choice movement with a long-term strategy. In the chapter, I argue that the factors influencing the change of law in Ireland have been present in Poland only to a small extent. To develop the argument, I will focus on the recent wave of pro-choice mobilisation in Poland under the umbrella of 'Black Protests' when thousands of women went on strike in the protest against introducing a complete abortion ban in 2016. I begin by analysing the reactions of the pro-choice movement in Poland to the success of the pro-choice mobilisation in Ireland, which served as an encouragement for the Polish movement on the one hand and a sign of caution for the right-wing politicians on the other.

'Ireland today, Poland tomorrow'? Reaction to results of Irish referendum

Ideas, discourses and frames tend to travel, mutate and diffuse when policy change adapted in one country fits to the political and societal context of another. This might take place when there is a set of shared values and ideas in a transnational space that leads to policy convergence (Paternotte and Kollman 2013) or a policy transfer with the use of "universal frames" which, for the case of abortion policies, usually relate to women's rights, medical and natural family framings of abortion (Boyle, Kim and Longhofer 2015). Transmission of scripts and plans of action might take place when the local conditions are similar, helping epistemic communities across the countries such as NGOs supporting women's rights seek international legitimacy (Ibid.). It is too early to assess the extent to which the results of the Irish referendum could facilitate liberalisation of Polish abortion law. However, when viewing the initial reaction in the Polish media, it is clear that both pro- and anti-choice circles recognise the similarity of local conditions as well as the possibility of transferring similar scripts to Poland.

The church, anti-choice lay organisations and media were clearly disappointed and found it difficult to interpret the reasons behind the Irish referendum results. The first reaction shared by the most prominent Catholic media in Poland was that the Irish referendum should serve as "a warning" (Gądecki 2018), "a lesson" for Polish Catholics (Falkowski 2018), or "a trigger for destruction of all the other values" (Bortkiewicz 2018). Catholic media also interpreted the Irish government's decision to hold the referendum as a plan to change the country's international "too Catholic" image (Ibid.). Ironically, the anti-choice circles recognised the influence of transnational networks and the diffusion of certain ideas. In this context, a leading conservative theologist said: "We live in a global world, in a global village, where all the good and all the bad things get transferred easily. The threat is even bigger in our country, especially that there are political forces and circles that facilitate such trendy ideas" (Ibid.). Ordo Iuris, a think tank behind the abortion ban proposed in 2016, took a similar standpoint on directly pushing for a further abortion ban when faced with the results of the Irish referendum. The think tank issued a statement that warned against the international community pressuring Poland to introduce "a supposedly universal right to abortion" (Kielmans-Ratyńska 2018). The legal experts from Ordo Iuris claimed that, since Poland remains one of the last countries in Europe that "provides the protection of life", we can expect "similar actions to be undertaken in Poland with the aim to change Polish legislation, as well as (or first of all) Polish public opinion" (Ibid.). Finally, for many, the results of the Irish referendum should additionally mobilise efforts to adopt a complete abortion ban (or at least limit the circumstances for legal abortion). One of the top church officials in Poland suggested that the result of the Irish Referendum "should encourage Poles to a more intensive protection of life, so that this situation does not repeat itself [in Poland]" (Gądecki 2018). The latter call relates to the abortion ban bill being currently 'frozen' in parliament (see below).

When it comes to pro-choice movement's reactions, the slogan 'Ireland today, Poland tomorrow' appeared almost immediately after the referendum results were confirmed (TS 2018). Like those in anti-choice circles, the liberal media in Poland emphasised similarities between these two countries, this time to express the hope that changes in Ireland meant that liberalisation of abortion law in Poland is also possible. From the perspective of the Polish pro-choice movements, three specific issues seemed to be most important for the Irish results: the decline of the Catholic Church in Ireland, solidarity with women that suffered because of the ban and gave their testimonies and the effective mobilisation of pro-choice organisations. First, the decline of the Catholic Church in Ireland was identified the most important condition facilitating the positive outcome of the referendum (Borowicz 2018; Gostkiewicz 2018; Szostkiewicz 2018). As noted by the editor of the biggest Polish news web portal, the strategies now employed by the church in Poland resemble the mistakes of the Irish church

(Gostkiewicz 2018). The columnist pointed to the revelations of child sexual abuse and paternity scandals among Irish clergy, as evidenced by the series of official reports (Ferns Report, Murphy Report, Ryan Report), and quoted in the text concrete examples of abuse, including physical and emotional violence against children (Ibid.). The same column refers to the Cloyne Report that described the ways in which the Dublin Archdiocese dealt with the abuse by not reporting abuse allegations and protecting the perpetrators (Ibid.). It also identified the Irish church's opposition to social and cultural changes as the reason for the institution losing church attendees or for the sharp decline in the number of church personnel (Szostkiewicz 2018). At the same time, the columnist cited the results of a survey (from 2017) on Polish attitudes towards legalising abortion: while 42% of respondents supported liberalising the existing abortion law, only 8% declared backing a complete abortion ban (Chrzczonowicz 2017). The columnist argued that by declaring an official support for a complete abortion ban, the Polish church was making the same mistakes: maintaining a conservative standpoint and not acknowledging a transformation of values in society (Szostkiewicz 2018).

Second, the commentators pointed to the testimonies of women who suffered because of the restrictive law, as well as the story of Savita Halappanavar and her death, which was repeatedly mentioned as an important example of a concrete victim of the previous law and a powerful reference for the pro-choice movement (Paciorek 2018). Third, the fact that Irish society opened the way for legalising abortion was also interpreted as a sign of the country fully accepting international human rights standards ("Irish women recognised as human beings" read the title of one of the texts) (Diduszko-Zyglewska 2018). Although less attention was paid to the concrete strategies of women's rights activists, some commentators viewed the success of the Yes campaign as the result of a broad coalition of the pro-choice movement, politicians from the major political parties and trade unions (Chrzczonowicz 2018). Irish society was praised for its ability to mobilise, especially the rush to go to Ireland to vote by those who live outside (#HomeToVote)(Diduszko-Zyglewska 2018). As a commentator in the left-wing journal *Political Critique* argued: "The campaign . . . is a lesson showing us how to turn society's anger into action, how to beat superstitions with facts, how to derive sparks of solidarity and enthusiasm from society" (Borowicz 2018).

In sum, it seems that there are solid reasons for applying similar types of strategies and ideational frames to the Polish case in order to push for liberalisation of abortion policy. Other political circumstances and factors would be necessary for Poland to follow the Irish path, and these are briefly analysed below. First, I briefly present some background information and basic facts in relation to the Polish abortion law.

Background and the current state of legislation

Unlike Ireland, Poland experienced a period when abortion on socio-economic grounds was permitted. Liberalisation of the law took place in 1956, when abortion on the grounds of "exceptionally difficult life conditions" became legal.[1] The Catholic Church strongly criticised such a policy. When the Communist regime collapsed, new political elites rejected the principle of gender equality, which they perceived as imposed by the totalitarian regime. An abortion ban was introduced in 1993, a couple of years after the collapse of state-socialism and came as a result of a so-called 'abortion compromise'. Under this law, still in force, legal abortion is possible in three specific situations: if the pregnancy constitutes a threat to the life or health of the mother, in case of severe and irreversible damage to the foetus, or if pregnancy is a result of a criminal act (rape). Thus, although the existing abortion law allows for the termination of a pregnancy in extraordinary circumstances, together with Malta and Ireland (before 2019), Poland belongs to the group of countries with the strictest of all European countries, as current regulations do not allow for abortion on the grounds of the difficult social or economic situation of a woman or abortion on demand.

Recent developments: new bills in parliament, basic facts and timeline

Although for many years the so-called 'abortion compromise' seemed to be resistant to change, this situation has evolved recently when the right-wing populist party, Law and Justice, won the presidential and parliamentary elections in 2015. Not even 6 months after the new right-wing populist government was formed in November 2015, an initiative to introduce a complete ban on abortion began. A bill, prepared and designed by the right-wing legal think-tank Ordo Iuris, was presented in March 2016 by the Committee of the Civic Initiative 'Stop Abortion', with the goal of collecting at least 100,000 signatures to be submitted to the Polish parliament as an official civic legal initiative.[2] The bill sought to remove all circumstances for legal abortion (Ordo Iuris 2018).

In response to this initiative, the pro-choice movement organised a series of protests in April 2016. After the first wave of protests was over, and the discussion seemed to move out of the public debate, the bill was officially submitted to the parliament on 5 July 2016, together with over 450,000 signatures collected by a group of anti-choice NGOs, often with the assistance of Catholic priests. Soon, a counter-initiative, the Committee for Legislative Action to 'Save the Women' was formed. The initiative proposed a draft law liberalising the existing abortion law, with the option of abortion on demand until the end of the 12th week of pregnancy, more direct access to contraception and a stronger emphasis on sexual education. The pro-choice initiative collected 215,000 signatures. Both bills were submitted to parliament and put to a vote in the fall 2016. When it came to the voting over the two bills at the end of September 2016, the bill 'Save the Women' was rejected and therefore excluded from any further proceedings, while at the same time the Sejm decided to continue proceedings with the complete abortion ban bill.

This led to the re-emergence of a mass protest against the abortion ban. The organisers, now gathered under the umbrella of the 'All Poland Women's Strike', called for a universal women's strike on Monday 3 October, under the slogans 'Black Monday' and 'Black Protest'. Three days later, the Law and Justice party decided to reject the drastic anti-abortion law: first by voting against it in Parliamentary Committee and then during the plenary session. A majority of the party's MPs voted to withdraw the bill from being further proceeded by the parliament, including Prime Minister Beata Szydło and Jarosław Kaczyński, a leader of the Law and Justice party.

The second attempt to initiate a change in the legislation was in 2017. A new bill was submitted to the Polish parliament, this time introducing a ban on abortion in the case of serious malformation of the foetus, supported by 830,000 signatures. The parliament decided to send the bill for further proceedings. Once again, the counter-bill liberalising the abortion law ('Save the Women') was also submitted, but the parliament rejected it, preventing any further proceedings from taking place. That event again mobilised Polish women to rally in the streets. Since that time, any official steps to adopt the bill banning abortion have been frozen.

What kind of political circumstances would support liberalisation of the abortion law in Poland? How is the abortion policy shaped by the voices of the various actors involved? Below, I will address these questions, taking into account the role of the Catholic Church and its circles, the role of party politics and the power of pro-choice mobilisation.

The church and its lay networks

The influence of the Catholic Church on the discourse surrounding abortion has often been analysed as an example of a political actor's impact on public policies (Fink 2009; Inglis 1998; Knill, Preidel and Nebel 2014). Popular interpretations of the Catholic Church's influential position identify it as the source of conservative worldviews, including gender roles, the definition and the role of marriage and the "sacredness" of the family (Mishtal 2015). In many countries, the Catholic Church has participated in strengthening nationalist discourses, serving as "chief signifier of nationalist identity" (Kozlowska, Béland and Lecours 2016); in Poland, it provides the blueprint for the ideals of the Polish patriot, as Pole equates to Catholic (Szelewa 2016). Thus, while the strong position and moral authority of the Catholic Church could block policy changes like the liberalisation of the abortion law, the opposite would take place if the position of the church were seriously undermined (Fink 2009). Catholic lay anti-choice organisations also play a major role here (Schreiber 2002). The role of the Catholic Church is a notable difference between Irish and Polish contexts because, as Scriven (this volume) shows, the Irish Catholic Church was neither as unified nor as fully mobilised against repeal as its historical position on the topic would indicate.

In Poland, by contrast, the Catholic Church has been very active and almost aggressive in pushing its anti-choice agenda using various channels of influence. Soon after the anti-abortion initiative was announced in March 2016, the Polish Episcopate issued an official statement in support, arguing that "it is not possible to keep the current compromise when it comes to the issue of protecting the unborn" (KEP 2018). When the initiative re-emerged later on, the church actively supported it through sermons, encouraging the mass attendees to add their signatures directly after the service, while also organising exhibitions showing dead and disfigured bodies of foetuses covered with blood. In addition to officially communicating the church's support for the bill, the church engaged its personnel and all local resources in order to achieve its goal, simultaneously strongly opposing liberalisation.

Partisan politics and the government's reaction

Partisan politics also have an impact on abortion policies, although this is limited, as abortion is considered a "moral policy issue" that often falls outside of the usual structure of political conflicts (Engeli 2009). The presence of Christian democratic parties has been shown to delay the adoption of laws permitting abortion, while in the countries with religious parties, the Catholic Church might act as an important veto player (Fink 2009). Irish political parties, who are not polarised on the basis of religion, sought to avoid overtly politicising abortion as a partisan issue. By contrast, the Law and Justice government's standpoint was initially quite welcoming towards the anti-abortion initiative, which met with declarations of support from Beata Szydło, then-Prime Minister (GW 2016), and the party leader, Jarosław Kaczyński (TVP INFO 2016).

At the first wave of protests in April 2016, however, it became clear that the government had not expected such an intense societal reaction. Soon, party leaders withdrew their strong statements of support. Instead, Kaczyński began to undermine one of the circumstances of legal abortion: the case of malformation of the foetus, labelling it "eugenics" (wPolityce 2016) and seeking more societal support. In addition, the scale of the second wave of protest in October 2016 was unanticipated and Law and Justice soon found the initiatives banning abortion inconvenient. After rejecting the bill, the party was criticised by anti-choice circles and the church. In order to shift attention from this criticism, the Prime Minister announced a governmental support program for families and mothers who decide to bear children "from so-called difficult pregnancies" (when the foetus is malformed) (TVN24 2016).

The law introducing the program, called 'Pro-Life', was adopted very quickly and included a special allowance for women who decided to give birth to children diagnosed as being a 'malformed foetus' during pregnancy, i.e. in a situation which would have allowed them to have a legal abortion. This one-off 'non-abortion' allowance amounts to 4000 PLN (approximately €921).

In summary, the political situation in Poland clearly did not facilitate liberalisation of the law because high ranking Law and Justice politicians supported the complete ban. Moreover, decisions were made in line with the signals coming from the church hierarchy. For example, when church officials started to express a somewhat softened standpoint on a complete abortion ban, one Law and Justice MP interpreted the Episcopate's softening position on abortion as "a mandate for rejecting the proposal" (Skarżyński 2016). At the same time, the party sought to navigate between the pressure of the church and the power of mass protest.

Pro-choice mobilisation

The impact of pro-choice mobilisation, usually centred around feminist (women's) organisations, has the potential to counterbalance and eventually dominate the discourse on reproductive rights, this time from the perspective of women's rights. Feminist influence in both Ireland and Poland has met with mixed responses and developed in difficult conditions within societies dominated by Catholic morality (see Connolly, this volume). The ideal female roles were inspired by the figure of the Virgin Mary (Titkow 2007). The second wave of feminism had a moderate and selective impact on various groups of women in both countries (Kiely and Leane 2014; Szelewa 2014). In general, one could expect stronger and more resourceful women's organisations to play a major role in pushing liberal abortion law on the agenda, while weak or dispersed movements do not facilitate a positive change (Staggenborg 1991). Just as the restriction of access to abortion in Poland represented one of the most radical expressions of the post-communist remasculinisation, it also 'gave birth' to the feminist movement in post-1989 Poland, despite the absence of feminist initiatives in many other East European countries (Korolczuk and Saxonberg 2015). The Polish pro-choice movement has had success in mobilising enormous street demonstrations, and yet it has not been able to access the institutional channels of influence that the Irish pro-choice movement leveraged for change. Furthermore, the Irish movement successfully advanced progressive change on the country's abortion laws, while the Polish movement has been forced into a defensive stance against repeated efforts to narrow an already extremely restrictive law.

Mass feminist mobilisation took place in Poland recently as a reaction to the new initiatives to introduce a complete abortion ban in 2016. The first protest took place on 3rd April in front of the Polish parliament's building in Warsaw, and was repeated one week later, this time under the umbrella of a coalition called 'Regaining Choice'. Both events took place on Sundays and included other forms of protests, such as attending Sunday mass but leaving in great numbers at the moment when priests read the official letter from the Episcopate about the "protection of life" (KEP 2016). Social media became crucial for centralisation of the efforts: first via an all-Poland Facebook page *Dziewuchy Dziewuchom* ('Gals for Gals') and through an effort to populate Beata Szydło's Facebook page with thousands of women ironically informing the Prime Minister about the details of their menstruation cycle with the hashtag #*TrudnyOkres* (#ToughPeriod) (Newsweek 2016). As such, they demonstrated their resistance to the government intervening in personal choices about women's sexual and reproductive health.

The second wave of protest was even more intense. A smaller demonstration first took place in front of the parliament building, as protest spread through social media marked by the hashtag *#czarnyprotest* (#blackprotest), with thousands of women wearing black clothes and posting their photos on Facebook and Instagram. Because this form of protest became so popular, the organis- ers, now gathered under the umbrella of 'All Poland Women's Strike', decided to use it and called for a universal women's strike on Monday 3 October under the label 'Black Monday' (and 'Black Protest'). Altogether, 143 rallies and demonstration were registered on that date in over 100 cities and towns in Poland, with the esti- mated number of participants ranging from 100,000 to almost one million, including solidarity demonstrations and marches organised in many cities around the world (Korolczuk 2016: 91, quoting CBOS 2016). It is important to stress that the Black Protests in 2016 allowed for the development of certain organisational capacities, networks and resources that were then mobilised later on. However, such women's organisations and the potentially empowering legacy of Black Protests has dissipated, at least to some extent, while some major activities have been discontinued.

Conclusions

Although the results of Irish referendum received attention world- wide, women's organisations in countries like Poland, where access to abortion is very limited (or non-existing), welcomed the news from Ireland enthusiastically. There are important differ- ences, however, in the two countries: the political situation, with right-wing populist parties forming the government in Poland; and it is much less likely that change in legislation on abortion in Poland would happen after a national referendum. This has an impact on the selection of influencing activities. Hence, while canvassing was an important strategy in the Irish case with refer- endum (see McDonald et al., this volume), this strategy would be less effective in Poland, where the parliament makes the decision about changing the law on this matter.

Some important conclusions can be drawn for the Polish pro-choice movement. Just as the Irish pro-choice mobilisation was multitiered, flexible and sought to represent the multiple faces of the women's movement in Ireland, the mobilisation of the movement in Poland was ad hoc, becoming divided shortly after the main wave of protests in 2016. While the Irish movement used several different channels of influence, the most prevalent activity among Polish women's pro-choice organisations was direct activism, including one-day street protests, rallies, demonstrations and sharing on social media, while much weaker emphasis was put on continuing the work in between the protests and on using various other influencing activities. While existing analyses focus on answering the question how the Black Protest was possible in the first place (Korolczuk 2016), a bigger question arises about the long-term meaning of this mobilisation. Since there were some expectations that the success of the Black Protest might translate into some political force, none of this happened. Although the protests were officially organised by the feminist organisations, this did not increase an overall support for feminism as such; only 5% of Polish women would identify themselves as feminists (Pacewicz 2018).

And yet, it is clear that women would take to the streets again if the parliament decided to proceed with the bill banning abortion in the case of foetal malformation. This is perhaps the reason why Law and Justice MPs are preventing the bill from entering the official legislative pathway, although they are being pressured by church officials and the initiators of the Bill. The Black Protest was the biggest instance of protest organised in Poland since 1989, and for many women it was the first time in their life to participate in a rally. The issue of the right to abortion has returned to the centre of public debate and it seems that now, after 25 years, the 'abortion compromise' might soon be challenged. It is perhaps a good moment for the movement in Poland to restructure, professionalise, use various sorts of influencing activities, strengthen their visibility, use next year's (2019) election campaign to provoke debates on the access to safe abortion and to slowly build further capacities and resources to repeat the Irish success story.

Notes

1 Act of 27 April 1956 on the conditions of legalizing the termination of pregnancy, Journal of Laws 1956, no 12, item 61.
2 Such legislative procedure is possible in Poland and if the initiators collect at least 100,000 signatures, the bill must proceed in parliament and be put to the vote at least once.

Bibliography

Abrams, D. and Travaglino, G.A. 2018. Immigration, political trust, and Brexit: testing an aversion amplification hypothesis. *British Journal of Social Psychology*, 57(2):310–326.

Adamus, E.P. 2018. *A sad day*. 26 May 2018. https://edmundadamus. wordpress.com/2018/05/26/a-sad-day-2 [Accessed: 12 October 2018].

Adey, P. 2004. Surveillance at the airport: surveilling mobility/mobilizing surveillance. *Environment & Planning A*, 36(8):1365–1380.

Ahmed, S. 2004. *The Cultural Politics of Emotion*. Edinburgh: Edinburgh University Press.

Aiken, A., Gomperts, R. and Trussell, J. 2017. Experiences and characteristics of women seeking and completing at-home medical termination of pregnancy through online telemedicine in Ireland and Northern Ireland: a population-based analysis. *BJOG: An International Journal of Obstetrics & Gynaecology*, 124(8):1208–1215.

Aiken, A.R. 2017. *Opening statement to the Joint Oireachtas Committee on the Eighth Amendment to the Constitution*. Paper presented at Presentation to the Joint Oireachtas Committee on the 8th Amendment, Dublin, 11 October 2017. https://data.oireachtas.ie/ie/oireachtas/committee/dail/32/ joint_committee_on_the_eighth_amendment_of_the_constitution/ submissions/2017/2017-10-11_opening-statement-professor-abigail-aiken-university-of-texas_en.pdf.

Alive. 2018. *We may do any evil to achieve what we want*. (July/August 2018).

Alliance for Choice. 2018a. *About x-ile project: our mission*. www.x-ileproject.com/about.

Alliance for Choice. 2018b. *Access to abortion care for Northern Irish confirmed*. 8 August 2018. www.alliance4choice.com/repeal-58/59/2018/8/ access-to-abortion-care-for-northern-irish-confirmed.

Alliance for Choice. 2018c. *Alliance for Choice on Secretary of State Northern Ireland's response to parliamentary question on abortion from Stella Creasy MP*. 9 May 2018. www.alliance4choice.com/news/2018/5/ alliance-for-choice-on-secretary-of-state-northern-irelands-response-to-parliamentary-question-on-abortion-from-stella-creasy-mp.

Alliance for Choice. 2018d. *CEDAW list of Issues for GB and Northern Ireland 2018*. 2 August 2018. www.alliance4choice.com/repeal-58/59/2018/8/cedaw-list-of-issues-for-gb-and-ni-2018.

Alliance for Choice. 2018e. *A central booking system for Northern Irish abortion seekers*. 6 March 2018. www.alliance4choice.com/news/2018/3/a-central-booking-system-for-northern-irish-abortion-seekers.

Alliance for Choice. 2018f. *YES for Ireland*. 26 May 2018. www.alliance4choice.com/news/2018/5/yes-for-ireland.

Altheide, D. and Schneider, C. 2013. *Qualitative Media Analysis*. 2nd ed. London: Sage.

Ammerman, N.T. 2010. The Challenges of pluralism: locating religion in a world of diversity. *Social Compass*, 57(2):154–167.

Amnesty International. 2015. Two-thirds majority in Ireland want abortion decriminalized. www.amnesty.org/en/latest/news/2015/07/two-thirds-majority-in-ireland-want-abortion-decriminalized.

Anderson, B. 1983. *Imagined Communities: Reflections on the Origin and Spread of Nationalism*. London: Verso.

Association of Catholic Priests. 2018. *ACP statement about the upcoming referendum on the 8th Amendment*. 4 May 2018. www.associationofcatholicpriests.ie/2018/05/acp-statement-on-the-upcoming-referendum-on-the-eight-amendment [Accessed: 28 November 2018].

Augé, M. 1992. *Non-Places: An Introduction to Anthropology of Supermodernity*. New York: Verso.

Baird, B. and Millar, E. 2018. More than stigma: interrogating counter narratives of abortion. *Sexualities*. Ahead of print. DOI: 10.1177/1363460718782966.

Barr, C. and Ó Corráin, D. 2017. Catholic Ireland 1740–2016. In Biagini, E. and Daly, M. (eds.). *The Cambridge Social History of Modern Ireland*. Cambridge: Cambridge University Press.

Barry, U. 1988. Abortion in the Republic of Ireland. *Feminist Review*, 29:57–63.

Bax, M. 1970. Patronage Irish style: Irish politicians as brokers. *Sociologische Gids*, 17(3):179–191.

BBC. 2017. Northern Ireland women to get free abortions in England. *BBC News*, 29 June 2017. www.bbc.co.uk/news/uk-politics-40438390.

BBC. 2018a. Rise in NI women going to England for abortions. *BBC News*, 7 June 2018. www.bbc.co.uk/news/uk-northern-ireland-44382514.

BBC. 2018b. Abortion pills prosecution challenge by NI mother adjourned. *BBC News*, 20 September 2018. www.bbc.co.uk/news/uk-northern-ireland-45550006.

BBC. 2018c. Abortion decriminalisation bill tabled in Commons. *BBC News*, 23 October 2018. www.bbc.co.uk/news/uk-politics-45955492.

Beaumont, C. 1997. Women, citizenship and Catholicism in the Irish free state, 1922–1948. *Women's History Review*, 6(4):563–585.

Beck, U. and Beck-Gernsheim, E. 2002. *Individualization: Institutionalized Individualism and its Social and Political Consequences*. London: SAGE.

Benford, R.D. and Snow, D.A. 2000. Framing processes and social movements: an overview and assessment. *Annual Review of Sociology*, 26(1):611–639.

Bilewicz, M., Mikołajczak, G. and Babińska, M. 2017. Speaking about the preborn. How specific terms used in the abortion debate reflect attitudes and (de)mentalization. *Personality and Individual Differences*, 111(C):256–262.

Binchy, W. 1977. Marital privacy and family law: a reply to Mr. O'Reilly. *Studies: An Irish Quarterly Review*, 66(264):330–335.

Binchy, W. 1992. New abortion regime has no effective limits. *The Irish Times*, 6 March 1992.

Binchy, W. 2018. Oireachtas Committee has opened the door to abortion for disability. *Irish Times*, 6 January 2018.

Bishop,C. 2012. Digital divide. *ArtForum*, 51(1):435–441. www.artforum.com/print/201207/digital-divide-contemporary-art-and-new-media-31944.

Bloomer, F. and Fegan, E. 2014. Critiquing recent abortion law and policy in Northern Ireland. *Critical Social Policy*, 34(1):109–120.

Boltanski, L. 2013. *The Foetal Condition: A Sociology of Engendering and Abortion*. Cambridge: Polity Press.

Borowicz, W. 2018. Płakaliśmy, ściskaliśmy się i wiwatowaliśmy [We cried, hugged each other and cheered]. *Political Criticism*. http://krytykapolityczna.pl/swiat/plakalismy-sciskalismy-sie-irlandia-referendum-aborcja.

Bortkiewicz, P. 2018. Referendum w Irlandii podważające wartość życia zostało przeprowadzone skutecznie, rodzi się więc pokusa, żeby niszczyć inne wartości [Referendum in Ireland was conducted effectively, hence the temptation to destroy other values]. *Radio Maryja*. www.radiomaryja.pl/informacje/tylko-u-nas-ks-prof-p-bortkiewicz-referendum-w-irlandii-podwazajace-wartosc-zycia-zostalo-przeprowadzone-skutecznie-rodzi-sie-wiec-pokusa-zeby-niszczyc-inne-wartosci.

Bowden, E. 2018. Northern Ireland abortion laws reform bid launched in Westminster. *Belfast Telegraph*, 11 October 2018. www.belfasttelegraph.co.uk/news/northern-ireland/northern-ireland-abortion-laws-reform-bid-launched-in-westminster-37406597.html.

Boyle, E.H., Kim, M. and Longhofer, W. 2015. Abortion liberalization in world society, 1960–2009 1. *American Journal of Sociology*, 121(3):882–913.

Bracken, L. 2017. The Assisted Reproduction Bill 2017: an analysis of proposals to regulate surrogacy in Ireland. *Northern Ireland Legal Quarterly*, 68(4):577–585.

Brennan, C. 2018. 'We should remove the Eighth Amendment' – Micheál Martin has changed his mind. [Online] *thejournal.ie*. Available at: www.thejournal.ie/micheal-martin-eighth-amendment-3804808-Jan2018/ [Accessed: 1 February 2019].

Briggs, L. 2018. *How All Politics Became Reproductive Politics: From Welfare Reform to Foreclosure to Trump*. Berkley, CA: University of California Press.

Brown, C.G. 2009. *The Death of Christian Britain: Understanding Secularisation, 1800–2000*. 2nd ed. Abingdon: Routledge.

Brown, D.T. 2011. *Ireland: A Social and Cultural History 1922–2002*. London: HarperCollins.

Browne, K. and Nash, C.J. 2014. Resisting LGBT rights where "we have won": Canada and Great Britain. *Journal of Human Rights*, 13(3):322–336.

Browne, K. and Nash, C.J. 2017. Heteroactivism: beyond anti-gay. *ACME*, 16(4):643–652.

Browne, K. and Nash, C.J. 2018. Resisting marriage equalities: the complexities of religious opposition to same sex marriage. In Bartolini, N., Mackian, S. and Pile, S. (eds.). *Spaces of Spirituality*. Abingdon: Routledge.

Browne, K., Nash, C.J. and Gorman-Murray, A. 2018. Geographies of heteroactivism: resisting sexual rights in the reconstitution of Irish nationhood. *Transactions of the Institute of British Geographers*, 43(4):526–539.

Buckley, J. 2018. Pastoral letter on the right to life. *Diocese of Cork and Ross*. http://corkandross.org/wp-content/uploads/2018/04/Pastoral-letter.pdf.

Burack, C. 2014. *Tough Love: Sexuality, Compassion, and the Christian Right*. Albany, NY: State University of New York Press.

Busardò, F.P., Gulino, M., Napoletano, S., Zaami, S. and Frati, P. 2014. The evolution of legislation in the field of medically assisted reproduction and embryo stem cell research in European Union members. *BioMed Research International*, 2014.

Byrne, S. 2018. Declan Ganley doesn't 'trust' politicians on repeal. *HeadStuff*. 2 May 2018. www.headstuff.org/topical/declan-ganley-repeal-the-eighth.

Cabinet Office. 2017. *Conservative and DUP Agreement and UK Government financial support for Northern Ireland: Confidence and Supply Agreement between the Conservative and Unionist Party and the Democratic Unionist Party*. London. www.gov.uk/government/publications/conservative-and-dup-agreement-and-uk-government-financial-support-for-northern-ireland.

Calkin, S. 2019a. Towards a political geography of abortion. *Political Geography*, 69:22–29.

Calkin, S. 2019b. Healthcare, Not Airfare! Art, Abortion and Political Agency in Ireland. *Gender, Place & Culture*, 26(3):338–361.

Calkin, S. and Freeman, C. 2018. Trails and technology: social and cultural geographies of abortion access. *Social & Cultural Geography*: 1–8. Ahead of print: 10.1080/14649365.2018.1509114.

Campbell, E. 2018. My experience of the Together For Yes (TFY) campaign. *Sexual and Reproductive Health Matters*. Blogpost. 10 October 2018. www.srhm.org/news/my-experience-of-the-together-for-yes-tfy-campaign/

Carey, M. 2017. *Mistrust: An Ethnographic Theory*. Chicago, IL: HAU Books.

Carroll, R. 2018. Cash-for-ash fiasco: Northern Ireland's Enron on Craggy Island. *The Guardian*, 28 September 2018. www.theguardian.com/uk-news/2018/sep/28/cash-for-ash-arlene-foster-accountable-but-not-responsible.

Catholic Church. 1994. *Catechism of the Catholic Church*. Dublin: Veritas.

CBOS. 2016. Polacy o prawach kobiet, 'czarnych protestach' i prawie aborcyjnym [Poles on women's rights, 'black protests' and abortion law]. www.cbos.pl/SPISKOM.POL/2016/K_165_16.PDF.

Catholics for Choice. 2018. *About our work*. www.catholicsforchoice.org/about-us/about-our-work [Accessed: 20 December 2018].

Catholics Together for Yes. 2018. "After we vote yes. . ." *Twitter*. Posted 1 May 2018. https://twitter.com/Catholics4yes/status/991410018892374027.

Central Statistics Office. 2017. *Census 2016 summary results – part 1*. www.cso.ie/en/csolatestnews/presspages/2017/census2016summaryresults-part1.

Choose Life 2018. *Pastoral messages*. www.chooselife2018.ie/category/news/pastoral-messages.

Chow, E.N.-L., Fleck, C., Fan, G.-H., Joseph, J. and Lyter, D.M. 2003. Exploring critical feminist pedagogy: infusing dialogue, participation, and experience in teaching and learning. *Teaching Sociology*, 31(3):259–275.

Chretien, C. 2018. Ireland votes to legalize abortion: 'a tragedy of historic proportions'. *LifeSite News*, 26 May 2018. www.lifesitenews.com/news/breaking-ireland-votes-to-legalize-abortion [Accessed: 12 October 2018].

Chrzczonowicz, M. 2017. Już 42 proc. Polaków za liberalizacją ustawy antyaborcyjnej. Nowy sondaż OKO.press [Already 42 per cent of Poles in support of liberalising the abortion law. New opinion poll of Oko.press]. *OKO.press*. https://oko.press/juz-42-proc-polakow-liberalizacja-ustawy-antyaborcyjnej-nowy-sondaz-oko-press.

Chrzczonowicz, M. 2018. Już oficjalnie: Irlandia powiedziała "Tak" prawu do aborcji. Za liberalizacją zagłosowało rekordowe 66 proc. [It's official: Ireland said "Yes" to the right to abortion. A record of 66 per cent in favour of liberalization]. OKO.press. https://oko.press/juz-oficjalnie-irlandia-powiedziala-tak-prawu-do-aborcji-za-liberalizacja-zaglosowalo-rekordowe-66-proc.

Clarke, R. and Jackson, M. 2018. Statement on the proposal to repeal the 8th Amendment to the Irish Constitution from the Archbishop of Armagh and the Archbishop of Dublin. *Church of Ireland*. www.ireland.anglican.org/news/7763/statement-on-the-proposal-to [Accessed: 6 February 2018].

Clifford, M. 2016. Government problems: kicking the can of responsibility down the road. *Irish Examiner*, 13 September 2018. www.irishexaminer.com/viewpoints/columnists/michael-clifford/government-problems-kicking-the-can-of-responsibility-down-the-road-420684.html.

Cloatre, E. and Enright, M. 2017. 'On the Perimeter of the lawful': enduring illegality in the Irish family planning movement, 1972–1985. *Journal of Law and Society*, 44(4):471–500.

Coakley, J. 2006. Society and political culture. In Gallagher, M.G. and Coakley, J. (eds.). *Politics in the Republic of Ireland*. Abingdon: Routledge.

Comaroff, J. and Comaroff, J.L. 2006. *Law and Disorder in the Postcolony*. Chicago, IL: University of Chicago Press.

Comaroff, J.L. 2009. Reflections on the rise of legal theology. *Social Analysis*, 53(1):193–216.

Comaroff, J.L. and Comaroff, J. 2009. Reflections on the anthropology of law, governance and sovereignty in a brave neo world. In Von Benda Beckmann, F. and Von Benda Beckmann, K. (eds.). *Rules of Law and Laws of Ruling: On the Governance of Law*. Farnham: Ashgate.

Commission on Assisted Human Reproduction. 2005. *Report of the Commission on Assisted Human Reproduction*. https://health.gov.ie/wp-content/uploads/2014/03/Report-of-The-Commission-on-Assisted-Human-Reproduction.pdf [Accessed: 19 December 2018].

Committee on the Elimination of Discrimination against Women. 2018. *Report of the inquiry concerning the United Kingdom of Great Britain and Northern Ireland under article 8 of the Optional Protocol to the Convention on the Elimination of All Forms of Discrimination against Women*.

Condit, C.M. 1990. *Decoding Abortion Rhetoric: Communicating Social Change*. Urbana, IL: University of Illinois Press.

Congregation for the Doctrine of the Faith. 1987. *Instruction on Respect for Human Life in Its Origin and on the Dignity of Procreation*. Rome. www.vatican.va/roman_curia/congregations/cfaith/documents/rc_con_cfaith_doc_19870222_respect-for-human-life_en.html [Accessed: 11 October 2018].

Congregation for the Doctrine of the Faith. 2008. *Instruction Dignitas Personae on Certain Biological Questions*. Rome. www.vatican.va/roman_curia/congregations/cfaith/documents/rc_con_cfaith_doc_20081208_dignitas-personae_en.html [Accessed: 12 October 2018].

Conlon, D. 2017. 'Huge lack of understanding' of abortion in Oireachtas. *The Irish Times*, 20 December 2017.

Connolly, L. [2001] 2003. *The Irish Women's Movement: From Revolution to Devolution*. London: Palgrave Macmillan.

Connolly, L. and O'Toole, T. 2005. *Documenting Irish Feminisms: The Second Wave*. Dublin: Woodfield Press.

Cooley, H. 2004. It all about the fit: the hand, the mobile screenic device and tactile vision. *Journal of Visual Culture*, 3(2):133–155.

Cotter, N. 2009. Experiences from a Constitutional State: Ireland's problematic embryo. In Culley, L., Hudson, N. and Van Rooij, F. (eds.). *Marginalized Reproduction: Ethnicity, Infertility and Reproductive Technologies*. London: Earthscan.

Cotter, N. 2010. *Parenthood pursuits: couples' experiences of infertility and its treatment. An Irish case study*. PhD Thesis. Dublin: Trinty College Dublin. www.tara.tcd.ie/handle/2262/85269.

Coyne, E. 2018. Catholic hospitals set to ban abortion. *The Times*, 25 July 2018. www.thetimes.co.uk/edition/ireland/catholic-hospitals-set-to-ban-abortion-v9zwkd2qk.

Cresswell, T. 1996. *In place/out of place: geography, ideology, and transgression.* Minneapolis, MN:University of Minnesota Press.

Crossley, N. 2002. *Making Sense of Social Movements.* Buckingham: Open University Press.

Crowley, U. and Kitchin, R. 2008. Producing 'decent girls': governmentality and the moral geographies of sexual conduct in Ireland (1922–1937). *Gender, Place & Culture*, 15(4):355–372.

de Londras, F. 2015. Constitutionalizing fetal rights: a salutary tale from Ireland. *Michigan Journal of Gender and Law*, 22(2):243–289.

de Londras, F. 2018. *Repeal the 8th, activism, social movements and constitutional change in Ireland.* https://constitutional-change.com/repeal-the-8th-activism-social-movement-and-constitutional-change-in-ireland.

de Londras, F., Conway, V., Enright, M., Fletcher, R. and McGuinness, S. 2018. *Amending the Health (Regulation of Termination of Pregnancy) Bill: 5 priority issues for the Seanad.* https://lawyers4choice.ie/2018/11/29/amending-the-health-regulation-of-termination-of-pregnancy-act-5-priority-issues-for-the-seanad.

de Londras, F. and Enright, M. 2018. *Repealing the 8th: Reforming Irish Abortion Law.* Bristol: Policy Press.

de Londras, F. and Markicevic, M. 2018. Reforming abortion law in Ireland: reflections on the public submissions to the Citizens' Assembly. *Women's Studies International Forum*, 70:89–98.

de Souza e Silva, A. 2006. From cyber to hybrid: mobile technologies as interfaces of hybrid spaces. *Space and Culture*, 9(3):261–278.

de Zordo, S. 2016. The biomedicalisation of illegal abortion: the double life of misoprostol in Brazil. *História, Ciências, Saúde-Manguinhos*, 23(1):19–36.

de Zordo, S., Mishtal, J. and Anton, L. 2016. *A Fragmented Landscape: Abortion Governance and Protest Logics in Europe.* Oxford: Berghahn Books.

Dean, J. 2005. Communicative capitalism: circulation and the foreclosure of politics. *Cultural Politics*, 1(1):51–73.

Derrida, J. 2008. *The Gift of Death, Second Edition; and Literature in Secret.* Chicago, IL: University of Chicago Press.

Devine, C. 2016. 'Putting blue paint over it won't make it go away'– protest held over the removal of Repeal the 8th mural at Temple Bar. *Independent.ie*, 26 July 2016. www.independent.ie/irish-news/news/putting-blue-paint-over-it-wont-make-it-go-away-protest-held-over-the-removal-of-repeal-the-8th-mural-at-temple-bar-34913753.html [Accessed: 11 October 2018].

Devlin, M. 2009. A woman's plight exposes our hypocrisy on abortion. *Irish Independent*, 10 September 2009.

DeWan, J. 2010. Abortion: let's ease the burden of silence and shame. *Irish Examiner*, 10 May 2010.

Diduszko-Zyglewska, A. 2018. *Irlandki ludźmi!* [Irish women recognized as people]. http://krytykapolityczna.pl/swiat/diduszko-referendum-irlandia-aborcja.

Doan, P.L. 2010. The tyranny of gendered spaces – reflections from beyond the gender dichotomy. *Gender, Place & Culture*, 17(5):635–654.

Dodge, M. and Kitchin, R. 2001. *Mapping cyberspace*. Abingdon: Routledge.

Doherty, C. and Redmond, S. 2015. The radicalisation of a new generation of abortion rights activists. In Quilty, A., Kennedy, S. and Conlon, C. (eds.). *The Abortion Papers Ireland: Volume 2*. Cork: Attic Press.

Donnan, H. and Wilson, T.M. 2006. *The Anthropology of Ireland*. Oxford: Berg Publishers.

Douglas, D.A. 2018. Vote was a scream for freedom: letters and editorial comment. *Irish Independent*, 28 May 2018.

Douglas, M. 2013. *Risk and Blame*. London: Taylor & Francis.

Dowd, M. 2018. Scarlet Letter in the Emerald Isle. *New York Times*, 19 May 2018. www.nytimes.com/2018/05/19/opinion/sunday/ireland-abortion-referendum.html.

Doyle, K. 2016. Kenny risks Independent support with abortion plan. *Irish Independent*, 12 April 2016. www.pressreader.com/ireland/irish-indepe ndent/20160412/283128543016466.

Drovetta, R. 2015. Safe abortion information hotlines: an effective strategy for increasing women's access to safe abortions in Latin America. *Reproductive Health Matters*, 23(45):47–57.

Duffy, D.N., Pierson, C., Myerscough, C., Urquhart, D. and Earner-Byrne, L. 2018. Abortion, emotions, and health provision: explaining health care professionals' willingness to provide abortion care using affect theory. *Women's Studies International Forum*, 71:12–18.

Duffy, R. 2018. Maser's Repeal the 8th mural is back up in Temple Bar (and it won't come down this time). *thejournal.ie*, 27 April 2018. www.thejournal. ie/amnesty-repeal-mural-3983467-Apr2018 [Accessed: 9 May 2018].

Duffy, R. 2016. Sitting down with Maser: the man and the artist behind the blue Repeal wall. *thejournal.ie*, 19 November 2016. www.thejournal.ie/ maser-interview-3089275-Nov2016 [Accessed: 9 May 2018].

Dunlap, C.J. 2008. Lawfare today: a perspective. *Yale Journal of International Affairs*, 3(1):146–154.

Dyck, J.J. 2009. Initiated distrust: direct democracy and trust in government. *American Politics Research*, 37(4):539–568.

Dyer, S., Chambers, G.M., de Mouzon, J., Nygren, K.G., Zegers-Hochschild, F., Mansour, R., Ishihara, O., Banker, M. and Adamson, G.D. 2016. International Committee for Monitoring Assisted Reproductive Technologies world report: assisted reproductive technology 2008, 2009 and 2010. *Human Reproduction*, 31(7):1588–1609.

Elections Ireland. 2018. *Regulation of Termination of Pregnancy (Repeal of 8th Amendment), Referendum of 25 May 2018*. https://electionsireland. org/results/referendum/refresult.cfm?ref=201836R.

Elkink, J.A., Farrell, D.M., Reidy, T. and Suiter, J. 2019 Forthcoming. The death of conservative Ireland? The 2018 abortion referendum. *Irish Political Studies*.

Engeli, I. 2009. The challenges of abortion and assisted reproductive technologies policies in Europe. *Comparative European Politics*, 7(1):56–74.

Enright, A. 2018. Personal stories are precious things and they made the difference. *Irish Times*, 28 May 2018. www.irishtimes.com/opinion/ anne-enright-personal-stories-are-precious-things-and-they-made-the-difference-1.3510189 [Accessed: 12 October 2018].

Enright, M. 2018a. 'The enemy of the good': reflections on Ireland's new abortion legislation. *Feminists@law*, 8(2):1–12.

Enright, M. 2018b. The American origins of proposed anti-choice amendments to the Health (Regulation of Termination of Pregnancy) Bill 2018. *Lawyers4Choice*. https://lawyers4choice.ie/2018/11/05/the-american-origins-of-proposed-amendments-to-the-health-regulation-of-termination-of-pregnancy-bill-2018.

Enright, M. 2018c. Abortion and the Citizen's Assembly: agonist futures? *IACL-AIDC Blog*, 5 December 2018. https://blog-iacl-aidc.org/blog/2018/ 12/5/abortion-and-the-citizens-assembly-agonist-futures-xb2x6.

Enright, M. and Cloatre, E. 2018. Transformative illegality: how condoms 'became legal' in Ireland, 1991–1993. *Feminist Legal Studies*, 26(3):261–284.

Enright, M., Fletcher, R., De Londras, F. and Conway, V. 2018. *Position paper on the updated general scheme of the Health (Regulation of Termination of Pregnancy) Bill*. https://lawyers4choice.files.wordpress. com/2018/08/position-paper-1.pdf.

Evans-Pritchard, E.E. 1976. *Witchcraft, Oracles and Magic among the Azande*. Abridged ed. Oxford: Clarendon Press.

Evans-Pritchard, E. E. and Gillies, E. 1976. Witchcraft, oracles and magic among the Azande. Abridged with an introduction by Eva Gillies ed. Oxford: Clarendon Press.

Fagan, K. 2018. "Word of the day. . ." *Twitter*. Posted 11 May 2018. https:// twitter.com/karen_de_facto/status/994889685238460416.

Falkowski, P. 2018. Lekcja dla Polski [Lesson for Poland]. *Nasz Dziennik* https://wp.naszdziennik.pl/2018-05-30/297573,lekcja-dla-polski.html.

Fan, S.P., Liberman, Z., Keysar, B. and Kinzler, K.D. 2015. The exposure advantage: early exposure to a multilingual environment promotes effective communication. *Psychological Science*, 26(7):1090–1097.

Farmer, A. 2018. Lies that swung the Irish vote. *The Conservative Woman*, 2 June 2018. www.conservativewoman.co.uk/lies-that-swung-the-vote-for-irish-abortion [Accessed: 12 October 2018].

Farrell, D.M. 2014. 'Stripped down' or reconfigured democracy. *West European Politics*, 37(2):439–455.

Farrell, D.M., O'Malley, E. and Suiter, J. 2013. Deliberative democracy in action irish-style: the 2011 We the Citizens pilot Citizens' Assembly. *Irish Political Studies*, 28(1):99–113.

Farrell, D.M., Suiter, J. and Harris, C. 2018. 'Systematizing' constitutional deliberation: the 2016–18 citizens' assembly in Ireland. *Irish Political Studies*, 34(1):112–123.

Fegan, E. and Rebouche, R. 2003. Northern Ireland's abortion law: the morality of silence and the censure of agency. *Feminist Legal Studies*, 11(3):221–254.

Fegan, J. 2018. I had no real interest in politics, until this' – Ireland's accidental abortion activists. *The Guardian*, 22 May 2018. www.theguardian.com/world/2018/may/22/ireland-abortion-vote-accidental-activists-eighth-amendment.

Ferraretti, A.P., Pennings, G., Gianaroli, L., Natali, F. and Magli, M.C. 2010. Cross-border reproductive care: a phenomenon expressing the controversial aspects of reproductive technologies. *Reproductive BioMedicine Online*, 20(2):261–266.

Ferree, M.M., Gamson, W.A., Gerhards, J. and Rucht, D. 2002. *Shaping abortion discourse: democracy and the public sphere in Germany and the United States*. Cambridge: Cambridge University Press.

Ferriter, D. 2010. *The Transformation of Ireland 1900–2000*. London: Profile Books.

Field, L. 2018. The abortion referendum of 2018 and a timeline of abortion politics in Ireland to date. *Irish Political Studies*, 33(4):608–628.

Fink, S. 2009. Churches as societal veto players: religious influence in actor-centred theories of policy-making. *West European Politics*, 32(1):77–96.

Fischer, C. 2016. Gender, nation, and the politics of shame: Magdalen laundries and the institutionalization of feminine transgression in modern Ireland. *Signs: Journal of Women in Culture and Society*, 41(4):821–843.

Fitzgerald, G. 2014. *Just Garret: Tales from the Political Front Line*. Dublin: Liberties Press.

Fletcher, R. 1998. "Pro-life" absolutes, feminist challenges: the fundamentalist narrative of Irish abortion law 1986–1992. *Osgoode Hall Law Journal*, 36(1):1–62.

Fletcher, R. 2001. Post-colonial fragments: representations of abortion in Irish law and politics. *Journal of Law and Society*, 28(4):568–589.

Fletcher, R. 2005. Reproducing Irishness: race, gender, and abortion law. *Canadian Journal of Women and the Law*, 17(2):365–404.

Fletcher, R. 2015. Civic feminism and voluntary abortion care: a story of ESCORT's contribution to reproductive justice. In Quilty, A., Kennedy, S. and Conlon, C. (eds.). *The Abortion Papers Ireland: Volume 2*. Cork: Cork University Press.

Fletcher, R. 2016. Negotiating strangeness on the abortion trail. In Harding, R., Fletcher, R. and Beasley, C. (eds.). *ReValuing Care in Theory, Law and Policy: Cycles and Connections*. Abingdon: Routledge.

Fletcher, R. 2018. #RepealedThe8th: translating travesty, global conversation, and the Irish abortion referendum. *Feminist Legal Studies*, 26(3):233–259.

Fletcher, R., McGuinness, S., Conway, V., de Londras, F. and Enright, M. 2018. *Briefing paper on the Health (Regulation of Termination of Pregnancy) Bill, 2018: making the legislation work, delivering on the referendum*. https://lawyers4choice.files.wordpress.com/2018/10/hrtop_briefing_final.pdf.

Freeman, C. 2017. The crime of choice: abortion border crossings from Chile to Peru. *Gender, Place & Culture*, 24(6):851–868.

Freitag, M. and Ackermann, K. 2016. Direct democracy and institutional trust: relationships and differences across personality traits. *Political Psychology*, 37(5):707–723.

Gądecki, S. 2018. Intensywniej brońmy życia [Let's defend life more intensively]. *Nasz Dziennik*. https://naszdziennik.pl/wiara-kosciol-w-polsce/197857,intensywniej-bronmzycia.html.

Gallagher, M. 2018. Analysis of the abortion (8th Amendment) referendum. *Irish Politics Forum*, 31 May 2018. https://politicalreform.ie/2018/05/31/on-the-second-8th-amendment-referendum-may-2018.

Galligan, Y. 1998. *Women and Politics in Contemporary Ireland: From the Margins to the Mainstream*. London: Pinter.

Gardner, C.B. 1995. *Passing By: Gender and Public Harassment*. Berkeley, CA: University of California Press.

Gentleman, A. 2016. Northern Irish women on abortion: 'people feel they can't trust anyone. *The Guardian*, 8 April 2016. www.theguardian.com/world/2016/apr/08/northern-ireland-abortion-women-culture-suspicion-fear-prosecution-belfast.

Gianaroli, L., Ferraretti, A.P., Magli, M.C. and Sgargi, S. 2016. Current regulatory arrangements for assisted conception treatment in European countries. *European Journal of Obstetrics and Gynecology*, 207: 211–213.

Gibbon, P. and Higgins, M. 1974. Patronage, tradition and modernisation: the case of the Irish 'gombeenman'. In Clapham, C. (ed.). *Private Patronage and Public Power: Political Clientelism in the Modern State*, Ann Arbor, MI: University of Michigan.

Gillon, R. 2001. Is there a 'new ethics of abortion'? *Journal of Medical Ethics*, 27:ii5–ii9.

Gilmartin, M. and Kennedy, S. 2018. Mobility, migrants and abortion in Ireland. In Macquarrie, C., Bloomer, F., Pierson, C. and Stettner, S. (eds.). *Crossing Troubled Waters: Abortion in Ireland, Northern Ireland, and Prince Edward Island*. Prince Edward Island, Canada: Island Studies Press.

Ginsburg, F.D. and Rapp, R. 1995. *Conceiving the New World Order: The Global Politics of Reproduction*. Berkeley, CA: University of California Press.

Girvin, B. 1993. The referendums on abortion 1992. *Irish Political Studies*, 8(1):118–124.

Girvin, B. 1994. Moral politics and the Irish abortion referendums, 1992. *Parliamentary Affairs*, 47(2):203–221.

Girvin, B. 1996. Abortion politics: public policy in cross-cultural perspective. In Githens, M. and Mcbride Stetson, D. (eds.). *Abortion Politics: Public Policy in Cross-cultural Perspective*. New York: Routledge.

Gizzo, S., Noventa, M., Quaranta, M., Venturella, R., Vitagliano, A., Gangemi, M. and D'Antona, D. 2016. New frontiers in human assisted reproduction – from research to clinical practice: several considerations (review). *Molecular Medicine Reports*, 14(5):4037–4041.

Gloppen, S. and St. Clair, A.L. 2012. Climate change lawfare. *Social Research*, 79(4):899–930.

Gomes, J. 2018. The Big Lie that swayed the Irish referendum. *Medium*, 1 June 2018. https://medium.com/@jules.gomes/the-big-lie-that-swayed-the-irish-referendum-1d0c625559ee [Accessed: 12 October 2018].

González Vélez, A. and Jaramillo, I. 2017. Legal knowledge as a tool for social change. *Health and Human Rights*, 19(1):109–118.

Gostkiewicz, M. 2018. Jak jeden z najbardziej katolickich krajów Europy stracił wiarę, a Kościół - władzę [How one of the most Catholic countries in Europe has lost its faith]. [Online] http://weekend.gazeta.pl/weekend/1,152121,23466259,jak-jeden-z-najbardziej-katolickich-krajow-europy-stracil-wiare.htm.

Government of Ireland. 2018 [31]. "Health (Regulation of Termination of Pregnancy) Act." https://data.oireachtas.ie/ie/oireachtas/act/2018/31/eng/enacted/a3118.pdf [Accessed: 2 September 2019].

Government of the United Kingdom of Great Britain and Northern Ireland and Government of Ireland. 1998. *The Belfast Agreement*. Belfast.

Graham, L. 2018. *A comment from the president the MCI on the forthcoming referendum in the Republic of Ireland*. www.irishmethodist.org/news/17-may-2018/comment-president-mci-forthcoming-referendum-republic-ireland [Accessed: 14 December 2018].

Gray, S. 2018. Ireland: the fight isn't over. It just gets harder. *LifeSite News*, 31 May 2018. www.lifesitenews.com/opinion/ireland-the-fight-isnt-over.-it-just-gets-harder [Accessed: 12 October 2018].

Grimen, H. 2009. Power, trust, and risk. *Medical Anthropology Quarterly*, 23(1):16–33.

Grzymała-Busse, A. 2015. *Nations under God: How Churches Use Moral Authority to Influence Policy*. Princeton, NJ: Princeton University Press.

The Guardian. 2018. Activists take 'abortion pills' during pro-choice rally in Belfast. *The Guardian*, 31 May 2018. www.theguardian.com/world/2018/may/31/pro-choice-activists-take-abortion-pills-belfast-protest.

Guttmacher Institute. 2018. *Abortion worldwide 2017: unequal progress and unequal access*. www.guttmacher.org/report/abortion-worldwide-2017.

GW. 2016. Beata Szydło: Jestem za całkowitym zakazem aborcji [Beata Szydło: I support a complete abortion ban]. *Gazeta Wyborcza*, 31 March 2016. http://wyborcza.pl/1,75398,19841921,beata-szydlo-jestem-za-calkowitym-zakazem-aborcji.html?disableRedirects=true.

Halloran, M. 2018. Repeal mural will 'no doubt' go up on private wall space, says Taoiseach. *The Irish Times*, 24 April 2018. www.irishtimes.com/news/politics/oireachtas/repeal-mural-will-no-doubt-go-up-on-private-wall-space-says-taoiseach-1.3473018 [Accessed: 11 October 2018].

Haraway, D. 1991. *Simians, Cyborgs, and Women: The Reinvention of Women*. New York: Routledge.

Health Services Executive. 2013. *Investigation of Incident 50278 from time of patient's self-referral to hospital on the 21st of October 2012 to the patient's death on the 28th of October 2012*. Dublin: The Stationary Office.

Healy, G., Sheehan, B. and Whelan, N. 2016. *Ireland Says Yes: The Inside Story of How the Vote for Marriage Equality Was Won*. Kildare: Merrion Press.

Healy, S. 2017. Pro-abortion groups call for reforms: travelling art exhibition highlights need for law reform. *The Sligo Champion*, 10 January 2017.

Henchion, C. 2018. *After the Referendum Abortion in Ireland*. Paper presented at FIAPAC Conference, Nantes, France, 15 September 2018.

Hesketh, T. 1990. *The Second Partitioning of Ireland? The Abortion Referendum of 1983*. Dublin: Brandsma Books.

Hill-Collins, P. 2009. It's All In the Family: Intersections of Gender, Race, and Nation. *Hypatia*, 13(3):62–82.

Holborow, M. 2018. Ireland's abortion victory: women's lives, the liberal agenda and the radical left. *International Socialism*. http://isj.org.uk/irelands-abortion-victory.

Holc, Janine P. 2004. The purest democrat: fetal citizenship and subjectivity in the construction of democracy in Poland. *Signs*, 29(3):755–782.

Holland, K. 2013. *Savita: the Tragedy that Shook the Nation*. Dublin: Transworld Ireland.

Holland, K. 2018. Project Arts Centre told to remove 'Repeal the 8th' mural from wall. *The Irish Times*, 20 April 2018. www.irishtimes.com/news/social-affairs/project-arts-centre-told-to-remove-repeal-the-8th-mural-from-wall-1.3468694 [Accessed: 9 May 2018].

Holmquist, K. 2008. Stories of adoption that need to be heard. *The Irish Times*, 16 September 2008.

hooks, b. 1994. *Teaching to Transgress: Education as the Practice of Freedom*. New York: Routledge.

hooks, b. 2010. *Teaching Critical Thinking: Practical Wisdom*. New York: Routledge.

Hosford, P. 2013. Billboard company discontinues Youth Defence campaign after Rape Crisis Centre incident. *thejournal.ie*, 25 July 2016. www.thejournal.ie/admobile-company-drops-youth-defence-after-rape-crisis-incident-969637-Jun2013 [Accessed: 26 July 2016].

Hosford, P. 2018. Repeal The Eighth mural returns to Temple Bar. *thejournal.ie*, 9 April 2018. www.thejournal.ie/repeal-the-eighth-mural-returns-3948627-Apr2018 [Accessed: 11 October 2018].

Hug, C. 1998. *The Politics of Sexual Morality in Ireland*. London: Palgrave Macmillan.

Humphreys, J. 2016. Why Ireland's citizens' assembly is a model for Europe. Unthinkable: deliberative democracy experiment shows Ireland 'trusts its citizens, instead of fearing them. *The Irish Times*, 27 November 2016. www.irishtimes.com/culture/why-ireland-s-citizens-assembly-is-a-model-for-europe-1.2876808.

Hunt, C. 2015. We need to talk about all kinds of abortions. *Sunday Independent*, 8 February 2015.

Inglis, T. 1994. Women and the struggle for daytime adult education in Ireland. *Studies in the Education of Adults*, 26(1):50–66.

Inglis, T. 1998. *Moral Monopoly: The Rise and Fall of the Catholic Church in Modern Ireland*. 2nd ed. Dublin: University College Dublin Press.

Inglis, T. 2003. *Truth, Power and Lies: Irish Society and the Case of the Kerry Babies*. Dublin: University College Dublin Press.

Inglis, T. 2005. Origins and legacies of Irish prudery: sexuality and social control in modern Ireland. *Éire-Ireland*, 40(3):9–37.

Inglis, T. 2007. Catholic identity in contemporary Ireland: belief and belonging to tradition. *Journal of Contemporary Religion*, 22(2):205–220.

Inglis, T. and MacKeogh, C. 2012. The double bind: women, honour and sexuality in contemporary Ireland. *Media, Culture & Society*, 34(1):68–82.

Iona Institute. 2018. Pro-life movement must now take the long view as it has overseas. *Iona Institute Blog*, 29 May 2018. https://ionainstitute.ie/pro-life-movement-must-now-take-the-long-view-as-it-has-overseas [Accessed: 2 December 2018].

Irish Catholic Bishops Conference. 2018. *Statement of the summer 2018 general meeting of the Irish Catholic Bishops' Conference*. Maynooth. www.catholicbishops.ie/2018/06/13/statement-of-the-summer-2018-general-meeting-of-the-irish-catholic-bishops-conference.

Irish Examiner. 2018. 'I wouldn't like to attribute sin in this matter' – Fr D'Arcy reacts to Bishop's confession comments. *Irish Examiner*, 28 May 2018. www.irishexaminer.com/breakingnews/ireland/i-wouldnt-like-to-attribute-sin-in-this-matter--fr-darcy-reacts-to-bishops-confession-comments-845506.html.

Irish Family Planning Association. 2018. *Abortion in Ireland: Statistics*. www.ifpa.ie/Hot-Topics/Abortion/Statistics [Accessed: 1 September 2018].

Irish Independent. 2013. The secret histories. *Irish Independent*, 2 February 2013.

Irish Medical Council. 2004. *A guide to ethical conduct and behaviour*. www.medicalcouncil.ie/News-and-Publications/Publications/Professional-Conduct-Ethics/Ethical-Guide-6th-Ed-2004-.pdf.

Irish Medical Council. 2009. *Guide to professional conduct and ethics for registered medical practitioners*. www.medicalcouncil.ie/News-and-Publications/ Publications/Professional-Conduct-Ethics/Guide-to-Professional-Conduct-and-Behaviour-for-Registered-Medical-Practitioners-pdf.pdf.

Irish Medical Council. 2016. *Guide to professional conduct and ethics for registered medical practitioners*. www.medicalcouncil.ie/News-and-Publications/Reports/Guide-to-Professional-Conduct-and-Ethics-8th-Edition-2016-.pdf.

Irish Times. 1981. CAP opens new centre. *The Irish Times*, 8 December 1981.

IWLM. 1971. *The Irish Women's Liberation Movement examines the law in 1971*. http://womeninhistory.scoilnet.ie/content/unit6/IWLM.html.

Jackson, P. 1992. Abortion trials and tribulations. *The Canadian Journal of Irish Studies*, 18(1):112–120.

Jans, V., Dondorp, W., Goossens, E., Mertes, H., Pennings, G., Smeets, H. and de Wert, G. 2018. Of mice and human embryos: is there an ethically preferred order of preclinical research on new assisted reproductive technologies? *Human Reproduction*, 33(9):1581–1585.

Jiménez, A.C. 2011. Trust in anthropology. *Anthropological Theory*, 11(2):177–196.

Joas, H. 2013. *The Sacredness of the Person: A New Genealogy of Human Rights*. Washington, DC: Georgetown University Press.

Johnston, L. 2007. Mobilizing pride/shame: lesbians, tourism and parades. *Social & Cultural Geography*, 8(1):29–45.

Joint Oireachtas Committee on the 8th Amendment of the Constitution. 2017a. *Debate, Wednesday, 18 October 2017*. Dublin. www.oireachtas.ie/en/debates/debate/joint_committee_on_the_eighth_amendment_of_the_constitution/2017-10-18.

Joint Oireachtas Committee on the 8th Amendment of the Constitution. 2017b. *Report of the Joint Committee on the Eighth Amendment of the Constitution*. Dublin. https://data.oireachtas.ie/ie/oireachtas/committee/dail/32/joint_committee_on_the_eighth_amendment_of_the_constitution/reports/2017/2017-12-20_report-of-the-joint-committee-on-the-eighth-amendment-of-the-constitution_en.pdf.

Jones, R.K. and Henshaw, S.K. 2002. Mifepristone for early medical abortion: experiences in France, Great Britain and Sweden. *Perspectives on Sexual and Reproductive Health*, 34(3):154–161.

Kalia, A. 2018. "Shrouded in shame": the young women on either side of Ireland's abortion debate. *The Guardian*. 30 January 2018. www.theguardian.com/inequality/2018/jan/30/ireland-abortion-referendum-debate-young-women.

Katigbak, E.O. 2017. Manifesting shame in a Philippine migrant village. *Emotion, Space and Society*, 22:36–42.

Kelleher, O. 2018. Church defends pro-life speaker at anniversary Mass. *Irish Examiner*, 19 April 2018. www.irishexaminer.com/ireland/church-defends-pro-life-speaker-at-anniversary-mass-469615.html.

Kelly, F. 2018. Yes vote shows overwhelming desire for change that nobody foresaw. *The Irish Times*, 25 May 2018.

Kenny, Ciara. 2016. March for Choice goes global with protests planned for 25 cities. *Irish Times*. www.irishtimes.com/life-and-style/abroad/generation-emigration/march-for-choice-goes-global-with-protests-planned-for-25-cities-1.2796837.

Kennedy, F. 2002. Report – Abortion Referendum 2002. *Irish Political Studies*, 17(1):114–128.

KEP. 2018. *Komunikat w sprawie pełnej ochrony życia człowieka* [Statement on the full protection of life]. Warsaw: Polish Episcopal Conference.

Kielmans-Ratyńska, R. 2018. Wpływ wyników irlandzkiego referendum na Polskę i ruch pro-life [Impact of the Irish referendum on Poland and pro-life movement]. *Ordo Iuris*. https://ordoiuris.pl/ochrona-zycia/wpIyw-wynikow-irlandzkiego-referendum-na-polske-i-ruch-pro-life-analiza-ordo-iuris.

Kiely, E. and Leane, M. 2014. Pre-baby boom women's attitudes and responses to second wave feminism in Ireland. *Women's Studies International Forum*, 44(1):172–183.

King, L. 2002. Demographic Trends, pronatalism, and nationalist ideologies in the late twentieth century. *Ethnic and Racial Studies*, 25(3):367–389.

Kinzler, K. 2016. The superior social skills of bilinguals. *New York Times*, 11 March 2016. www.nytimes.com/2016/03/13/opinion/sunday/the-superior-social-skills-of-bilinguals.html [Accessed: 12 October 2018].

Knill, C., Adam, C. and Hurka, S. 2015. *On the Road to Permissiveness?: Change and Convergence of Moral Regulation in Europe*. Oxford: Oxford University Press.

Knill, C., Preidel, C. and Nebel, K. 2014. Brake rather than barrier: the impact of the Catholic Church on morality policies in Western Europe. *West European Politics*, 37(5):845–866.

Knox, K.B. 2017. Airports "to ban pro-life group protests". *Irish Independent*, 28 June 2017.

Kolirin, L. 2018. Polls show broad support for Northern Ireland abortion reform. *CNN International*, 9 October 2018. https://edition.cnn.com/2018/10/09/health/northern-ireland-abortion-polls-intl/index.html.

Komito, L. 1984. Irish clientelism: a reappraisal. *The Economic and Social Review*, 15(3):173–194.

Konc, J., Kanyó, K., Kriston, R., Somoskői, B. and Cseh, S. 2014. Cryopreservation of embryos and oocytes in human assisted reproduction. *BioMed Research International*. DOI: 10.1155/2014/307268.

Korolczuk, E. 2016. Explaining mass protests against abortion ban in Poland: the power of connective action. *Zoon Politicon*, 7(26):91–113.

Korolczuk, E. and Saxonberg, S. 2015. Strategies of contentious action: a comparative analysis of the women's movements in Poland and the Czech Republic. *European Societies*, 17(4):404–422.

Kozlowska, I., Béland, D. and Lecours, A. 2016. Nationalism, religion, and abortion policy in four Catholic societies. *Nations and Nationalism,* 22(4):824–844.

Kuhar, R. and Paternotte, D. 2017. *Anti-Gender Campaigns in Europe: Mobilizing against Equality.* London: Rowman & Littlefield.

Kushnir, V.A., Barad, D.H., Albertini, D.F., Darmon, S.K. and Gleicher, N. 2017. Systematic review of worldwide trends in assisted reproductive technology 2004–2013. *Reproductive Biology Endocrinology,* 15(6).

Laffoy, M. 2017. First report and recommendations of the Citizens' Assembly: the Eighth Amendment of the Constitution. *An Thionól Saoránach.* www.citizensassembly.ie/en/The-Eighth-Amendment-of-the-Constitution/Final-Report-on-the-Eighth-Amendment-of-the-Constitution/Final-Report-incl-Appendix-A-D.pdf.

Lang, A. 2007. But is it for real? The British Columbia Citizens' Assembly as a model of state-sponsored citizen empowerment. *Politics & Society,* 35(1):35–70.

Leduc, L. 2002. Opinion change and voting behaviour in referendums. *European Journal of Political Research,* 41(6):711–732.

Lee, J.J. 1989. *Ireland 1912–1985: Politics and Society.* Cambridge: Cambridge University Press.

Liisberg, S. and Pedersen, E.O. 2015. Introduction. trust and hope. In Liisberg, S., Pedersen, E.O. and Dalsgård, A.L. (eds.). *Anthropology and Philosophy: Dialogues on Trust and Hope.* Oxford: Berghahn Books.

Liisberg, S., Pedersen, E.O. and Dalsgård, A.L. 2015. *Anthropology and Philosophy: Dialogues on Trust and Hope.* Oxford: Berghahn Books.

Littlejohn, R. 2018. Shameless Shami's call for Ulster to impose abortion rights shows her contempt for democracy. *Daily Mail,* 29 May 2018. www.dailymail.co.uk/debate/article-5780725/RICHARD-LITTLEJOHN-Shameless-Shamis-contempt-democracy.html [Accessed: 12 October 2018].

Lorde, A. 2007. The transformation of silence into language and action. *Sister Outsider: Essays and Speeches.* Berkeley, CA: Crossing Press.

Loscher, D. 2017. Poll highlights public's lack of trust in politicians. *The Irish Times,* 9 February 2017. www.irishtimes.com/news/ireland/irish-news/poll-highlights-public-s-lack-of-trust-in-politicians-1.2968437.

Loughlin, E. 2016. TDs slam planned citizens' assembly as a 'charade'. *Irish Examiner.* 14 June 2016. www.irishexaminer.com/ireland/tds-slam-planned-citizens-assembly-as-a-charade-410190.html.

Loughlin, E., McConnell, D., Ó Cionnaith, F. and Baker, N. 2018. Institutional misogyny: Dr Scally says culture of paternalism left 221 women in dark on smears. *Irish Examiner,* 13 September 2018. www.irishexaminer.com/breakingnews/ireland/institutional-misogyny-dr-scally-says-culture-of-paternalism-left-221-women-in-dark-on-smears-868653.html.

Lowe, P. 2016. *Reproductive Health and Maternal Sacrifice: Women, Choice and Responsibility.* New York: Springer.

Lucie-Smith, A. 2018. Theresa May celebrates abortion in Ireland. What was she thinking? *Catholic Herald*, 28 May 2018. http://catholicherald. co.uk/commentandblogs/2018/05/28/theresa-may-celebrates-abortion-in-ireland-what-was-she-thinking [Accessed: 12 October 2018].

Luddy, C. 2017. Family, sex and the law. In Biagini, E. and Daly, M. (eds.). *The Cambridge Social History of Modern Ireland*. Cambridge: Cambridge University Press.

Luhmann, N. 1979. *Trust and Power*. New York: Wiley.

Luibhéid, E. 2006. Sexual regimes and migration controls: reproducing the Irish nation-state in transnational contexts. *Feminist Review*, (83):60–78.

Luibhéid, E. 2013. *Pregnant on Arrival: Making the Illegal Immigrant*. Minneapolis, MN: University of Minnesota Press.

Luker, K. 1985. *Abortion and the Politics of Motherhood*. Berkeley, CA: University of California Press.

Lynch, R.N. 1974. The National Committee for Human Life Amendment Inc.: its goals and origins. *Catholic Lawyer*, 20(4):303–308.

MacQuarrie, C., Pierson, C., Stettner, S. and Bloomer F. (eds.). 2018. *Crossing Troubled Waters: Abortion in Ireland, Northern Ireland, and Prince Edward Island*. Prince Edward Island, Canada: Island Studies Press.

Mahon, E. and Cotter, N. 2014. Assisted reproductive technology – IVF treatment in Ireland: a study of couples with successful outcomes. *Human Fertility*, 17(3):165–169.

Marecek, J., Macleod, C. and Hoggart, L. 2017. Abortion in legal, social, and healthcare contexts. *Feminism & Psychology*, 27(1):4–14.

Martin, A.K. 1999. Death of a nation: transnationalism, bodies and abortion in the late twentieth-century Ireland. In Mayer, T. (ed.). *Gender Ironies of Nationalism Sexing the Nation*, Abingdon: Routledge.

Martin, E. 2013a. Archbishop Eamon Martin's closing address at the novena in the parish of Saint Patrick, Dundalk. [Online] *Irish Catholic Bishop's Conference* www.catholicbishops.ie/2013/05/09/archbishop-eamon-martins-closing-address-novena-parish-saint-patrick-dundalk.

Martin, E. 2013b. Message to priests and parishes from Archbishop Martin concerning Catholic teaching on the dignity of human life and regarding abortion. *Irish Catholic Bishop's Conference*. www.catholicbishops. ie/2013/01/11/message-priests-parishes-archbishop-martin-catholic-teaching-dignity-human-life-abortion.

Martin, E. 2018. 'Being missionary disciples' – homily of Archbishop Eamon Martin for the Armagh diocesan pilgrimage to the National Marian Shrine in Knock. *Archdiocese of Armagh*. www.catholicbishops.ie/2018/05/27/being-missionary-disciples-homily-of-archbishop-eamon-martin-for-the-armagh-diocesan-pilgrimage-to-the-national-marian-shrine-in-knock.

Massey, D.B. 2005. *For Space*. London: SAGE.

McAuliffe, M. and Kennedy, S. 2017. Defending Catholic Ireland. In Kuhar, R. and Paternotte, D. (eds.). *Anti-Gender Campaigns in Europe: Mobilizing against Equality*. London: Rowman & Littlefield.

McAvoy, D. 2018. The people of Ireland have voted Yes to repeal the Eighth Amendment [Press release]. *Both Lives Matter*, 27 May 2018. https://bothlivesmatter.org/the-people-of-ireland-have-voted-yes-to-repeal-the-eighth-amendment [Accessed: 12 October 2018].

McAvoy, S. 2015. The Catholic Church and fertility control in Ireland: the making of a dystopian regime. In Quilty, A., Kennedy, S. and Conlon, C. (eds.). *The Abortion Papers Ireland: Volume 2*. Cork: Attic Press.

McCafferty, N. 1984 [1983]. Caoineadh mhná na hEireann [The weeping of the women of Ireland]. *In Dublin*, 22 September 1983. Reprinted in McCafferty, N. *The Best of Nell: A Selection of Writings Over Fourteen Years*. Dublin: Attic Press.

McCafferty, N. 2016. *Nell*. Dublin: Penguin.

McCarthy, A. 2000. Irish women harder on themselves than British. *The Irish Times*, 4 July 2000.

McDonagh, M. 2018. What really happened in Ireland's abortion referendum? *The Spectator*, 26 May 2018. https://blogs.spectator.co.uk/2018/05/what-really-happened-in-irelands-abortion-referendum [Accessed: 12 October 2018].

McDonnell, O. and Murphy, P. 2018. Mediating abortion politics in Ireland: media framing of the death of Savita Halappanavar. *Critical Discourse Studies*, 16(1):1–20.

McDonough, C. 2018. Believers must dry their tears and burn bright. *The Irish Catholic*, 31 May 2018.

McDowell, L. and Sharp, J.P. 1997. *Space, Gender, Knowledge: Feminist Readings*. London: Arnold.

McEvoy, J. and O'Leary, B. 2013. *Power Sharing in Deeply Divided Places*. Philadelphia, PA: University of Pennsylvania Press.

McGarrigle, S. 2018. Priest Martin McVeigh who sparked church walk out when discussing abortion referendum at First Holy Communion mass defends himself. *Irish Mirror*. 23 May 2018. www.irishmirror.ie/news/irish-news/priest-martin-mcveigh-who-sparked-12579321.

McGee, H. 2018. How the Yes and No sides won and lost the abortion referendum. *Irish Mirror*. 27 May 2018. www.irishtimes.com/news/politics/how-the-yes-and-no-sides-won-and-lost-the-abortion-referendum-1.3509924.

McGill, M. 2018. Saying 'Yes' to repeal in rural Ireland. *missmarymcgill.com*, 11 March 2018. https://missmarymcgill.com/2018/03/11/saying-yes-to-repeal-in-rural-ireland.

McGreevy, R. 2018. Citizens' Assembly is an example to the world, says chairwoman. [Online] *The Irish Times*. www.irishtimes.com/news/ireland/irish-news/citizens-assembly-is-an-example-to-the-world-says-chairwoman-1.3539370 [Accessed: 1 February 2019].

McGuinness, S. and Uí Chonnachtaigh, S. 2011. Implications of recent development in Ireland for the status of the embryo. *Cambridge Quarterly of Healthcare Ethics*, 20(3):396–408.

McIntyre, A. 2014. Doctrine of double effect. In Zalta, E.N. (ed.). *The Stanford Encyclopedia of Philosophy.* Winter 2014.

McIvor, M. 2018. Human rights and broken cisterns: counterpublic Christianity and rights-based discourse in contemporary England. *Ethnos:* 1–21.

McMahon, A. 2018. Varadkar backs Yes vote saying Ireland should 'trust women and trust doctors'. [Online] *The Irish Times.* www.irishtimes. com/news/politics/varadkar-backs-yes-vote-saying-ireland-should-trust-women-and-trust-doctors-1.3469913 [Accessed: 2 February 2019].

McNeely, N., Morrow, T. and Gribben, T. 2018. PCI outlines Eighth Amendment referendum position. *The Presbyterian Church in Ireland.* www.presbyterianireland.org/News/2018-News-Archive/April-2018/PCI-outlines-Eighth-Amendment-referendum-position.aspx [Accessed: 4 December 2018].

Messerschmidt, J.W., Martin, P.Y. and Messner, M.A. 2018. *Gender Reckonings: New Social Theory and Research.* New York: New York University Press.

Millar, E. 2017. *Happy Abortions: Our Bodies in the Era of Choice.* London: Zed Books Limited.

Minihan, M. 2017. Was Citizens' Assembly best way to deal with abortion question? *The Irish Times,* 29 April 2017. www.irishtimes.com/news/politics/was-citizens-assembly-best-way-to-deal-with-abortion-question-1.3065226 [Accessed: 10 November 2018].

Mishtal, J. 2015. *The Politics of Morality: The Church, the State, and Reproductive Rights in Postsocialist Poland.* Athens, OH: Ohio University Press.

Mitchell, S. 2012. The government must address the legal deficiencies on abortion. *The Sunday Business Post,* 11 March 2012.

Moane, G. and Quilty, A. 2012. Feminist education and feminist community psychology: experiences from an Irish context. *Journal of Community Psychology,* 40(1):145–158.

Morgan, L. and Roberts, E. 2012. Reproductive governance in Latin America. *Anthropology & Medicine,* 19(2):241–254.

Morgan, L. and Michaels, M. 1999. *Fetal Subjects, Feminist Positions.* Philadelphia, PA: University of Pennsylvania Press.

Morin, K. 2013. Distinguished Historical geography lecture: carceral space and the usable past. *Historical Geography:* 1–21.

Morozov, E. 2012. *The Net Delusion: How not to Liberate the World.* London: Penguin.

Muehlenberg, B. 2018. This is what evil looks like. *CultureWatch,* 28 May 2018. https://billmuehlenberg.com/2018/05/28/this-is-what-evil-looks-like [Accessed: 12 October 2018].

Mullally, U. 2018. *Repeal the 8th.* London: Unbound.

Mulligan, A. 2011. Frozen embryo disposition in Ireland after Roche v Roche. *Irish Jurist,* 46:202–210.

Murray, C. 2016. The Protection of Life During Pregnancy Act 2013: suicide, dignity and the Irish discourse on abortion. *Social & Legal Studies*, 25(6):667–698.

Murray, S. 2017. Why this pro-life TD is calling for regulated access to abortion pill. *Independent.ie*, 12 December 2017. www.independent.ie/irish-news/politics/why-this-prolife-td-is-calling-for-regulated-access-to-abortion-pill-36400233.html [Accessed: 24 September 2018].

Nachtigall, R.D., Becker, G., Friese, C., Butler, A. and MacDougall, K. 2005. Parents' conceptualization of their frozen embryos complicates the disposition decision. *Fertility and Sterility*, 84(2):431–434.

Nash, C. 2002. Embodied Irishness: gender, sexuality and Irish identities. In Graham, B. (ed.). *In Search of Ireland: A Cultural Geography*. Abingdon: Routledge.

Nash, C.J. and Browne, K. 2015. Best for society? Transnational opposition to sexual and gender equalities in Canada and Great Britain. *Gender, Place & Culture*, 22(4):1–17.

Nash, C.J. and Browne, K. 2019 Forthcoming. Resisting the mainstreaming of LGBT equalities in Canadian and British Schools: sex education and trans school friends. *Environment and Planning C*.

Nash, C.J. and Gorman-Murray, A. 2016. Digital technologies and sexualities in urban space. In Brown, G. and Browne, K. (eds.). *Routledge Research Companion to Geographies of Sex and Sexualities*. Abingdon: Routledge.

Nebel, K. and Hurka, S. 2015. Abortion: the impossible compromise. In Knill, C., Adam, C. and Hurka S. (eds.). *On the Road to Permissiveness?: Change and Convergence of Moral Regulation in Europe*. Oxford: Oxford University Press.

Newman, J. 2018. How the Irish were manipulated into voting for abortion. *The Conservative Woman*, 27 May 2018. www.conservativewoman.co.uk/how-the-irish-were-manipulated-into-voting-for-abortion [Accessed: 12 October 2018].

Newsweek 2016. *Trudny okres dla rządu, kobiety trollują premier na Facebooku - Polska* [Tough period for the government]. www.newsweek.pl/polska/trudny-okres-dla-rzadu-kobiety-trolluja-premier-na-facebooku/lk24m6s.

Ní Aodha, G. 2018. Bishop says Catholics who voted Yes have sinned and should go to confession. *thejournal.ie*, 28 May 2018. www.thejournal.ie/bishop-catholics-who-voted-yes-sinned-4039904-May2018.

Norris, P. 2006. Did the media matter? agenda-setting, persuasion and mobilization effects in the British general election campaign. *British Politics*, 1(2):195–221.

Nussbaum, M. 2004. *Hiding from Humanity: Disgust, Shame, and the Law*. Princeton, NJ: Princeton University Press.

Ó Broin, C, 2017. Debunking the most common 'alternative facts' about the Irish language. *thejournal.ie*, 9 April 2017. www.thejournal.ie/readme/

column-debunking-the-most-common-alternative-facts-about-the-irish-language-3329361-Apr2017 [Accessed: 9 April 2019].

O'Brien, B. 2018. Compassion's role in voting on 8th Amendment. *The Irish Times*, 5 May 2018. www.irishtimes.com/opinion/compassion-s-role-in-voting-on-eighth-amendment-1.3484429.

O'Brien, C. 2018. You can't paint over an issue, but you can paint over an artwork! *The Project Arts Centre*, 20 April 2018. https://projectartscentre.ie/cant-paint-issue-can-paint-artwork-maser-mural-update [Accessed: 9 May 2018].

O'Brien, J. 2018. Catholic Ireland says, 'Yes, we trust women'. *Boston Globe*, 30 May 2018. www.bostonglobe.com/opinion/2018/05/30/catholic-ireland-says-yes-trust-women/HGdWxdBnQyKdWAj8Cs5WkN/story.html [Accessed: 9 April 2019].

Observer. 2018. The Observer view on the Irish referendum result. [Online] *Observer editorial*. www.theguardian.com/commentisfree/2018/may/26/the-observer-view-on-the-irish-referendum-result [Accessed: 5 February 2019].

O'Callaghan, J. 1998. Censorship of indecency in Ireland: a view from abroad. *Cardozo Arts & Entertainment Law Journal*, 16(1):53–80.

O'Carroll, J.P. 1991. Bishops, knights – and pawns? Traditional thought and the Irish abortion referendum debate of 1983. *Irish Political Studies*, 6(1):53–71.

O'Connell, M. 2018. Repealed the Eighth. *British Journal of Midwifery*, 26:428–433.

O'Hara, L. 2016. *Street harassment: creative place-based interventions*. Paper presented at Conference of Irish Geographers, Dublin, Ireland, 5–7 May 2016.

O'Mahony, C. 2017. This kind of "help" isn't what most frightened women need. *Irish Independent*, 28 June 2017.

O'Neill, L. 2016. Well, I have news for you. I am a feminist. And I am angry. *Irish Examiner*, 5 March 2016.

Ordo Iuris. 2018. *Komitet Inicjatywy Ustawodawczej Stop Aborcji zarejestrowany* [Stop Abortion Committee registered]. https://ordoiuris.pl/ochrona-zycia/komitet-inicjatywy-ustawodawczej-stop-aborcji-zarejestrowany.

O'Regan, M. 2017. Abortion referendum should be held 'as early as possible', says Tánaiste. *The Irish Times*, 4 May 2017.

O'Regan, M. 2018. Repeat of Kerry babies case unlikely in modern Ireland. *The Irish Times*, 16 January 2018. www.irishtimes.com/news/ireland/irish-news/repeat-of-kerry-babies-case-unlikely-in-modern-ireland-1.3357782.

O'Reilly, E. 1992. *Masterminds of the Right*. London, Ontario: Attic Press.

O'Reilly, K. 2018. Spring pastoral letter from Archbishop Kieran O'Reilly. *Archdiocese of Cashel and Emily*, May 2018. https://cashel-emly.ie/wp-content/uploads/2018/04/Spring-Pastoral-letter-2018.pdf.

O'Sullivan, K. 2016. Maser Artwork subject to planning permission to be taken down. *The Project Arts Centre*, 25 July 2016. http://projectartscentre.

ie/maser-artwork-subject-planning-permission-taken [Accessed: 26 July 2016].

O'Sullivan-Latchford, D. 2018. Pro-life advocates are highlighting the weakness of arguments to repeal the Irish Constitution's 8th Amendment, which recognises the equal right to life of the unborn child and the mother. *EWTN Ireland*. www.ewtnireland.com/prayer-campaigning-intensify-irelands-abortion-referendum-draws-near.

O'Toole, F. 2014. Why Ireland became the only country in the democratic world to have a constitutional ban on abortion. *The Irish Times*, 26 August 2014.

Pacewicz, K. 2018. Tylko 5 proc. Polek uważa się za feministki, choć ich postulaty popiera większość [Only 5% of Polish women consider themselves feminists, although majority supports the feminist postulates].*Wysokie Obcasy*. www.wysokieobcasy.pl/wysokie-obcasy/7,163229,23952656,tylko-5-proc-polek-uwaza-sie-za-feministki-choc-postulaty.html.

Paciorek, M. 2018. Kobiety w Irlandii będą mogły przerwać niechcianą ciążę. [Women in Ireland will be allowed to terminate their pregnancy]. *Radio TOK FM*. www.tokfm.pl/Tokfm/7,103094,23454663,historyc zne-zwyciestwo-kobiet-w-referendum-w-irlandii-beda.html.

Paternotte, D. and Kollman, K. 2013. Regulating intimate relationships in the European polity: same-sex unions and policy convergence. *Social Politics*, 20(4):510–533.

Petchesky, R. 1984. *Abortion and Woman's Choice: The State, Sexuality, and Reproductive Freedom*. London: Longman.

Pileggi, V., Holliday, J., De Santis, C., Lamarre, A., Jeffrey, N., Tetro, M. and Rice, C. 2015. Becoming scholars in an interdisciplinary, feminist learning context. *Feminist Teacher*, 26(1):29–52.

Polletta, F. and Lee, J. 2006. Is telling stories good for democracy? Rhetoric in public deliberation after 9/11. *American Sociological Review*, 71(5):699–723.

Pollitt, K. 2014. *Pro: Reclaiming Abortion Rights*. London: Picador.

Power, J. 2017. Number of abortion pills seized by Irish customs declines. *The Irish Times*, 24 April 2017. www.irishtimes.com/news/health/number-of-abortion-pills-seized-by-irish-customs-declines-1.3059156 [Accessed: 24 September 2018].

Präg, P. and Mills, M.C. 2017. Cultural determinants influence assisted reproduction usage in Europe more than economic and demographic factors. *Human Reproduction*, 32(11):2305–2314.

Precious Life. 2018a. *170 British and Irish Politicians call on Westminster to interfere in Northern Ireland abortion laws*. https://preciouslife. com/news/585/170-british-and-irish-politicians-call-on-westminster-to-interfere-in-ni-abortion-laws.

Precious Life. 2018b. *Abortion racism*. https://preciouslife.com/news/597/abortion-racism-billboard-markets-abortion-to-black-women-as-selfcare.

Precious Life. 2018c. *I think it is very much directed towards eliminating Down syndrome: debate on screening in Wales.* www.preciouslife.com/news/573/i-think-it-is-very-much-directed-towards-eliminating-down-syndrome-debate-on-screening-in-wales.

Precious Life. 2018d. *MP shows scan of unborn daughter in Parliament.* www.preciouslife.com/news/578/mp-shows-scan-of-unborn-daughter-in-parliament.

Precious Life. 2018e. *Precious Life "determined to keep fighting" against abortion in Northern Ireland.* www.preciouslife.com/news/560/precious-life-determined-to-keep-fighting-against-abortion-in-northern-ireland.

Precious Life. 2018f. *Precious Life accuse abortion MPs of endangering the peace process.* [Press release]. www.preciouslife.com/news/583/press-release-precious-life-accuse-abortion-mps-of-endangering-the-peace-process.

Precious Life. 2018g. *Precious life to Irish Abortion Minister – stop interfering.* www.preciouslife.com/news/586/precious-life-tells-irish-abortion-minister-to-stop-interfering-in-n-ireland-affairs.

Precious Life. 2018h. *Precious Life to say "civil rights begin in the womb" at civil rights commemoration.* www.preciouslife.com/news/588/press-release-precious-life-to-say-civil-rights-begin-in-the-womb-at-civil-rights-commemoration-march.

Precious Life. 2018i. *Thousands stand 'together for life' at the All Ireland Rally for Life at Stormont.* www.preciouslife.com/news/582/thousands-stand-together-for-life-at-the-all-ireland-rally-for-life-at-stormont.

Probyn, E. 2005. *Blush: Faces of Shame.* Minneapolis, MN: University of Minnesota Press.

Provost, C. and Ros Rebollo, R. 2018. A historic victory for women's rights': how the world responded to Ireland's abortion referendum. *Open Democracy.* www.opendemocracy.net/5050/claire-provost-rocio-ros-rebollo/world-reaction-ireland-historic-vote-abortion-rights.

Quilty, A., Kennedy, S. and Conlon, C. 2015. *The Abortion Papers Ireland: Volume 2.* Cork: Attic Press.

Quinn, D. 2013. Legislating for X Case is just beginning of this saga. *Independent.ie*, 12 July 2018. www.independent.ie/opinion/columnists/david-quinn/legislating-for-x-case-is-just-beginning-of-this-saga-29414364.html.

Qvortrup, M. 2014. *Referendums around the world: the continued growth of direct democracy.* London: Palgrave Macmillan UK.

Qvortrup, M. 2018. *Government by referendum (pocket politics).* Manchester: Manchester University Press.

Radicc, M. 2018. Putting the public in public art: an ethnographic approach to two temporary art installations. *City & Society*, 30(1):45–67.

Raftery, M. 2006. Babies born in shame. *The Irish Times*, 12 January 2006.

Rally for Life. 2018. *Previous rallies*. https://rallyforlife.net/previous-rallies.

Rao, R. 2014. The locations of homophobia. *London Review of International Law*, 2(2):169–199.

Reddy, W.M. 2001. *The Navigation of Feeling: A Framework for the History of Emotions*. Cambridge: Cambridge University Press.

Reidy, T. 2018. Liberal Frontier: Abortion referendums in Ireland. In Brunn, S.D. and Kehrein, R. (eds.). *Handbook of the Changing World Language Map*. New York: Springer.

Rigney, T. 2018. Referendum on the Eighth Amendment. *The Irish Times*, 21 May 2018.

Ring, E. 2010. I was very angry. I felt let down, maltreated. *Irish Times*, 29 January 2010.

Ring, E. and Ó Cionnaith, F. 2018. Abortion debate: all publicly funded hospitals to provide legal health services, says Health Minister. *Irish Examiner*, 26 July 2018. www.irishexaminer.com/ireland/abortion-debate-all-publicly-funded-hospitals-to-provide-legal-health-services-says-health-minister-473045.html.

Roberts, D. 1999. *Killing the Black Body: Race, Reproduction, and the Meaning of Liberty*. New York: Vintage.

Rohlinger, D.A. 2006. Friends and foes: media, politics, and tactics in the abortion war. *Social Problems*, 53(4):537–561.

Romero, C. 2018. Ireland's historic chance to trust women. *The Hill*, 31 March 2018. http://thehill.com/opinion/healthcare/380862-irelands-historic-chance-to-trust-women.

Rose, G. 2016. Rethinking the geographies of cultural 'objects' through digital technologies: Interface, network and friction. *Progress in Human Geography*, 40(3):334–351.

Rossiter, A. 2009. *Ireland's Hidden Diaspora: The 'Abortion Trail' and the Making of a London-Irish Underground, 1980–2000*. London: IASC Press.

Roth, R. 2003. *Making Women Pay: The Hidden Costs of Fetal Rights*. New York: Cornell University Press.

RTÉ. 2018. Result is culmination of quiet revolution, says Varadkar. *RTÉ News*, 26 May 2018. www.rte.ie/news/eighth-amendment/2018/0526/966132-reaction.

RTÉ-Universities. 2016. *General election exit poll, 26 February 2016*. https://static.rasset.ie/documents/news/rte-exit-poll-report.pdf.

RTÉ-Universities. 2018. *Thirty-sixth Amendment to the Constitution Exit Poll, 25th May, 2018*. https://static.rasset.ie/documents/news/2018/05/rte-exit-poll-final-11pm.pdf.

Ryan, L. 1996. 'The massacre of innocence' infanticide in the Irish Free State. *Irish Studies Review*, 4(14):17–20.

Ryan, S. 2018. Priest tells St Vincent de Paul to remove clothing bank from church car park in row over Eighth campaign. *Independent.ie*, 31 May 2018. www.independent.ie/irish-news/priest-tells-st-vincent-de-paul-to-remove-clothing-bank-from-church-car-park-in-row-over-eighth-campaign-36963884.html [Accessed: 12 December 2018].

Sanger, C. 2016. Talking about abortion. *Social & Legal Studies*, 25(6):651–666.

Sanger, C. 2017. *About Abortion: Terminating Pregnancy in Twenty-First Century America*. Cambridge, MA: Harvard University Press.

Saunders, P. 2018. Ireland votes to legalise abortion – a desperately sad day. *National Right to Life News Today*, 27 May 2018. www.nationalrighttolifenews.org/news/2018/05/ireland-votes-to-legalise-abortion-a-desperately-sad-day [Accessed: 12 October 2018].

Saurette, P. and Gordon, K. 2016. *The changing voice of the anti-abortion movement: the rise of "pro-woman" rhetoric in Canada and the United States*. Toronto: University of Toronto Press.

Save the 8th 2018a. *8 Reasons to Vote No*. www.save8.ie/8-reasons [Accessed: 10 September 2018].

Save the 8th 2018b. *Save the 8th statement on pro-life speakers at Catholic masses*. www.save8.ie/save-the-8th-statement-on-pro-life-speakers-at-catholic-masses [Accessed: 4 December 2018].

Scheer, M. 2012. Are emotions a kind of practice (and is that what makes them have a history)? a Bourdieuian approach to understanding emotion. *History and Theory*, 51(2):193–220.

Scheper-Hughes, N. 1979. *Saints, Scholars and Schizophrenics: Mental Illness in Rural Ireland*. Berkeley, CA: University of California Press.

Scherz, C. 2010. 'You aren't the first and you won't be the last': Reflections on moral change in contemporary rural Ireland. *Anthropological Theory*, 10(3):303–318.

Schreiber, R. 2002. Injecting a woman's voice: conservative women's organizations, gender consciousness, and the expression of women's policy preferences. *A Journal of Research*, 47(7):331–342.

Sethna, C. and Doull, M. 2012. Accidental tourists: Canadian women, abortion tourism, and travel. *Women's Studies*, 41(4):457–475.

Sheldon, S. 1997. *Beyond Control: Medical Power and Abortion Law*. London: Pluto Press.

Sheldon, S. 2016. How can a state control swallowing? The home use of abortion pills in Ireland. *Reproductive Health Matters*, 24(48):90–101.

Sheldon, S. 2018. Empowerment and privacy? Home use of abortion pills in the Republic of Ireland. *Signs*, 43(4):823–849.

Side, K. 2006. Contract, charity, and honourable entitlement: social citizenship and the 1967 Abortion Act in Northern Ireland after the Good Friday Agreement. *Social Politics: International Studies in Gender, State & Society*, 13(1):89–116.

Side, K. 2016. A geopolitics of migrant women, mobility and abortion access in the Republic of Ireland. *Gender, Place & Culture*, 23(12):1788–1799.

Sills, E.S. and Murphy, S.E. 2009. Determining the status of non-transferred embryos in Ireland: a conspectus of case law and implications for clinical IVF practice. *Philosophy, Ethics, and Humanities in Medicine*, 4(1):8.

Simpson, C. 2018. Theresa May said she does not back abortion decriminalisation plan. *The Irish News*, 23 November 2018. www.irishnews.com/news/northernirelandnews/2018/11/23/news/theresa-may-said-she-does-not-back-abortion-decriminalisation-plan-1491367.

Singer, E. 2018. Realizing abortion rights at the margins of legality in mexico. *Medical Anthropology*, 38(2):167–181.

Sinnott, R. 1995. *Irish Voters Decide: Voting Behaviour in Elections and Referendums since 1918*. Manchester: Manchester University Press.

Sinnott, R. 2002. Cleavages, parties and referendums: relationships between representative and direct democracy in the Republic of Ireland. *European Journal of Political Research*, 41(6):811–26.

Skarżyński, S. 2016. Wpadka Krystyny Pawłowicz [Krystyna Pawłowicz's failure]. *OKO.press*. https://oko.press/wpadka-krystyny-pawlowicz-chciala-ratowac-a-pograzyla-pis.

Smeaton, J. 2018a. Pro-life leader explains how Catholic bishops destroyed the Irish conscience. *LifeSite News*, 28 May 2018. www.lifesitenews.com/news/pro-life-leader-explains-how-catholic-bishops-destroyed-the-irish-conscienc [Accessed: 12 October 2018].

Smeaton, J. 2018b. We will not be giving in to despair. We will start again now. *Society for the Protection of Unborn Children*, 26 May 2018. www.spuc.org.uk/news/press-releases/2018/may/ireland-referendum-result [Accessed: 12 October 2018].

Smyth, A. 1992. *The Abortion Papers Ireland Volume 1*. Dublin: Attic Press.

Smyth, A. 1995. States of change: reflections on Ireland in several uncertain parts. *Feminist Review*, (50):24–43.

Smyth, A. 2018. *Unseen voices: representations, interpretations and reconstruction*. Paper presented at New Perspectives Postgraduate Symposium on the Humanities, Maynooth, Ireland, 13 October 2018.

Smyth, L. 1998. Narratives of Irishness and the problem of abortion: the X Case 1992. *Feminist Review*, (60):61–83.

Smyth, L. 2002. Feminism and abortion politics: choice, rights, and reproductive freedom. *Women's Studies International Forum*, 25(3):335–345.

Smyth, L. 2006. The cultural politics of sexuality and reproduction in Northern Ireland. *Sociology*, 40(4):663–680.

Smyth, L. [2005] 2016. *Abortion and Nation: The Politics of Reproduction in Contemporary Ireland*. Abingdon: Routledge.

Society for the Protection of Unborn Children. 2018. Pro-abortion MPs must stop bullying Northern Ireland [Press release]. *Society for the Protection of Unborn Children*, 28 May 2018. www.spuc.org.uk/news/press-releases/2018/may/proabortion-mps-must-stop-bullying-northern-ireland [Accessed: 12 October 2018].

Spreng, J.E. 2015. *Abortion and Divorce Law in Ireland*. Jefferson, NC: McFarland & Company.

Staggenborg, S. 1991. *The Pro-Choice Movement: Organization and Activism in the Abortion Conflict*. Oxford University Press.

Stake, J.E. and Hoffmann, F.L. 2001. Changes in student social attitudes, activism, and personal confidence in higher education: the role of women's studies. *American Educational Research Journal*, 38(2):411–436.

Statz, M. and Pruitt, L. 2018. To recognize the tyranny of distance: a spatial reading of whole woman's health v. Hellerstedt. *Environment and Planning A: Economy and Space*, 51(5):1106–27.

Staunton, C. 2018. The regulation of stem cell research in Ireland: from the Commission on Assisted Human Reproduction to the Assisted Human Reproduction Bill 2017. *Medical Law International*, 18(1):35–58.

Stein, A. 2001. *The Stranger Next Door: The Story of a Small Community's Battle over Sex, Faith, and Civil Rights*. Boston: Beacon Press.

Subset. 2018. *Grey Area Project*. https://store.subset.ie/pages/grey-area-exhibition-ii [Accessed: 11 October 2018].

Suiter, J., Farrell, D.M. and O'Malley, E. 2016. When do deliberative citizens change their opinions? Evidence from the Irish Citizens' Assembly. *International Political Science Review*, 37(2):198–212.

Suiter, J. and Reidy, T. 2013. It's the campaign learning stupid: an examination of a volatile Irish referendum. *Parliamentary Affairs*, 68 (1):182–202.

Sunstein, C.R. 1996. Social norms and social roles. *Columbia Law Review*, 96(4):903–968.

Sutherland, P. 2018. Legal advice on the 8th Amendment. *Irish Times*, 13 January 2018.

Szelewa, D. 2014. The second wave of anti-feminism? Post-crisis maternalist policies and the attack on the concept of gender in Poland. *Gender, Rovne, Prilezitosti, Vyzkum*, 15(2):33–47.

Szelewa, D. 2016. Killing 'unborn children'? the Catholic Church and abortion law in Poland since 1989. *Social & Legal Studies*, 25(6):741–764.

Szostkiewicz, A. 2018. Kościół w Polsce idzie tą samą drogą, co wcześniej irlandzki [Polish Church follows the Irish Church]. *Gra w Klasy: Blog Adama Szostkiewicza*. https://szostkiewicz.blog.polityka.pl/2018/05/27/aborcja-irlandia-polska.

Sztompka, P. 1997. *Trust, Distrust and the Paradox of Democracy*. Berlin: WZB.

Takeshita, C. 2012. *The Global Biopolitics of the IUD: How Science Constructs Contraceptive Users and Women's Bodies*. Cambridge, MA: MIT Press.

Taylor, C. 2011. Obama tells Dublin crowd America 'will stand by you.' [Online] *Irish Times*. www.irishtimes.com/news/obama-tells-dublin-crowd-america-will-stand-by-you-1.876964.

Taylor, G. 1985. *Pride, Shame, and Guilt: Emotions of Self-Assessment*. Oxford: Clarendon Press.

Thompson, C. 2005. *Making Parents: The Ontological Choreography of Reproductive Technologies*, Cambridge, MA: MIT Press.

Thomsen, S.R. and Suiter, J. 2016. Candidates, parties and constituency relations: a study in irish clientelism. In Elkink, J.A. and Farrell, D. (eds.). *The Act of Voting: Identities, Institutions and Locale*. Abingdon: Routledge.

Thomson, J. 2016. Abortion and same-sex marriage: how are non-sectarian controversial issues discussed in Northern Irish politics? *Irish Political Studies*, 31(4):483–501.

Throsby, K. 2004. *When IVF Fails: Feminism, Infertility and the Negotiation of Normality*. Basingstoke: Palgrave MacMillan.

Titkow, A. 2007. *Tożsamość polskich kobiet: ciągłość zmiana konteksty* [The identity of Polish women: continuity, change, context]. Warsaw: IFIS PAN.

Trounson, A. and Mohr, L. 1983. Human pregnancy following cryopreservation, thawing and transfer of an eight-cell embryo. *Nature*, 305(5936):707–709.

TS. 2018. Wyniki referendum aborcyjnego w Irlandii w komentarzach internautów [Results of the Irish referendum commented by the internet users]. *Tygodnik Solidarność*, 26 May 2018. www.tysol.pl/a19679-Wyniki-referendum-aborcyjnego-w-Irlandii-w-komentarzach-internautow.

Turley, K.V. 2018. Ireland's old order has been swept away for a new order that kills children. [Online] *LifeSite News*. www.lifesitenews.com/opinion/irelands-old-order-has-been-swept-away-for-a-new-order-that-kills-children [Accessed: 12 October 2018].

Turloughmore, C. 2018. No pro-lifers at airports? *Irish Independent*, 9 February 2018.

TVN24. 2016. *Trzy zobowiązania rządu w sprawie ochrony życia* [Three government's commitments relating to the protection of life]. www.tvn24.pl/r/681687.

TVP INFO 2016. *PiS za całkowitym zakazem aborcji?* [PiS supporting a complete abortion ban?]. www.tvp.info/24679362.

Uslaner, E.M. 2002. *The Moral Foundations of Trust*. Cambridge: Cambridge University Press.

van Maren, J. 2018a. Ireland has fallen – and the battle is just beginning. *LifeSite News*, 27 May 2018. www.lifesitenews.com/blogs/ireland-has-fallenand-the-battle-is-just-beginning [Accessed: 12 October 2018].

van Maren, J. 2018b. 'This is not the end': an Irish pro-lifer's open letter to his homeland *LifeSite News*, 4 June 2018. www.lifesitenews.com/opinion/looking-for-hope-for-ireland-youll-find-it-here [Accessed: 12 October 2018].

Waitt, G., Figueroa, R. and McGee, L. 2007. Fissures in the rock: rethinking pride and shame in the moral terrains of Uluru. *Transactions of the Institute of British Geographers*, 32(2):248–263.

Warnock, M. 1984. *Report of the Committee of Inquiry into Human Fertilisation and Embryology*. Department of Health and Social Security. www.

bioeticacs.org/iceb/documentos/Warnock_Report_of_the_Committee_
of_Inquiry_into_Human_Fertilisation_and_Embryology_1984.pdf
[Accessed: 10 October 2018].

Weingarten, K. 2016. Shame before the law: effects of abortion regulation.
In Mendible, M. (ed.). *American Shame: Stigma and the Body Politic*.
Bloomington, IN: Indiana University Press.

Whitty, N. 1993. Law and the regulation of reproduction in Ireland:
1922–1992. *University of Toronto Law Journal*, 43(4):851–888.

Wilken, R. 2008. Mobilizing place: mobile media, peripatetics, and the
renegotiation of urban places. *Journal of Urban Technology*, 15(3):39–55.

Woliver, L. 2010. *The Political Geographies of Pregnancy*. Champaign, IL:
University of Illinois Press.

wPolityce. 2016. *Jarosław Kaczyński o manifestacjach KOD, miejscu dla
pomników 10/04, aborcji i. . . rodeo. Sprawdź, co powiedział szef PiS!*
[Jarosław Kaczyński on the KOD manifestations, place of the 10/4
monuments, abortion and rodeo. Check out what the PiS boss said!].
W Polityce [On Politics]. https://wpolityce.pl/polityka/289247-wsieci-
jaroslaw-kaczynski-o-manifestacjach-kod-miejscu-dla-pomnikow-1004-
aborcji-i-rodeo-sprawdz-co-powiedzial-szef-pis.

Yuval-Davis, N. 1997. *Gender and Nation*. London: SAGE.

Zebracki, M. 2017. Queerying public art in digitally networked space.
ACME: An International E-Journal for Critical Geographies, 16(3):
440–474. www.acme-journal.org/index.php/acme/article/view/1354.

Zebracki, M. and Palmer, J.M. 2018. Introduction to special issue: urban
public art: geographies of co-production. *City & Society*, 30(1):5–13.

Index